The Kingdom of Kush

DEREK A. WELSBY

The Kingdom of Kush

THE NAPATAN
AND MEROITIC EMPIRES

PUBLISHED FOR THE TRUSTEES
OF THE BRITISH MUSEUM
BY BRITISH MUSEUM PRESS

© 1996 The Trustees of the British Museum

Published by British Museum Press
A division of The British Museum Company
46 Bloomsbury Street, London WC1B 3QQ

British Library Cataloguing in Publication Data
A catalogue record for this book is available from the British Library

ISBN 0 7141 0986 X

Designed by John Hawkins
Typeset by Southern Positives and Negatives (SPAN), Lingfield, Surrey
Printed in Great Britain by The Bath Press, Avon

Frontispiece The lion god Apedemak. Relief on the wall
of his temple at Naqa. (D. A. Welsby)

Contents

Acknowledgements

A number of colleagues have assisted me in the task of writing this book by their willingness to discuss certain points and by furnishing unpublished information. Chief among these I would like to thank Patrice Lenoble, David Edwards, Pamela Rose, Tim Kendall and Stephen Quirke. Vivian Davies read most of an early draft and made many helpful suggestions. Especial thanks must go to my editor Carolyn Jones for her diligent reading of the text and for the numerous comments she made.

Most of the photographs were taken by the writer. The others are reproduced here with the permission of the Ashmolean Museum and the Griffith Archive, Oxford; The National Trust (through the good offices of Mr T. Mitchell); Liverpool University; The National Corporation for Antiquities and Museums, Khartoum; and the Trustees of the British Museum. Dr P. Lenoble, Dr T. Kendall and Dr J. Alexander kindly allowed the writer to use their photographs (figs 13, 28 and col. pl. 1 respectively).

Introduction

The area immediately to the south of the Ancient Egyptian frontier at Aswan was known, certainly by the time of the Old Kingdom, as the land of Wawat. Wawat was a land of great wealth on account of the prolific gold mines that lay within its territory. Further to the south was the land of Kush which is most frequently referred to in Egyptian inscriptions with the epithet 'miserable' or 'wretched', even after the territory had been incorporated within the Egyptian Empire. 'Kush' is used in a geographical sense, its inhabitants being referred to as the Nehesy,[1] the people who inhabited the river valley, as opposed to the Medjay who occupied the wadis in the Eastern Desert.

The origin of the term Kush is unknown, but it does not appear to be an Egyptian word.[2] The earliest form of the word can be transliterated as 'Kas' and thereafter it appears most frequently as 'Kash'.[3] Today it is most often rendered as Kush.

That it was a term acceptable to the indigenous rulers of the area during the Second Intermediate Period is clear from an inscription found at Buhen recording the construction of a temple of Horus 'to the satisfaction of the ruler of Kush'.[4] This Kingdom of Kush has been equated by archaeologists and historians with the Kerma culture, so named after the largest urban complex known in the area. The scale and character of the buildings on that site, together with the extremely rich burials in the cemetery 4 km to the east, indicate that this was the centre of a rich and powerful kingdom. The kingdom was destroyed during the Egyptian territorial expansion early in the XVIIIth Dynasty and the site of Kerma lapsed into political obscurity.

The subject of this book could be called the Second Kingdom of Kush. The people thought of themselves as Kushites. One of the earliest kings whose name we know is Kashta, a throne name meaning 'The Kushite'. To the classical authors of the Greek, Hellenistic and Roman world the kingdom and the geographical area were called Ethiopia, and the people Ethiopians – meaning 'burnt-faced persons'. The use of this term in a modern context, however, is rather confusing as the Kushites and the peoples occupying the Ethiopian highlands had very little in common.

During the XXVth Dynasty (c.747–656 BC), at a time when the Kushites ruled Egypt, at least one inscription refers to Kush by the old Egyptian term for the area south of the frontier, Ta Sety, meaning 'the Land of the Bow'.[5] In Kushite royal inscriptions the kings refer to themselves as 'the King of Upper and Lower Egypt' even long after the Kushites had been expelled from Egypt.

Today the most common designation of the area occupied by the Kingdom of Kush is Nubia. The name Nubia derives from a people known as the Noba or Nuba who moved into the Nile Valley, apparently from the south-west, over a period of centuries and ultimately filled the power vacuum created by the collapse of the Kushite state. In modern Egypt and Sudan, Nubia is defined as the area occupied by the Nubians, a distinct cultural group among the peoples of those countries. Prior to the flooding of parts of the Nile valley by the construction of the dams at Aswan, the Nubians lived between Aswan and el Debba downstream of the Fourth Cataract. Archaeologists, however, use the term Nubia to cover the indeterminate area which was controlled by the Ancient Egyptians, by the kings based at Kerma, by the Kushites, and later by the kings of the medieval Christian states. Where used in this book Nubia designates this geographical area and should not be related to the modern Nubians or the earlier Noba.

It has been common for much of this century for archaeologists to divide the history of Kush into two phases, the Napatan and the Meroitic. Reisner, who first coined these terms, wrote '... the Meroitic Kingdom of Ethiopia is culturally and politically merely a continuation of the Napatan Kingdom of Ethiopia.'[6] Later scholars have made much of the distinction between the two periods based on a number of factors. The date assigned to this 'cultural change' has been related to the location of the royal burial grounds, whether at Napata or at Meroe. Reisner noted in the light of his statement quoted above that 'it was therefore to be expected that the first king's tomb at Meroe would approximate in its structure, reliefs, inscriptions, burial chambers and funerary furniture [to] the last preceding king's tomb at Napata ...'. The history of Kush is a continuum and it is not desirable arbitrarily to divide it into periods. In this book the terms Napatan and Meroitic are avoided wherever possible, except for the designation Meroitic for the indigenous language of Kush.

As will be described elsewhere, the significance of the move of the royal burial ground from el Kurru to Nuri and then to Meroe is unclear. It is known that the major political centre of the kingdom lay at Meroe long before the royal burial ground was moved there. There are certainly significant differences between Kushite culture when one looks at the early and late periods, but this was a gradual process of change fuelled by the assimilation of influences principally from Egypt. We have no idea whether the local cultures of Napata and of Meroe were distinct and there is no reason to assume that these hypothetical local cultures influenced the rulers of Kush to such a degree that the move of the seat of power from one to another brought a concomitant change in Kushite culture throughout the realm.

Ideally this book should provide a balanced account of the history of the Kingdom of Kush and of the lifestyle of its inhabitants throughout its thousand-year history. Such an aim has been attempted, but the result cannot claim total success. Although the material remains of the Kushites are to be found over a vast tract of the Nile valley, we know, relatively speaking, very little about them compared with many of the other great civilisations of the ancient world.

Consideration of the Kushites alongside such giants of the ancient world as the

Greeks, Romans and Egyptians is justified on account of the longevity of the kingdom and of its size, if for no other reasons. At the time when Rome was a small village on the banks of the Tiber and the Greek city states held sway over minuscule territories, the Kushites ruled an empire stretching from the central Sudan to the borders of Palestine. The Kingdom of Kush outlived the Greek city states and the period of Macedonian hegemony over vast tracts of the ancient world, and co-existed with the rise, heyday and much of the period of decline of the Roman Empire.

With the expulsion of the Kushites from Egypt at the hands of the Assyrians, the Kushite kingdom became peripheral to the Mediterranean world and increasingly found itself at the end of a cul-de-sac in the Nile valley, the exit to which was always blocked by a strong power to the north. Thus, little interest was taken in Kush by its literate northern neighbours. The paucity of information from external sources is particularly serious on account of a similar lack of written records from the kingdom itself. Only at Qasr Ibrim have significant amounts of documents, generally written on papyrus, been recovered. These, together with inscriptions on stone and on pottery, would still form an invaluable source of information were it not for the fact that we cannot yet read the language. A number of inscriptions, particularly royal inscriptions of early date, are written in Egyptian and can thus be understood, but until the Meroitic language is deciphered much of what the Kushites thought about themselves, their world and their gods will remain a mystery to us.

In the absence of written sources, we have to rely heavily on archaeological data. This data is extremely difficult to handle and interpret. To write a general account of the Kushites one must make a considerable number of interpretations from the observed evidence, often with very little opportunity of checking whether the conclusions reached are correct or not.

In some fields of study archaeological data is more useful than in others. In the field of architecture, for example, we can actually observe the buildings, frequently in extremely good states of preservation. We can understand how they were built and often how they were used. We can also observe the development of Kushite architecture through time and note how it was influenced by changes in the architecture of its neighbours. When we try to obtain an idea of what life was actually like for the inhabitants of Kush, and what were the hopes, fears and aspirations of the inhabitants, we are on much shakier ground.

It is hoped that this book will not only instil an interest in a civilisation that flourished on the middle Nile for over a millenium, but will also lead to an appreciation of the intriguing problems facing the historian and archaeologist when attempting to understand an ancient culture. Studying the Kingdom of Kush is like a detective story in which a number of disparate and often apparently contradictory facts must be woven into a coherent and plausible narrative of events. It is these very problems which make the study so exciting and rewarding.

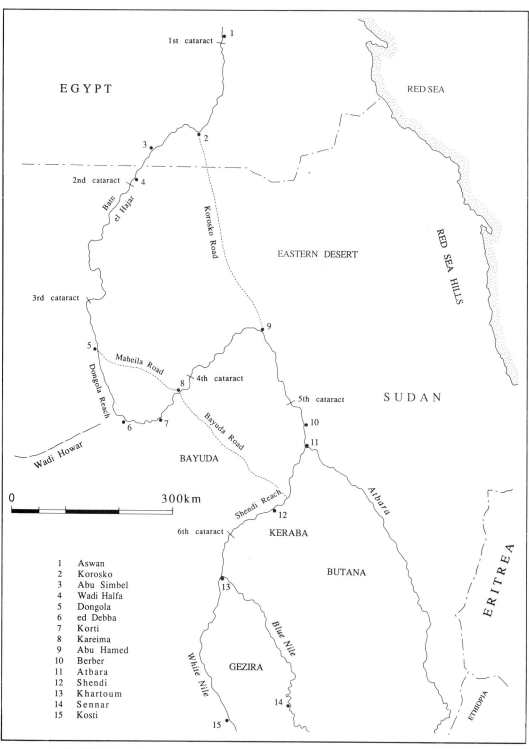

1st cataract

EGYPT

RED SEA

2

3

2nd cataract

4

Batn el Hajar

Korosko Road

EASTERN DESERT

RED SEA HILLS

3rd cataract

9

5

Maheila Road

8

4th cataract

SUDAN

Dongola Reach

5th cataract

10

11

6

7

Bayuda Road

BAYUDA

Atbara

Wadi Howar

0   300km

Shendi Reach

12

6th cataract

KERABA

BUTANA

ERITREA

1   Aswan
2   Korosko
3   Abu Simbel
4   Wadi Halfa
5   Dongola
6   ed Debba
7   Korti
8   Kareima
9   Abu Hamed
10 Berber
11 Atbara
12 Shendi
13 Khartoum
14 Sennar
15 Kosti

13

Blue Nile

White Nile

GEZIRA

14

ETHIOPIA

15

1 *The Nile Valley from Sennar to Aswan.*

CHAPTER ONE

The Early
History of Kush

The Nile is the only river to cross the Sahara, thereby providing a corridor for travel from the Mediterranean basin into central Africa across the largest desert on earth. The waters of the river allow an almost continuous strip of cultivation to extend across the desert, making it possible for sedentary peoples to live in the midst of this most inhospitable of regions.

However, it should not be imagined that the productivity of the Nile valley is consistent throughout its length. Although the river in its upper reaches is important for communications, life in the southern rainbelt does not rely exclusively on the river. As one moves to the north the climate becomes progressively more arid and the importance of the river is enhanced until it is the only life-sustaining feature. In the driest part of the valley, where there is virtually no rainfall whatsoever, all sedentary human settlement, at least since the end of the last great pluvial period, has been confined to the river banks.

The Nile valley is famed for its agricultural productivity which allowed the development of the mighty power of Pharaonic Egypt and today sustains a very large population in the Arab Republic of Egypt. However, it is principally the Delta and the wide flood plain of Upper Egypt which sustains Egypt. Upstream of Aswan the river valley is much less hospitable and for a length of 160 km through the Batn el Hajar (the Belly of the Rocks) there are only isolated pockets of arable land along the river banks and on the islands.

The presence of six cataracts between central Sudan and southern Egypt makes the Nile far from ideal as a waterway for communications. The valley also does not provide a good land route as the river's winding course is vastly longer than more direct routes across the desert. Therefore, much of the north-to-south movement (and vice versa) left the river valley for at least part of the journey; those areas which were bypassed became backwaters. The ultimate fate of the Kushites may have been that eventually the whole of the Middle Nile became a backwater when trade from south to north abandoned the valley completely and took to the Indian Ocean and the Red Sea.

Until the predynastic period (c.5000–3100 BC) there was no major power, as far as we are aware, in the Nile valley. Late in predynastic times power bases developed in the valley to the north of the First Cataract which rapidly led to the establishment of a strong centralised state on the lower Nile. This power base has ensured the territorial integrity of Egypt throughout history and it is only on rare occasions and for relatively short periods that parts of the valley north of Aswan have been ruled separately. To the south the physical barriers along the Nile, the lack of geographical homogeneity and the gradual change in climate and rainfall have tended to fragment rather than unify. Attempts to control vast tracts of the river have rarely succeeded and such control has only been exercised by three powers: Kush, the Turko-Egyptians and the Anglo-Egyptians.

Although the agricultural potential of the valley for several hundred kilometres to the south of the First Cataract is poor, the ancient Egyptians were soon attracted to the area in their quest for good quality stone and for the mineral resources of the area. As early as the IVth Dynasty (*c.*2613–2494 BC) diorite was being quarried in the desert to the west of the much later temples at Abu Simbel and at the same period a settlement was established at Buhen on the Second Cataract for the exploitation of copper reserves in the area.[1] Gold, however, held the biggest attraction and the gold mines in the Wadis el Allaqi and Gabgaba acted as a magnet to the rulers of the north for three thousand years.

The area also had considerable economic importance, as whoever controlled the Middle Nile controlled the flow of goods from the regions to the south. These goods were largely funnelled along the Nile valley before the dramatic rise of maritime trade in the later first millenium BC and of cross-desert trade in the Islamic period. The presence of a rich source of materials to the south and of a massive consumer market to the north led, during the third millenium BC, to the development of a powerful state astride the trade route whose capital lay at Kerma, a little upstream of the Third Cataract. Throughout the Middle Kingdom (2040–1750 BC) the pharaonic frontier lay on the Second Cataract with the massive fortresses built by the Egyptians perhaps designed to protect the transhipment and portage of goods through this, the worst of the cataracts of the Nile.

During the Second Intermediate Period (*c.*1750–1650 BC) centralised power in Egypt was broken by the rise to power of the Hyksos in the Delta. The rulers of Kerma took advantage of the situation, entered into diplomatic relations with the Hyksos, and proceeded to occupy the Egyptian Second Cataract fortresses and to expand their power well to the north. The hapless pharaohs could do little to counter this aggression but, with the defeat of the Hyksos and the reunification of Egypt by Amosis (1570–1546 BC), it was not long before the Egyptians sought their revenge. The Egyptian New Kingdom campaigns in Nubia were designed to remove the most powerful of the middlemen who sat athwart the route to the south. The power of Kerma was crushed and the Egyptians advanced upriver at least as far as Kurgus near the Fifth Cataract, where inscriptions were set up commemorating a royal presence under the pharaohs Thutmose I and III. An Egyptian military installation has also been claimed here although this has never been verified.[2] It is presumably no coincidence that the most southerly evidence for the extent of the Kerma kingdom lies precisely in this region.

As at the end of the Middle Kingdom it was the weakness of Egypt at the end of the

New Kingdom (after 1086 BC) which resulted in the loss of control over the lands to the south of the First Cataract. This may have been a very gradual process, of which we know few details. How much the indigenous inhabitants of the regions were able to contribute to the expulsion of the Egyptians is equally unclear. One of the major Egyptian cult centres at Napata fell into ruin and we may legitimately doubt whether any survivals of the Egyptian colonial period remained by the ninth century BC throughout much of Nubia.

The el Kurru cemetery and its chronology

It is from this time that we have the first evidence of the Kushite state, thanks to the work of the eminent Egyptologist George A. Riesner. In 1918 he began the excavation of a cemetery at el Kurru, 12 km downstream from the Egyptian centre at Napata. A sequence of burials, clearly of a royal nature, was discovered, including some of the pharaohs of the XXVth Dynasty who were well known to ancient historians. The earliest 'royal' burial, which occupied the prime site in the cemetery atop a small rise, was designated Ku.Tum.1. It is with the occupant of this tomb that the history of Kush begins. The name of the individual in this grave is unknown, which in itself does not pose problems. However, the grave is undated and this has led to considerable difficulties. Indeed it may be said that the absence of a reliable chronology for the Kingdom of Kush is one of the most serious problems facing the development of research. This point will be returned to below. Of more immediate relevance is the antecedents of the 'first' ruler of Kush.

Reisner was of the opinion that he had excavated the grave of the earliest Kushite ruler.[3] But what evidence is there for this? No written source can be used to add support, so we have to rely entirely on the archaeological evidence. That this individual was the first to be buried in the cemetery seems logical on account of the position which his grave occupies. However, there can be no certainty that this is the first royal burial ground. Throughout the history of Kush the royal burial grounds moved from el Kurru to Nuri, back to el Kurru, to Nuri, to el Kurru yet again, then to Meroe south cemetery, and finally to Meroe north cemetery. The few burials at Jebel Barkal are difficult to fit into the sequence. The significance of the presence of a pyramid associated with the name of Taharqo at Sedeinga remains unexplained.[4]

Many other tumuli cemeteries are known in the middle Nile valley, most of which have never been examined archaeologically and remain undated. It is possible that there are royal burials pre-dating those at el Kurru which remain to be recognised. The location of the earliest known Kushite royal burials at el Kurru is particularly interesting as it would appear to highlight the discontinuity from the New Kingdom, when the vicinity of Jebel Barkal has been thought to have been the religious and administrative focus of the area. However, the importance of Jebel Barkal during the New Kingdom may have been overstated.[5] A recent re-examination of the excavation notes of Reisner has shown that there was a settlement at el Kurru of sufficient importance to have had a defensive wall.[6] This presumably was the early capital of Kush, the area owing its importance to the wide tracts of irrigable land here, as extensive as that around Jebel Barkal. It was only with the acceptance of Egyptian religious ideology and the re-emergence of Jebel Barkal as a major cult centre, that the focus of attention shifted to the Barkal area and royal burials began at Nuri a few kilometres upstream. The loss of Egypt, which elevated the Temple of Amun at Barkal to the position of pre-eminence in the Kushite realm, will have served to enhance the importance of Jebel Barkal.

The early development of the Kingdom of Kush is unknown to us. Reisner's chronological scheme has been recently re-examined, but the evidence is ambiguous. It has spawned two widely diverging interpretations of the early history of Kush. Reisner and his supporters favour a 'short' chronology where the royal burials at el Kurru, prior to the historically dated king Piye, are assumed to consist of six rulers, the other graves being those of members of the royal family. Why Reisner opted for this interpretation is nowhere clearly stated. He writes, 'For reasons the details of which would now take too much time, I divide the sixteen graves into six generations ...'. 'If we calculate the six generations of ancestors at 20–30 years each ... [and] ... if we take the beginning of Piankhy's [Piye's] reign at about 740 BC, we get 860–920 BC for the date of the oldest ancestor, he of Ku.Tum.1.'[7] The proponents of the 'long' chronology believe that many more of the graves are those of rulers and, therefore, that the time span involved must be considerably greater.

The recent study of Reisner's records and of the somewhat scanty material remains from his excavations of the tombs under discussion here, all of which have been very badly robbed, suggested that Reisner's original interpretation more adequately fits the observed facts than does the 'long' chronology. Caution is required, as much of the evidence is ambiguous at best and contradictory at worst. The 'short' chronology provides an explanation for the discontinuity of Egyptianising traits in the early burial customs of the Kushite rulers. However, it demands an acceptance of the fact that the rulers had a marked predilection for, and access to, old Egyptian objects of types which had long been out of production.

The 'long' chronology helps to fill the gap between the period of Egyptian domination of Nubia and the rise of the Kingdom of Kush. As with the 'short' chronology, the chronological data upon which it is based is derived from the objects of Egyptian manufacture associated with the tombs. The divergence of opinion results from our very imprecise knowledge of the dating of artefacts at this time. Some seem to date to the late New Kingdom and Third Intermediate Period (to about the eleventh and tenth century BC), others to a little before the XXVth Dynasty (*c*.747–656 BC). The scholarly arguments concerning the chronology of the burials at el Kurru are far from over.[8]

The limits of Kushite control

The territorial expansion of the early Kushite state is shrouded in mystery. Fundamental points at issue concern the origin of the early Kushite rulers. Did they come from the area of el Kurru or did they originate in, and control, another area of the later Kushite Empire, and move into (invade and conquer) the el Kurru region? The excavations of a cemetery of 105 tumuli at Debeira East, north of the Second Cataract, may shed some light on this problem.[9] These tumuli are very similar in a number of respects to the earliest tumuli at el Kurru and the contents of the graves are also very similar to those within Ku.Tum.1. Much of this material consists of Egyptian imports which, as with the similar material from the el Kurru tumulus, can be dated to the late New Kingdom. Amongst this material is a type of very distinctive squat jar which has only been noted at these two sites. A close relationship between the two sites, which lie several hundred kilometres apart, seems likely although its significance is unclear. One suggestion is that the first ruler to be buried at el Kurru moved south to avoid renewed aggression by the Egyptians into northern Nubia.[10]

Some scholars have suggested that the ruling clan buried at el Kurru came from the Meroe region, others that they were the descendants of one of the princely families who governed the area on behalf of the Egyptian administration during the New Kingdom. Reisner's view that the earliest Kushite rulers were of Libyan origin[11] is now totally discarded.

How soon was Kushite control of the area to the north and south of el Kurru established? We know from the historical sources that under Kashta, the Kushites were able to move north into Egypt. His predecessor, Alara, certainly controlled Kawa.[12]

Further evidence for contact between the far north of Nubia and the area at the downstream end of the Fourth Cataract comes from Qasr Ibrim. Part of a building, dated by the analysis of associated camel dung by the radiocarbon method to the late tenth or ninth century BC, has been compared with the early Kushite palace B100 at Jebel Barkal.[13] Six phases of defences pre-date the temple built by Taharqo at Ibrim in the earlier seventh century BC. A radiocarbon date from the phase 3 mud brick curtain wall indicates that it is broadly contemporary with the 'palace'. However, the evidence available is not sufficient to allow us to identify the builders of these defences and of the palatial structure. Likewise the pottery, which may be contemporary with these structures, does not allow us to recognise the presence of the Kushites on the site at this time.[14]

No historical sources are known which shed light on the very early territorial expansion of the Kushite state. The activities of Osorkon II (*c.*874–850 BC) and Takeloth II (*c.*850–825 BC) in northern Nubia together with the revival of the title 'Viceroy of Kush' can be linked with Egyptian inscriptions found as far south as Wadi Halfa and Semna.[15] Such a deep penetration into Nubia was presumably short-lived. Any military conflict between Egypt and Kush in the ninth century was of short duration. In 827 BC gifts from the Egyptian pharaoh to the Temple of Amun at Karnak included 'the gold of Khenet-hen-nefer'; the name frequently used during the New Kingdom for the area around Napata,[16] suggesting that there were diplomatic and/or trading relations presumably between the Kushite king and Egypt. In the present state of our knowledge Kushite penetration north of Kawa before the reign of Kashta cannot be proven.

The earliest evidence for the Kushites in the south comes from Meroe where burials in the south and west cemeteries contain objects contemporary with a number of XXVth Dynasty rulers.[17] A sphinx of King Aspelta has been recovered from Defeia close to Khartoum.[18] Further artefacts of the early Kushite date come from the cemetery at Jebel Moya over 200 km to the south of Khartoum.[19] As with the northern expansion of the kingdom the details and chronology are very poorly known. The early Kushites did not live in a vacuum and, therefore, the expansion of their domains could only be achieved at the expense of the indigenous inhabitants who must have lost their independence.

The early rulers

The early Kushite rulers are very shadowy figures and only one is known to us by name before the Kushite expansion into Egypt under Kashta. Alara is mentioned on a much later inscription set up by Taharqo which implies that there was a temple of Amun at Kawa in his reign to which he entrusted the safety of his family.[20] Alara's veneration of the Egyptian god Amun can be compared with the archaeological evidence for Egyptian influence on Kushite funerary rites and burial customs observed in the contemporary burials at el Kurru. Another inscription from Kawa, of a king named Ary, records the construction of a new temple of Amun on the site. The identity of this king is unclear, but recent studies have strongly argued that he either predates Alara or is the same person.[21] The Egyptianisation of the Kushite élite was to be given considerable impetus by the physical control the Kushites were to exercise over Egypt during the XXVth Dynasty. This, however, should be seen as the culmination of a period of acculturation the motives for which, at an early stage in the development of the Kushite state, can only be guessed.

Although the activities of the Kushite kings in Egypt are known in some detail, the contemporary situation in the rest of the kingdom is little understood. The inscriptions that survive relate principally to building activities. According to Reisner the earliest Kushite structure known at Jebel Barkal is Temple B800, built by Kashta or his immediate predecessor, now known to be Alara.[22]

Piye seems to have been the first to refurbish and enlarge the old Egyptian Temple of Amun at Jebel Barkal. At the commencement of this work at least one room in the temple had lost its roof,[23] suggesting that the New Kingdom cult of Amun had ceased to exist before its re-establishment by the early Kushite rulers. Piye considerably enlarged the temple, extending it towards the river by the construction of a large hypostyle hall entered through a massive pylon. He may also have been responsible for the enlargement of Temple B800. He is credited with the construction of a large building adjacent to the latter temple, which is almost certainly to be identified as a palace. The arrangement of the temple and palace conform exactly to the long-established Egyptian practice. The palace is set to the right (starboard) side as one leaves the temple and the main axis of the palace lies perpendicular to the long axis of the temple, the axes meeting at the outer doorway of the temple.[24] This also puts the 'palace' in the same position relative to the extended Temple B500, the Temple of Amun.

These activities at Jebel Barkal indicate the importance of the site as a religious centre. As the earliest Kushite royal burial ground known to us lies at el Kurru, it is reasonable to suggest that el Kurru was the major centre during the early history of Kush. We know very little of the settlement there apart from the presence of a defensive circuit and monumental buildings.[25] The use of the ancestral burial ground may have long outlasted the secular importance of the town, the original reason for its location. Taharqo, by choosing to be buried closer to Jebel Barkal, may have simply been accepting the shift of the seat of political power to Barkal. As far as we are aware, the eclipse of the settlement at el Kurru was total and that site appears to have had no importance whatsoever in the later Kushite period.

At Kawa, Shebitqo restored the New Kingdom temple built by Tutankhamun and constructed a new temple close by. His successor Taharqo was also active at Kawa, firstly clearing sand from and restoring a temple on the site and then by the construction of a large temple of Amun.[26] Temples of almost identical plan, and therefore probably also built by Taharqo, have been excavated at Sanam across the river from Jebel Barkal, and at Tabo on Argo Island 30 km to the north of Kawa.[27] Taharqo continued the expansion of the Temple of Amun B500 at Jebel Barkal, and appears to have been active at Sedeinga. There an inscription bearing the king's cartouche has been found associated with a small pyramid.[28] The king was almost certainly buried at Nuri, where he constructed a massive pyramid, so the function of the edifice at Sedeinga is unclear. He also built the earliest known Kushite temple at Qasr Ibrim, as well as temples at several other sites in Lower Nubia.[29]

There is no evidence for building, or any other activity, to the south of Sanam. This may reflect a lack of interest in the southern part of the kingdom when the centre of operations and imperial aspirations were focused on Egypt and beyond. Equally it may be the result of an absence of territorial control of the area to the south. The earliest evidence for occupation at Meroe is now dated to the tenth century BC[30] and graves contemporary with the reign of Piye in the southern cemetery have been claimed by Reisner.[31] At no other major Kushite centre in the south is there any hint of such early occupation.

The Kushite kings in Egypt were 'Lords of the Two Lands' and their buildings, activities and adoration of the Egyptian gods followed the established practices. They sought to integrate rather than to change, although their predilection for archaising forms of art and expression is worthy of note. There is nothing that is distinctly Kushite about the architecture of their monuments, and posterity – by according them the title of the XXVth Dynasty – reflects their success at being accepted amongst the rightful rulers of Egypt.

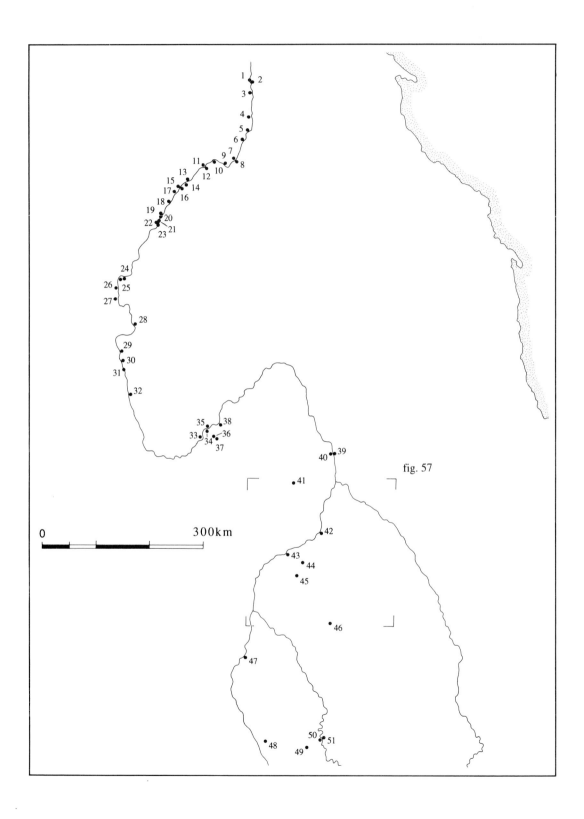

fig. 57

0   300km

CHAPTER TWO

The Heyday of Kush

The effects of the control of Egypt on the Kushites must have been substantial, although it would appear that the rulers were already imbued with a considerable amount of Egyptian culture and they entered Egypt not as conquering barbarians but as champions of the age-old traditions of the Pharaohs. It is, therefore, not easy to assess the impact of the Egyptian adventure on Kushite civilisation. Certainly the rulers will have become familiar with the grandeur of the monuments of Pharaonic Egypt. It therefore comes as no surprise to note that most of the earliest monumental buildings constructed by the Kushite rulers in Nubia were built at this time. The Pharaohs of the XXVth Dynasty had access to vast resources of wealth, allowing them to indulge in building activities far in excess of what their immediate predecessors undertook. Indeed the greatest Kushite builder of them all was Taharqo who ruled at this time.

The history of Kush within her own borders can be written very quickly. It is much to be lamented just how little we know of Kushite history from the ninth year of the reign of Tanwetamani (c.655 BC), when the Kushites finally lost control of Egypt, to the fourth century AD when Kush as an independent political entity came to an end. Military activities undertaken by the Kushites against Egypt and invasions mounted

Opposite 2 *The Kushite Empire after the withdrawal from Egypt.*

1 Philae	14 Jebel Adda	29 Tumbus	42 Meroe
2 Shellal	15 Ballana	30 Kerma	43 Wad ben Naqa
3 Dabod	16 Qustul	31 Tabo	44 Musawwarat es
4 Kalabsha	17 Faras	32 Kawa	Sufra
Wadi Kitna	18 Argin	33 el Kurru	45 Naqa
5 Dakka	19 Buhen	34 Sanam Abu Dom	46 Jebel Qeili
6 Maharraqa	20 Meinarti	35 Jebel Barkal	47 el Kawa
7 Areika	21 Gaminarti	36 Umm Ruweim 1	48 Jebel Tomat
8 Wadi el Arab	22 Mirgissa	Umm Ruweim 2	49 Jebel Moya
9 Shablul	23 Meili	37 Umm Kuweib	50 Sennar
10 Derr	24 Amara East	Umm Khafur	51 Abu Geili
11 Karanog	25 Missiminia	38 Nuri	
12 Qasr Ibrim	26 Sedeinga	39 Dangeil	
13 Arminna West	27 Soleb	40 Jebel Nakharu	
Ash Shaukan	28 Kedurma	41 Fura Wells	

from Egypt will be recounted in Chapter 3. We have no indication whether any of these invasions had any repercussions on the kingdom. We might postulate that a successful invasion from the north would, at the very least, have had a destabilising effect on the incumbent of the throne. We have no hint that the loss of Egypt by Tanwetamani seriously affected the position of the king. How long he survived the ignominy of defeat is unknown, but he was buried with all the customary honours in the ancestral burial ground at el Kurru.

The rulers and their chronology

It is thought that after Tanwetamani there were approximately sixty Kushite rulers. Of these we know the names of many and the deeds of a handful. Kushite kings are most frequently recognisable as builders; historical inscriptions are extremely rare and those in the Meroitic language can only be understood in the most general terms. There has been a good deal of controversy over the number of rulers, the order of their reigns and, particularly, their dates.

The first attempt to draw up a 'king list' was made by George Reisner, the excavator of the royal tombs at el Kurru, Nuri, Jebel Barkal and Meroe. His approach was first to take those rulers for which an absolute chronology was available and then to arrange the other rulers within the chronological framework provided.[1]

The reign of Taharqo is the only one where we can be certain both of its starting date and of its duration. He ascended the throne in 690 BC and ruled for twenty-six years.[2] Tanwetamani succeeded Taharqo and was certainly on the throne for a minimum of nine years.

The 'fixed' chronological pegs used to form the framework have varied over the years. Some have been discarded, others discarded and reinstated, and new ones have come into play. Among some of the frequently quoted chronological pegs are the following:

Aspelta
It has been assumed that Aspelta was on the throne when Psammetik II launched his invasion of Kush in 594 BC. This is based on the destruction of the royal statues in the Temple of Amun at Jebel Barkal, where the latest statues are of Aspelta. It was assumed that the temple was sacked by the troops of Psammetik II.[3] It is now thought that the destruction of these statues has nothing whatsoever to do with a foreign invasion, yet the date for Aspelta is still accepted.

Arkamani
Arkamani is assumed to be the king known to the Greeks as Ergamenes and the written sources have been interpreted as suggesting that he lived in the later half of the third century BC.

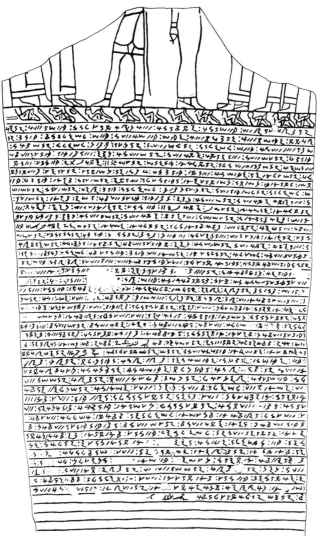

3 *Stela of Amanitore and Akinidad from Hamadab.*
(After Griffith 1917)

Amanirenas and Akinidad

On the great stela from Hamadab (fig. 3), a little to the south of Meroe, commemorating the rulers Amanirenas and Akinidad, there appears to be a reference to military activities against the Romans which are assumed to relate to the historically attested conflict in the 20s BC.

Tqrrmn

A graffito on the wall of the Temple of Isis at Philae records an embassy sent by King Tqrrmn (identified as Teqerideamani) to the Romans in the third year of the reign of the emperor Trebonianus Gallus, who ruled from AD 251 to 253.

Aezana inscription

The final snippet of chronological information is the Aezana inscription which can be dated to around AD 350 and may indicate the survival of the Kushites at that time, but does not furnish us with the name or status of the ruler.

The fixed points in the chronological framework are very sparse indeed and in many cases are questionable. Reisner used the technique of seriation, familiar to prehistoric studies, in an attempt to arrange not the rulers but the tombs of individuals who are thought to have been rulers into what he considered to be a logical sequence of development. Certainly one can observe in general terms developments in the architecture of the tombs and their superstructures and in the objects which are buried within them. For the lengths of individual reigns Reisner postulated that the larger and richer the tomb, its fittings and its pyramid, the longer was the reign of the incumbent.[4]

Criteria for recognising the tombs of rulers as opposed to those of other members of the royal family can be ambiguous. This is made even more complicated by the frequent destruction of the primary burials so that we are not even certain of the sex of the individual; and as there appear to have been, at least on some occasions, ruling queens, the possibilities for misidentification are considerable. Many objects of foreign manufacture are found in the royal tombs and approximate date-ranges for these can sometimes be offered. However, unfortunately it is their presence in Kushite royal tombs which is often held to be their most closely 'dated' occurrence. This is clearly a circular argument.

A critical problem is posed by the demolition of pyramids and their offering chapels during the life of the Kushite state. How frequently this occurred is unknown but it has been noted in a few cases, as at Beg.N.53 at Meroe, where blocks reused in later structures testify to the one-time existence of otherwise unknown monuments.[5] How many rulers have suffered *damnatio memoriae* in this way and thus have disappeared from history? The effect that such an occurrence would have on the chronology of the rulers of Kush can hardly be imagined. Such destruction of tomb monuments must be of historical significance and may reflect dynastic rivalry of which we are totally ignorant.

A further difficulty is how the royal cemeteries relate to each other. As a result of the survival of the historical sources on the XXVth Dynasty, which establish the order of succession, we are able to recognise that, although Taharqo forsook the ancestral burial ground at el Kurru for a virgin site at Nuri, his successor Tanwetamani was interred at el Kurru. But for the historical record, it would certainly have been assumed that Taharqo followed Tanwetamani.

Incidentally, this casts an interesting light on the contemporary perception of Taharqo who, largely on account of his building activities, appears to have been the mightiest of the Kushite Pharaohs. This was presumably not the view held in the immediate aftermath of his death. Tanwetamani may have been trying to disassociate himself from Taharqo whom he may have tried, not unreasonably, to blame for the débâcle which led to the loss of Egypt.

4 *Pyramids at Jebel Barkal. (D. A. Welsby)*

Reisner's seriation of the royal burials provides a logical sequence of rulers through-out the use of the cemetery at Nuri. With the move to Meroe, however, the situation becomes very complex. Problems are caused by the presence of pyramids at Jebel Barkal a little to the northwest of the sacred mountain (fig. 4). Architecturally these can be divided into two distinct groups, both of which can be closely paralleled at Meroe. That the Jebel Barkal pyramids, some of which certainly cover the burials of ruling kings and queens, are broadly contemporary with the similar monuments at Meroe seems inescapable. The significance of this observation has led to a number of expla-nations, none of which appear to be at all convincing. Reisner assumed that the Barkal royal tombs related to two royal dynasties at Napata independent from that at Meroe. A number of facts make this interpretation implausible. The son of a ruling queen, who was buried at Jebel Barkal, is interred at Meroe.[6] Arnekhamani, who has been thought to have been buried at Barkal, built a temple (fig. 5) to the Lion God Apedemak at Musawwarat es Sufra 60 km to the south-west of Meroe.[7] Although throughout Kushite history there was a tendency for rulers and their families to be buried in the

5 *The Lion Temple at Musawwarat es Sufra. (D. A. Welsby)*

cemeteries occupied by their predecessors, this was not an invariable rule. We simply do not know why certain rulers opted to be buried elsewhere.

Reisner wrote in 1923: 'Personally I feel that the main outlines of the chronology of the whole kingdom are now so well established that they form a basis for a reconstruction of the obscure dating of Ethiopia.'[8] However, what emerges from this short foray into the minefield of Kushite chronology is that nothing is certain and the whole chronological edifice could be seriously weakened at any time by the discovery of new evidence. We are, however, indebted to Reisner, and to the later scholars who have sought to refine his arguments, for providing us with some semblance of order. The lack of a secure chronology is only keenly felt when one seeks to relate events in Kush directly with those in the outside world. Otherwise a relative chronology is sufficient for us to recognise developmental trends in a wide range of Kushite activities and products.

Kings and queens

Although most of the rulers of Kush were male, there is clear evidence for the presence of queens on the throne, and there is no reason to suspect that they were not ruling in their own right. On occasion there may have been joint rulers and certainly on a number of temple reliefs the king and queen both occupy a prominent position. The equal status of King Natakamani and Queen Amanitore is indicated by her regalia, by the activities she is shown to be performing and, most graphically, in the crowning ceremony.[9] On the pylon of the temple built by these rulers at Naqa, the king and queen are of equal stature and assume identical poses on either side of the doorway as they smite their enemies (fig. 6).

In the Bible there is a reference in Acts 8:27 to a 'eunuch of great authority under Candace, queen of the Ethiopians'. A number of other ancient sources record the Kandake, the female ruler of Kush, the title being on occasion mistaken for the ruler's

6 *The pylon of the Lion Temple at Naqa. (D.A. Welsby)*

name. Another ancient source informs us that the Kandake was the king's mother, although this may be interpreted to mean the mother of the crown prince, i.e. the mother of the next king.[10] Of the ruling queens a number inherited the throne on the deaths of their husbands, the king. This does not appear to have been the case with Queen Shanakdakhete, the first ruling queen known to us, and Queen Amanishakheto. Reliefs depicting these queens incorporate special iconography designed to integrate these women into the kingship ideology and to establish their legitimacy in this essentially male office.[11]

Co-regencies have been suggested for a number of XXVth Dynasty rulers and for several later monarchs.[12] In no case is the evidence clear and we know of a number of occasions where the new ruler occupied a vacant throne. There has been some dispute as to whether Shebitqo associated Taharqo with him on the throne in the later years of his reign, but this is now doubted. The other supposed instances of co-regencies are also open to re-interpretation.[13]

Owing to our ignorance of familial relationships within the Kushite royal family or families it is difficult to formulate the rules of succession which were followed. A consideration of the chronology of the earliest Kushite rulers together with the genealogy of their consorts and with the royal ancestors recorded on the stela of Aspelta suggests that only two generations separate Alara from the individual buried in Ku.Tum.1. This would suggest that brother succeeded brother and would shorten the short chronology even further.[14]

The evidence we have indicates a rather ad hoc system, even within the very restricted time span of the XXVth Dynasty. It is neither the son of the reigning king nor the son of his queen who automatically assumes power. The system is, therefore, neither patrilineage nor matrilineage. However, the importance of the matrilineal line is stressed on a number of occasions, most notably by Aspelta, who traces his ancestors back through seven generations of the female line.[15] On occasion it may have been more politic to claim descent from one particular monarch rather than from another, but, if so, the details behind this reasoning elude us. Over the whole history of Kush a number of different claims to legitimate succession may have been developed, used and discarded. It would be extremely surprising if extra-legal claims to the throne did not also occur and successful usurpers would have quickly thrown up a smoke-screen behind which their propaganda machines will have glossed over their methods of obtaining power.

The historian Diodorus, writing in the first century BC, provides an interesting insight into the stability of the Kushite monarchy. He records that it was customary among the Ethiopians (Kushites) for the comrades of the king to commit suicide on his death. 'And it is for this reason ... that a conspiracy against the king is not easily raised among the Ethiopians, all his friends being equally concerned both for his safety and their own.'[16]

A number of inscriptions shed light on the nature of the succession of particular kings. Taharqo, on an inscription found at Kawa, describes how he was invited to join

King Shebitqo, since the king 'loved him more than all his brethren'. The inscription further states that 'I [Taharqo] received the crown in Memphis after the Hawk had soared to heaven'.[17] Taharqo does not appear to have been the son of Shebitqo and his exact relationship to him is unclear.

The circumstances surrounding the accession of Aspelta are recounted on an inscription set up by that king at Jebel Barkal (fig. 7).[18] Although Aspelta was the brother of the recently deceased king, he was not the only claimant to the throne, being only one amongst the 'royal brethren'. On the death of the king it is clear that there was no obvious successor. A group of twenty-four great officers of the kingdom appear to have been in charge during the interregnum.[19] Perhaps as a politic measure rather than as the norm, they first consulted the army, which was assembled at Napata. However, the army, we are told, although stating that the new king should come from within its ranks (if this is the correct interpretation of 'our lord abideth amongst us') was unable to decide. The choice was then left to Amun, i.e. to the priests of Amun. Still all did not go smoothly, as at the initial stage of the selection process none of the royal brethren was 'chosen by Amun'. Aspelta was then taken from among the royal brethren, presumably after a lot of behind-the-scenes wrangling, and presented to Amun.

On the inscription much is made by Aspelta of his royal ancestry, which presumably set him apart from the other candidates. There may have been more material considerations which swayed the priests of the Temple of Amun. The onerous nature of the deal which Aspelta entered into may account for the friction that has been thought to have later developed between him and those same priests. As we knew nothing of the other candidates, it is difficult to be certain that Aspelta was the strongest of the eligible princes and that this was the criterion used to decide the succession.[20]

Diodorus reported that the candidates for kingship were chosen by the priesthood, the priests selecting the most valorous of the Kushites, the final decision being made by the god.[21] The general principle of allowing the god to choose the new ruler from among the most suitable men echoes the events surrounding the accession of Aspelta.

An inscription of Irike-Amanote at Kawa records that he was at Meroe 'residing among the king's brethren' when King Talakhamani died. The moment of the king's death seems to have been taken as an opportunity for the desert tribe of the Rhrhs to revolt. As with the succession of Aspelta, it is clear from this inscription that there was no designated successor and that there was considerable confusion in the interregnum. In this potentially dangerous situation it was the army which was the arbiter of royal power, entering the palace and presenting the throne to Irike-Amanote.[22] Was this an exceptional situation where prompt action was required in the face of a military threat? It is clear that the priority was for a supreme commander to take control of the army.

The evidence we have suggests that, even with a 'legal' succession, there were no hard and fast rules for the choice of the next monarch and this can only have led to confusion and potential or actual conflict during the transfer of power.

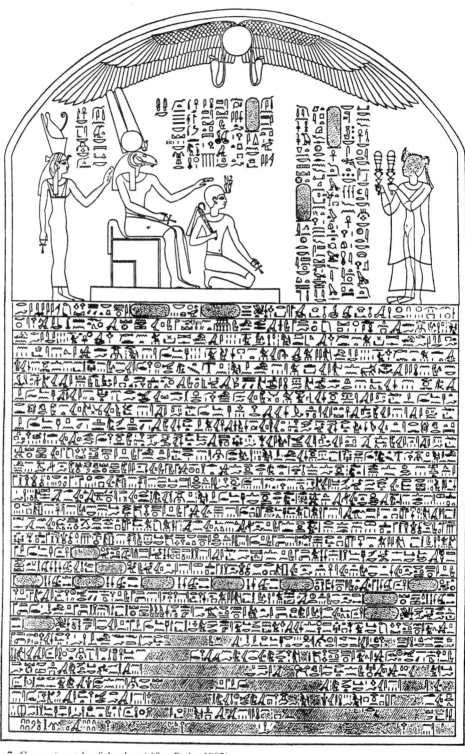

7 *Coronation stela of Aspelta. (After Budge 1907)*

Opposite 8 *Bronze statuette of Taharqo, from Kawa, showing the double uraeus. (BM, EA 63595)*

The royal insignia

In reliefs, sculpture and wall painting a wide range of insignia denote kingship and the status of other members of the royal family. Chief among these are the crowns, of which twenty-two different types have been noted.[23] The most characteristic and uniquely Kushite crown consisted of a skullcap, perhaps of metal or leather, with a diadem supporting two *uraei* (sacred serpents) and with streamers falling down the back (fig. 8). The double *uraei* have caused much comment. Only the pharaoh Akhenaten and very rarely a few post-XXVth Dynasty Egyptian kings are shown similarly attired, although for royal women it is much more common.

Why the Kushites adopted this unusual iconography is unknown, although it is firmly rooted in Egyptian tradition. It is clear that the two *uraei* are another way of representing the union of Upper and Lower Egypt, more familiarly depicted by the combination of the White and Red crowns. A number of the double *uraei* actually wear these crowns, proving that there is no attempt to symbolise the union of Egypt and Kush. The provision of the two *uraei* is by no means universal and a number of Kushite kings have a single *uraeus* and sometimes no *uraeus* at all.[24]

A number of royal ladies of the earlier Kushite period are depicted on reliefs with a headdress consisting of three long plumes each springing from the small figure of a goddess, Tfenet(?), Isis and Nephthys (fig. 9). Ladies of lesser importance only had one plume.[25] Clothing was also an important feature of royal insignia (see below).

The ruler and the priesthood

The important role of the priests of Amun at Jebel Barkal in the accession of Aspelta has been already discussed. Many scholars have accepted that subsequently Aspelta and the priesthood were in conflict. A second stela of Aspelta recounts how he imposed his nominee, Mediken, wife of Anlamani, as high priestess.[26] This in itself need not reflect animosity. It may have been the prerogative of the king to honour the wife of his predecessor in this way. At an earlier date, during the XXVth Dynasty, the person chosen to be the god's wife of Amun (high priestess) at Thebes was a political appointee, usually a close female relative of the king.[27] At Kawa and elsewhere a number of inscriptions record kings appointing female members of their families to important priesthoods.

The main evidence adduced to support the theory of conflict between the crown and the priesthood at this time is twofold. At Jebel Barkal the king's name was removed from his two stelae. However, a stela, probably from across the river at Sanam, and reliefs on the walls of the Temple of Amun at that site have not been so mutilated. A situation has been envisaged where the king and priests sat facing each other across the river, the king being impotent to prevent the mutilation of his stelae at Barkal.[28] This does seem rather implausible.

Another inscription from Jebel Barkal, known as the Excommunication Stela, has

Opposite **9** *Lady with plumes, from Kawa.* (*BM, EA 1771*)

had the royal name removed. Which ruler erected this stela is unknown. This has not prevented scholars ascribing the text to Aspelta and using it as further evidence for this conflict. This stela records that, in the second year of the reign, the king forbade a group, presumably of priests, to enter the temple on account of the terrible deed they had planned there, the slaying of a man without the command of Amun.[29]

The removal of the royal names of Piye and Aspelta may be related to the wanton destruction of the statues of Kings Taharqo, Tanwetamani, Senkamanisken, Anlamani and Aspelta. These statues, the latest of which is that of Aspelta, were removed from Temple B500, the main Amun temple, and dumped, some in a room on the north side of Temple B800 and others in a pit immediately outside the doorway of Temple B500.[30] Is this evidence of the wrath of the priests of Amun against some of the most important and powerful champions of Amun, against the men who had conquered and held Egypt and who had built, enlarged and endowed numerous temples of Amun from Napata to Thebes and beyond? The destruction seems more likely to reflect an intense desire to strike from the historical record a hated dynasty and the most likely motive for that is the accession of a rival dynasty to the throne. Why only the royal names and not the whole stelae were destroyed remains a mystery. Perhaps it was sacrilegious to remove any inscription set up to Amun, whosoever was the dedicator. That the name of Piye was reinstated on his stelae at Barkal,[31] while that of Aspelta was not, is particularly interesting.

There can be little doubt that there was later conflict between the ruler and the religious establishment. The Excommunication Stela, although rather obscure in its meaning, may be interpreted as a king's reaction to a plot to bring about his assassination by a group of priests. Whether this was an 'extra-legal' assassination or was connected with the practice of regicide, but carried out against a king who was not yet ready to join his father Amun, is unknown.

The practice of regicide in Kush is recorded by the Greek historian Diodorus. The priests of Meroe were apparently able to decide when the king should die and by the force of tradition the king accepted their decision as having divine authority. He recounts how Ergamenes [Arkamani] and his troops entered the sacred precinct and slew the priests, putting an end to their historic power.[32] It is particularly interesting to note the prominence given to the religious establishment at Meroe, and not that at Jebel Barkal. The veracity of Diodorus' statement has been doubted, but there is no other evidence to bear on this question one way or the other.

The removal of the royal burial ground from Nuri, a little upstream and across the river from the Temple of Amun, to Meroe must have been a statement of some significance and cannot have been viewed with equanimity by the priesthood at Barkal. Whether it represented an attempt to distance the monarchy from the traditional seat of religious authority in the Kushite state is unknown. It cannot have been a move towards a secular state as the divine mandate claimed by all Kushite rulers for their kingship came from Amun. For a ruler to eschew his close relationship with Amun would have been unthinkable.

The coronation procession

On the east wall of the hypostyle hall in the Temple of Amun built by Taharqo at Kawa is an inscription of Irike-Amanote. After relating the details surrounding the accession of the king it states that the king journeyed from his residence at Meroe to the major religious centres of the realm where he was confirmed in his position of sovereignty and where he swore obedience to his father Amun in the many local guises of the god. There is no mention of the first ceremony taking place in a temple of Amun at Meroe. The Amun Temple M.260, which today is one of the more prominent ruins on the site, developed into the second largest Amun temple in Kush. This building has now been dated to the late third or second century BC[33] and thus was not in existence at the time of the extant coronation inscriptions. Although there is evidence for a much earlier temple of Amun within the Royal Enclosure,[34] this was presumably not accorded a status on a par with the religious institutions in the north.

The king's journey will have taken him on the road across the Bayuda desert, the shortest route between Meroe and Napata. After the ceremonies at Napata he moved on to Krtn, Gematon (Kawa) and Pnubs. Pnubs has usually been identified as Tabo, where there is an Amun temple built probably by Taharqo. However, the discovery at Kerma[35] of the burial of Penamun, priest of Amun at Pnubs, may call this into question. A large religious complex at Kerma, the 'Kom of the Bodegas', dating to the New Kingdom and Kushite periods, has yet to be investigated. The location of Krtn is not known, but it is thought to lie downstream of Napata, perhaps near Korti.[36]

Taharqo had enlarged the Temple of Amun at Jebel Barkal. He built a large temple to Amun at Kawa, and the almost identical temples at Sanam and at Tabo are probably also his work. The temple at Kawa was presumably that visited during the coronation ceremonies. One might, therefore, suggest that the temples at Sanam and Tabo were also built to perform a similar role. Why Sanam and perhaps Tabo are not mentioned in this inscription and on the other coronation stelae is unclear.

These inscriptions indicate that there was a number of equally important centres in the kingdom and that, to receive the divine mandate to rule, a monarch had to visit them all. This calls into question the relevance of the long dispute among modern scholars as to the whereabouts of the capital during the various phases of Kushite history. The importance of the earliest capital at el Kurru seems, on present evidence, to have lapsed. During the XXVth Dynasty Memphis in Egypt was apparently a royal residence and hence a 'capital' of the state.

The coronation journeys reflect the peripatetic movements of the court. The capital of the state was where the royal court happened to be at any one time and the large number of royal palaces dotted throughout the realm indicate that it was constantly shifting. The move from one residence to another may have been on a regular basis dictated by the traditional presence of the king at religious festivals. One of the most important of these, the celebration of the New Year and of the start of the inundation, probably took place at Meroe.[37] After the withdrawal from Egypt there is epigraphic and/or archaeological evidence for royal palaces at Wad ben Naqa, Musawwarat es Sufra, Meroe, Jebel Barkal/Napata, Sanam(?), Krtn, Kawa and Pnubs.[38] Others may yet await recognition. It is interesting to note that, on his stela from Jebel Barkal, Harsiyotef records that he built the house of the king at Napata which had 'become in such a state of ruin that no man can enter therein'.[39]

To an extent, the location of the royal necropolis is not directly related to the seat of political power. As far as we are aware no Kushite monarch was buried in Egypt during the XXVth Dynasty, although the kings must have spent a considerable time on the lower Nile. However, it may be correct to say that royal burials are only found in the vicinity of royal residences. It is now known that the other-worldly importance of el Kurru is related to its probably having been the first 'capital' of Kush. The burial there of a king and his consort, probably in the fourth century BC,[40] may indicate that it retained its temporal importance longer than has been thought. El Kurru should perhaps be considered as a candidate for the location of Krtn with its royal palace. The choice of burial ground probably reflects dynastic traditions.

The rulers as builders

The rulers of Kush were the guardians of the state religion and to them fell the responsibility for the construction and upkeep of the houses of the gods. Although many temples must have been very wealthy and their priesthoods will no doubt have been responsible for routine maintenance, royal inscriptions make much of the piety of the ruler as demonstrated by his building activities. Taharqo laments the state of the Temple of Amun at Kawa, and work of clearing the sacred roadway to the temples there is recorded by Irike-Amanote.[41] Harsiyotef is recorded to have rebuilt a ruined temple at Napata.[42] Kings are also credited with the construction of royal palaces and of their own tombs and funerary monuments.

Royal building activities, on buildings other than an individual's own funerary monument, are directly attested from the reign of Piye until the second century AD. Among the most prolific builders were Taharqo in the early seventh century BC and Natakamani and Amanitore, who lived around the time of Christ. Taharqo's building activities were confined to the northern part of the kingdom, from Sanam north into Egypt. Most of Natakamani and Amanitore's known buildings lie in the Keraba, the western part of the area lying between the rivers Nile and Atbara.

The earliest ruler to have been active in the south was Aspelta, who built temples at Meroe and probably another at Defeia, a few kilometres to the north-east of Khartoum.[43] The most southerly monumental building known to date, perhaps a temple of Mut, Hathor or Isis,[44] may have stood at Soba East where a sandstone block, bearing a relief of the head of Hathor on two faces, has been found.[45] Of the two sphinxes known from the site, one bears a cartouche containing a partly preserved name of a ruler who may have reigned in the second century AD.[46]

Politics and administration

All the evidence indicates that throughout Kushite history the political system used to govern was monarchic. The possible influence of the priesthood of Amun on the ruler has already been noted. The relationship of the monarchs to their peers will presumably have varied depending on the strength of any particular monarch and of the aristocracy. Delegation of authority to other members of the royal family will likewise have varied over time.

It may be assumed that members of the royal family were closely associated with the running of the state. We know that Taharqo led the armies of Kush before he ascended to the throne, as did Akinidad seven centuries later. Aspelta sent his son Khariuwt to Kaned, the location of which is unknown, 'to administer it'.[47]

No ancient source informs us in detail about the administration of Kush. However, this does not mean that we are totally ignorant of the organisation of the administration. On the stela of Aspelta the following officials are noted:

'six trusty captains in the middle of the army of the king
six trusty captains [who are] commandants of the fortress(es)
six overseers (secretaries) of the archives
six nobles [who are] chief treasurers of the royal palace'[48]

These were presumably the most prominent at court, and they were chosen to oversee the election of the new king.

In the northern part of the kingdom it was the practice, particularly in the late second and third centuries AD, for officials to record their careers on their tombstones. We are thus able to identify a large number of administrative posts, to gain some idea of their relative status and, in some cases, of their function. It is evident that there was a complex administrative infrastructure in place. The precise meaning of a number of the titles noted below, however, is unknown.

The area between the Second Cataract and the Ptolemaic/Roman frontier appears to have been an administrative unit as early as the first half of the first century BC and was under the control of a *pesto* (viceroy). At that time the residence of the *pesto* was at Faras, but in the first century AD it was moved north to the vicinity of Karanog. The *pesto*, who at least in the third century AD appears to have held office for a term of three years, was appointed by and was responsible directly to the king. It was not uncommon for a retired *pesto* to be promoted to the higher rank of *pqr* or *pqr qori-s*, which was held at Meroe.

The *pesto* acted as the king's representative in the northern province and was presumably responsible for the day-to-day running of the province and for the mundane contacts with the foreign power to the north. The very high status of this office is confirmed by the presence of royal incumbents. In the late first century BC the 'crown prince' Akinidad was *pesto*. This may have been connected with the very special situation arising from the invasion of Kush by the Romans.

Special appointments could also be made by the king. Hllhror was one such official who, after serving as *pesto* in the north, was recalled to Meroe and then sent back to his old province as *qoreñ-lh*.[49]

A number of other upper echelon posts were held by the group who could aspire to the post of *pesto*. Beneath these were two further tiers of administrators. The lowest tier was made up of the local officials, whose titles are often qualified with a toponym, presumably the regional centres of administration, and these are to be found spaced equidistantly along the river valley. Among them are Derr, Karanog, Shablul, and Gezira Dabarosa. The middle tier of officials consisted of those involved in the civil administration of the royal and temple domains. Also included in this group are the middle priestly ranks.

The careers of Abratoye and Natemahar illustrate the diversity of posts which could be held, many of them concurrently.[50] Abratoye, who was buried at Karanog, was one of the most important figures in the third century AD. He is first active between the Second and Third Cataracts, when he is *tbqo* from Akilek to Sedeinga. He is then governor of Faras and *pelmos abd-li-s* ('general of the land'). At the same time he was probably also prophet of the sanctuary of the god Amanap at Qasr Ibrim and high priest or administrator in the dependent sanctuaries between Ibrim and Boqh. The culmination of his career was the post of *pesto*.

Natemahar spent his entire working life between the Second and Third Cataracts and resided at Sedeinga, where he died. During his career he held all the important civil and military posts in this area. He was *sleqeñ* of Sedeinga, *womnis kroro*, *athmo* of Amara, *aribet* of Sedeinga and *pelmos abd-li-s*. There was no *pesto* in this area, a *sleqeñ* being the highest official.

Of particular interest is the family of the Wayekiye, who seem to have been the most powerful group in Lower Nubia from the end of the second century AD to the late fourth. The first known member of the clan, Sesen, was a priest of Isis at Philae and later a royal scribe of Kush. The dual nature of the administration of the Dodekaschoinos by Rome and Kush is frequently indicated during the third century. By the middle of the century the posts held by the Wakekiye suggest that Kush was in full control of the whole of the area, and was conducting its administration and continuing business with Egypt as in the past.

Funerary stelae, apart from those associated with royal burials, are extremely rare in the south, perhaps largely the result of the fact that far fewer excavations have been conducted to the south of the Dal Cataract. Moreover, funerary stelae set up in the more southerly regions of the country rarely carry details of the career of the deceased. We are thus ignorant of the administrative posts held in those areas. This has led in the past to scholars assuming that Lower Nubia had a special status and that it was administered in a totally different and much more complex way than the rest of the kingdom. It is, however, just as likely that it is the types of funerary stelae that differ rather than the form of administration. Whatever the correct interpretation of the evidence, we are almost totally ignorant of how the southern regions of Kush were administered, if indeed the administration was different from that of the north.

A number of inscriptions indicate that the southern part of the kingdom was divided into nomes, as was the north, and it was the capitals of these nomes which were visited by the king during the coronation procession and presumably thereafter throughout the reign. The nomes, at least in some cases, do not appear to have embraced both sides of the river. The nome of Gematon (Kawa) extended at least as far north as Kerma. Pnubs, if it is correctly identified as Tabo, was set on a seasonal island midway between the two and was also a nome capital; its nome can only have lain on the opposite side of the river. Likewise Napata (Jebel Barkal) and Sanam, each with their large temples of Amun, may have been in different nomes. At least one further nome probably lay to the south of Meroe in the area known as 'the end of Kenset'.[51] The larger nomes were subdivided into smaller units. This system, following the Egyptian pattern, was probably first organised by Taharqo. On the form of the earlier administrative system we have no information.[52]

In the south the administration will have been faced with the problem of dealing with a large mobile population of transhumers (seasonal migrants) and nomads. Many of these groups may have spent a part of the year outside Kushite territory in their quest for fodder and water. The lifestyle of these peoples demands freedom of movement and they have frequently been a disruptive element in basically sedentary societies. Attempts can be made to adopt a preclusive frontier policy, whereby the nomads and transhumers are denied access, but this frequently produces a constant state of hostilities.

A more equitable solution is to allow these groups to move as the climatic conditions dictate, but to control those movements. In North Africa the Romans achieved this by controlling the oases and by blocking all but a few access routes into their provinces. The transhumers could thus be controlled and presumably taxed along these officially designated routes. The Kushites appear to have adopted a not dissimilar system. By the construction of hafirs (reservoirs) they would have determined the points at which the non-sedentary population was forced to congregate for a part of the year. The presence of the State at these hafirs was demonstrated by the construction of temples and the erection of statuary, some of it, as at Basa (fig. 10), clearly designed to demonstrate the military prowess of Kush.

Empire or confederacy?

The monolithic nature of the Kushite administration has recently been called into question. At issue is whether the ruler of Kush was only the most powerful among a number of kings who controlled directly areas within the Kushite state, or whether he ruled alone. The evidence summarised above strongly suggests that, at least in the area between the Meroe and the northern frontier, the Kushite king directly controlled his domains through his administrative machinery. On the periphery of the empire the situation may have been rather different, the Kushite ruler exercising varying degrees of control or influence over local potentates.

10 *Statue of a lion attacking a bound captive, from Basa.*
(Courtesy of the National Museum, Khartoum; photo D. A. Welsby)

The situation may have varied over time. In the earliest period a number of rulers may have assumed control simultaneously, but certainly by the XXVth Dynasty the rulers who were buried at el Kurru and Nuri had vanquished whatever other claims to kingship there may have been. During the latest phases of the kingdom local élites and intrusive elements in the population would have had greater opportunity to move towards independence, and it may be this trend which largely caused the break-up of the state. In the heyday of the kingdom such secessionist tendencies would have been held in check, except during the short-lived periods of disputed succession of which we are largely ignorant.

The army

The role of the army in the maintenance of the territorial integrity of the state of Kush must have been of great importance. It is, therefore, much to be regretted that we know virtually nothing of it. We are not even sure of the status of the army, whether it was a professional force like the Roman army or a peasant militia raised in times of need. Some professional element must have existed; that there was a permanent unit charged with the protection of the ruler seems highly likely.

In most ancient, and in many modern, societies the relationship between the army and the ruler is a close one. The ruler's authority, although legally derived 'from the gods', ultimately rests with the army. The most effective way to establish and maintain the bond between the ruler and the army is for the ruler, as commander in chief, to lead his army to victory. Even in a highly legalistic society, like that of the Romans, the maintenance of this bond was all important and great pains were taken to strengthen it. The potential power of a successful military commander, and the threat he could pose to the legitimate authority, were amply demonstrated during the later Roman Empire, as they had been by the immediate successors of Alexander the Great.

In this context it is very surprising to read on the great inscription of Irike-Amanote at Kawa that the new king remained behind in his palace while the army fought the Rhrhs.[53] Other kings, even before they had performed their coronation procession around the nomes of the realm, led the army on victorious campaigns against the tribal neighbours of the state.

The maintenance of the army's support can rely heavily on the success of the ruler or of his appointed lieutenant. On a number of occasions Kushite prowess on the field of battle left much to be desired, but we have no indication that this had political repercussions or that the army elevated a more suitable or bellicose person from among its own ranks to assume power.

There is a little evidence that members of the royal family held high military commands, but whether this was the norm is uncertain. Taharqo and Akinidad are the most famous of these warlords. It may have been Akinidad who had the unenviable job of facing the Roman armies of Augustus in the 20s BC – although there is considerable dispute as to whether he was actually a contemporary of these events.

A small number of military titles are known. In the sixth century BC perhaps the most important were the commandants of the fortress(es), who played a prominent role in the election of King Aspelta.[54] Whether the presence of six men with this title reflects the real existence at that time of fortresses within the kingdom is unclear. Several hundred years later we hear of a 'general of the land', a 'general of Meroe' (*pelmos Bedewe-te*) and of a '*strategos* of the water'. These upper echelon officers did not usually have a mixed civil and military career: it appears that both military and civil power was invested in the hands of one man only on rare occasions. Akinidad was *pesto* and commander concurrently. Bekemete appears to have followed a military career before being elevated to *pesto* in the mid–third century AD.[55] Of the lower ranks an inscription from Dakka mentions a 'chief of the bowmen'.[56]

The people to the south of Aswan played a prominent part in the battles fought by the Egyptian pharaohs. They were famed as archers, and this concentration on archery is a feature of Kushite armies. The stela of Harsiyotef records a number of campaigns in which the king sent out his bowmen to do battle with a variety of foes. Nastasen also sent his bowmen against the chief Kambasuten and against a number of rebel groups.[57] The Harsiyotef inscription also mentions the use of horsemen. Kushite cavalry may be depicted on the south wall of the podium at the Sun Temple, Meroe, where there are several galloping horsemen armed with lances and wearing some sort of helmet.[58] There is no evidence for the use of the camel in Kushite warfare and this may be compared with the rarity of *dromedarii* in the Roman army, which also operated in similar arid areas.[59]

Herodotus, writing in the fifth century BC, describes the Kushite soldiers who were part of the army of Xerxes as follows:

> The Ethiopians were clothed in panthers' and lions' skins, and carried long bows, not less than four cubits in length, made from branches of palm trees, and on them they placed short arrows made of cane; instead of iron, they were tipped with a stone, which was made sharp, and of that sort on which they engrave seals. Besides this they had javelins, and at the tip was an antelope horn, made sharp like a lance; they had also knotted clubs. When they were going into battle they smeared one half of their body with chalk, and the other half with red ocre.[60]

Archaeology graphically confirms some of Herodotus' observations. Although objects of copper-alloy and iron are known from early in the Kushite period, arrowheads of stone are a common find in royal tombs as well as in the more humble graves. Among the stones employed were flint, quartz and carnelian. Arrowheads of this type have also been found during the excavations of domestic buildings at Meroe.[61] Arrow shafts made of reed have also been recovered.

Over 400 years later Strabo, describing the Kushite troops that opposed the Roman army, noted that they were badly armed. Most were equipped with a large shield made of raw hides and hatchets. Some, however, had pikes or swords. Elsewhere he notes that the Kushites used bows of wood four cubits long and hardened by fire.[62]

Although a large number of Kushite graves containing weapons have been excavated, we have no direct evidence that the incumbents of those graves were members of the regular army or were even soldiers. Weapons have been found occasionally in the graves of children, and at Sanam in the grave of a fish![63]

The identity of a man buried with late Kushite pottery at Wadi es Sebua, who had an iron arrowhead still lodged in his thorax, is unknown.[64] Two other individuals who met a similar fate, one shot through the back, were buried in the cemetery at Karanog.[65]

From the weaponry recovered from graves the evidence for the importance of archery is overwhelming, although much of this ordnance may have been for hunting. As well as the stone arrowheads noted above, arrowheads of iron and copper-alloy are common. On a number of occasions a single copper-alloy head has been found with a large number made of iron. This has led one excavator to assign a ritual significance to the copper-alloy head: it perhaps had amuletic value to increase the power of the iron-tipped arrows.[66]

The metal arrowheads take a variety of forms (fig. 11). There are simple leaf-shaped designs; others have one or two barbs; there are rare examples of so-called Scythian arrowheads, which are of triangular section; and one has a four-edged blade.[67] Other examples have multiple barbs and may have been used as harpoons.

Arrowheads are usually tanged, although a few socketed examples are known. Some of the best-preserved arrows were found in the tomb beneath pyramid Beg.W.122 at Meroe. They consisted of an iron head set into a short hardwood shaft and held by an iron ferrule. The rest of the shaft was of reed into which the hardwood shaft was socketed. The special quiver provided for these arrows and the discoloration on the arrowheads have been thought to indicate that these were poisoned arrows.[68] This quiver is a

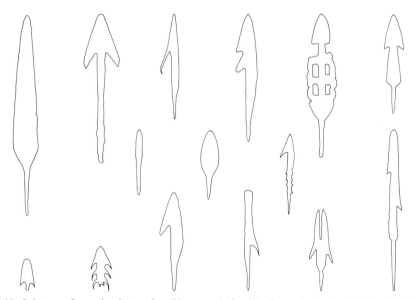

11 *Selection of arrowhead types from Karanog. (After Woolley and Randall-MacIver 1910)*

copper-alloy cylinder suspended from a chain and with bells attached. Other examples are of leather, often very elaborately decorated. Many examples are known dating to the end of the Kushite period or slightly beyond it.[69]

Remains of bows are very rare. In tomb Beg.W.106 at Meroe eight short tapering tubes of gold are decorated to represent the lashing towards the end of the bow and another of the same type was found in Beg.W.453.[70] A wooden bow, 640 mm in length and a maximum of 15 mm in section, and fragments of two others were found in the tomb of Queen Amanikhatashan (Beg.N.18) at Meroe.[71] As well as the long bows described by Strabo the composite bow is also seen on reliefs. This is particularly clear on a graffito at Musawwarat es Sufra, where Apedemak is dispatching very large single barbed arrows, with devastating force, from a composite bow into the back of a fleeing enemy.[72]

Closely connected with archery are small tapering stone rings which were used as archer's looses. These are of two main types. The ceremonial type is too large to have been functional. Examples are clearly visible on temple reliefs worn by kings, queens and gods. This type continued to be used beyond the end of the Kushite kingdom; very elaborate inlaid examples were recovered from the royal burials at Ballana.[73] The functional examples have frequently been found *in situ* on the thumb of the right hand in burials throughout Nubia.[74] Although most of the extant examples are of stone, one made of glass was recovered from tomb Beg.W.106 at Meroe, and wooden looses have been found at Jebel Adda and Qasr Ibrim.

The presence of the archer's loose implies the use of the Mongolian release, where the thumb holds the bowstring, rather than two or more fingers being used, as in the Mediterranean release. It has been suggested that the Mongolian release with the use of archer's looses was introduced into the Roman world from central Asia by the Huns in the later fourth century AD, although they were present on the middle Nile much earlier.[75]

Spear or lance heads, one of the latter with a hollow iron shaft,[76] are frequently recovered from graves, as well as rare examples of swords. A sword recovered from tomb Beg.W.134 at Meroe, unfortunately published without any measurements, appears to be a long thin weapon with parallel sides and with a pointed tip.[77] A similar weapon with a rounded pommel at the end of the hilt is depicted on a relief at the Sun Temple at Meroe in the right hand of a warrior, who wears the scabbard suspended by a strap high on his right side.[78] A clay mould found at Kawa[79] will have produced a very short sword or dagger with a blade approximately 265 mm in length.

Prince Arikhankharer is shown wielding an axe on a sandstone relief probably from Meroe,[80] and axe heads, albeit not of this type, have been found in Kushite graves. Among the types represented is a curious lunate form which may be of a ceremonial nature. One is depicted on a relief at the Sun Temple at Meroe, and examples have been recovered from graves at Meroe, Faras, Abu Geili and el Hobagi.[81]

There is very little evidence for the use of body armour by the Kushites. The war god Apedemak and a number of rulers are depicted on reliefs wearing what appears to be scale armour.[82] However, there is no evidence that this was actually armour. This type of costume is common in Egyptian iconography, particularly on representations of Amun, in contexts where the wearing of armour would not be apposite. No armour of this type has been recovered from excavation on Kushite sites. In grave G64 at Karanog robbers had used a cuirass to block up their entrance hole into the tomb. The most logical source for this cuirass was from among the grave goods in the tomb itself. The cuirass was made of leather with the hair left on the outer side. The leather has been worked up from within into a decorative relief pattern of knobs and bars.[83] The use of shields is noted in the ancient sources. Graffiti at Musawwarat es Sufra show warriors with large sub-rectangular shields.[84] Shield bosses have occasionally been identified in the archaeological record.

During the XXVth Dynasty the Kushites were faced with the problems of conquering walled cities. They cannot be expected to have had any expertise in this derived from their own experience and presumably made use of Egyptian experts. After the withdrawal from Egypt they would have had little occasion to practise siege warfare.

The area to the south of the Egyptian frontier was an important source of elephants for the armies of the Ptolemies, allowing them to match the Indian elephants of the Seleucids. It is likely that many of these animals came from the realm of the Kushites. Arrian records that before elephants were employed in warfare by the Macedonians and Carthaginians, they were used by the Ethiopians [Kushites] and the Indians.[85] There are also other references to the use made by the Ethiopians of war elephants and their prowess as mahouts, but whether we are justified in equating these Ethiopians with the Kushites is unclear. The elephant is depicted in Kushite art. At Musawwarat es Sufra reliefs of elephants are common. One of these shows a king riding an elephant. On the northwest wall of the Lion Temple a file of elephants leads prisoners on ropes (fig. 12).[86] Among the rare accounts of battles between Kushites and the outside world there is, however, no record of elephants being employed.

There is again no evidence that the chariot was used in a military context, although light two-wheeled horse-drawn vehicles are depicted in processions (fig. 75.4).[87]

It is difficult to assess the effectiveness of the Kushite army, as we have so few accounts of pitched battles and the information we have was written by the enemy and is hence inevitably biased. Although the final result of the clashes between Kushite and Assyrian armies was defeat for the Kushites, they did gain at least one victory over the Assyrians led by Esarhaddon in 674 BC.[88] Against the armies of Rome the Kushites seem to have made little impression. Strabo writes that in the engagement at Pselchis in 23 BC the Kushites soon fled, being both badly led and badly armed.[89]

Their earlier activities during the conquest of Egypt under the rulers of the XXVth Dynasty seem to have been marked with greater success, but here they were fighting local rulers and the operations may have been on a relatively small scale. The main threat to the Kushite state was that posed by nomadic raiding parties. To combat such assailants the Kushite bowman and horseman will have been ideal.

The success of the Kushite army can perhaps best be assessed by reference to the survival of their state for over a thousand years. Without an effective military force it is

12 *Prisoners leading elephants, Lion Temple, Musawwarat es Sufra. (After Hintze 1978)*

unlikely that this would have been feasible. As impediments to major invading armies from the north due credit, however, must also be given to the harsh nature of the country, the climate and the scarcity of water which defined closely predictable invasion routes.

The defence of the frontiers of Kush

The kingdom of Kush had a frontier of vast length relative to its area and was in this respect very similar to Egypt. However, the area of rich agricultural land at its disposal was considerably less than that of its northern neighbour. Its population was, therefore, probably much smaller and the potential threats to its frontiers greater.

Throughout their history the Kushites had to deal with a potential large-scale threat only on their northern frontier and the invasion route was clearly defined. It was, therefore, feasible to make provision for the defence of that frontier by placing garrisons in strongly fortified positions along the river. Towards the end of the life of the kingdom the Axumites may have posed a threat to the southern and south-eastern frontiers. In the rainlands of central Sudan the invasion routes are by no means as clearly defined and defence against a possible large-scale invasion would consequently have been much more difficult to mount; we have no evidence that such steps were taken.

However, the greatest problem facing the Kushites on their frontiers was not the threat of invasions which, as we shall see below, were extremely rare occurrences, but that of small-scale incursions. The epigraphic evidence for a number of these is discussed in Chapter 3. Such incursions could happen at any point along the frontier, small bands not being constrained by logistical factors, such as the presence of water, in the same way as a large army. It would thus have been impossible for the Kushites to have placed their army in frontier installations to provide a preclusive frontier in the same way that the Romans did in north-western Europe, for example.

In similar situations, where Rome was faced with a low-level threat from the semi-desert areas beyond her frontiers, as in the provinces of Numidia and Mauritania Caesariensis in North Africa, troops were concentrated in forts at regular intervals along the frontier. The linear barrier, the *Fossatum Africae* in Numidia, was designed to funnel the transhuming tribes into particular corridors, so that their movements across the frontier could be controlled. On the desert frontier of Tripolitania troops were placed at the oases, so as to block the major access routes from the south. In

Arabia troops were also concentrated in forts at regular intervals in the frontier zone.

In the Eastern Desert of Egypt, Roman military installations were built along the roads leading from the Nile valley to the Red Sea and a very limited military presence was maintained in the valley itself.

Treaties with the peoples beyond the frontier were the only guarantee of maintaining peace. In Egypt, as elsewhere, the Romans used diplomacy to ensure peace on the frontiers. The threat to Kush in the desert regions of the north will have been very similar to those faced by Egypt. To the south the problems of frontier security will have been more akin to those encountered by the Romans elsewhere in North Africa. However, the Kushite state could not have afforded a military organisation on a similar scale to that of Rome, and Kushite military installations and evidence for garrisons are virtually unknown. Presumably diplomacy was a major component of frontier policy, together with the occasional show of force. In the AD 60s, when Nero's centurions moved up the Nile beyond Meroe, the Kushite ruler was able to provide them with letters of recommendation to the 'kings' in the region they would enter, indicating the existence of diplomatic contacts between the Kushites and their southern neighbours, who had developed some degree of political organisation.

The historical sources hint at the gradual infiltration of Kushite territory by nomads and their absorption into the state. This may reflect the inability of the Kushites to keep these peoples out and highlights the vulnerability of the kingdom to outside pressure. It may only have been during the final decline of the Kushite state that fortified camps were built to the south-west of Meroe in an attempt to protect the heartlands of the empire from infiltration from Kordofan.

Military installations

The work by Reisner at el Kurru concentrated on the cemeteries, but he also undertook some excavations within the adjacent modern village, revealing structures which may be of early Kushite origin. Unfortunately these are not dated and even their exact location is now uncertain. They include a length of curtain wall with a semicircular projecting tower at the angle, which appears from Reisner's sketch plan to be faced with rough stone and rubble-filled. Elsewhere were two parallel walls, the inner of which was of much greater thickness, each pierced by gateways.[90]

The Royal City at Meroe was enclosed by a stout wall between 3.5 m and 7.75 m thick, constructed throughout of dressed stone blocks. At the angles and along the enceinte were boldly projecting towers, and similar towers may have flanked at least some of the gates. The necessity for these strong walls must have been short-lived as their defensive potential will have been seriously reduced by the construction of buildings against their exterior, including the Temple of Amun. These defences underwent a number of modifications including the addition of at least one gateway.[91] Well before the end of the Kushite period they were dispensed with altogether, being partly demolished and overbuilt in places. There is no evidence that any attempt

13 *Qasr Ibrim. (J. Alexander)*

was made to reinstate them in later, more unsettled times.

In the far north of the kingdom at Karanog, a substantial dwelling called the castle by the excavators, stood to a height of three stories.[92] It is one of at least two large buildings of this type in that settlement. Although it may have been defensible, this may not have been its primary function. It may be compared with the farmhouse-type current in Roman Tripolitania, which is contemporary and of similar plan. They appear to be a house type both well adapted to the climatic conditions and ideal for the ostentatious display of wealth and power. Their defensive capabilities may have been incidental.[93]

Across the river from Karanog, Qasr Ibrim (fig. 13), and Jebel Adda 40 km upstream, are thought to have been built and occupied as military installations. The first defences at Qasr Ibrim have been dated to the late eleventh or early tenth century BC by the radiocarbon dating of the chaff in their mud bricks. Who built these defences is uncertain, but they clearly pre-date the arrival of the Kushites in the area. The defences here had a long sequence of development which only came to an end when the Ottoman garrison abandoned the site in 1810. The first fortifications were built with an outer face of mud bricks, an inner face of stone and with a rubble core. The mud brick outer face was bonded with a pink mortar. Later constructions were of rubble work or of dressed sandstone blocks (fig. 14).[94] There can be no doubt that a number of the later modifications to those defences were undertaken by the Kushites. In 23 BC, when

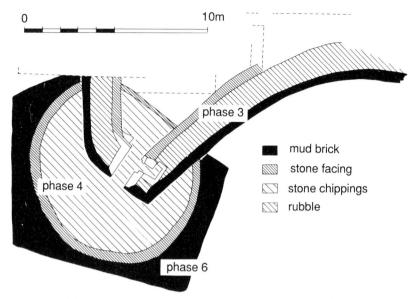

14 *Gateway and later tower at Qasr Ibrim. (After Horton 1991)*

Petronius captured the town, it was described as a strong city, although apparently it was captured at the first assault.[95]

The earliest occupation at Jebel Adda may have been entirely military in character. The site was defended by a massive mud brick wall, perhaps faced with rough sandstone blocks and with towers flanking the gate and spaced along the curtain wall. No wall was provided above the precipitous slope down to the river. Within the defended enclosure were a few signs of activity, consisting mostly of 'byres, storage pits and bins'. In the centre was a more substantial mud brick structure, which appeared to be a dwelling rather than a temple.[96] This phase has been dated to the third century AD, when the high proportion of males buried in the cemetery accompanied by weapons is further support for the military character of the site. As at Qasr Ibrim, there were numerous modifications to the defences, the latest being of dressed stone.

There are a number of other fortified settlements at Faras, Sheik Daud, Ikhmindi, Sabaqura and Kalabsha. Kalabsha and Sabaqura lie to the north of the frontier established by Augustus between the Kushites and Romans until the latter's withdrawal towards the end of the third century AD. All these sites have gateways of identical type. The narrow gate-opening is in the side wall of a projecting square tower, the passageway then turning through a right angle before entering the enceinte. The similarity of these installations suggests that they are broadly contemporary.[97] The defences at Faras are thought to be Kushite;[98] those at the other sites to be of early medieval date! An inscription from Ikhmindi records that the defences were set up 'for the protection of men and beasts' by Tokiltoeton, king of the Nobadae. It further mentions Josephios Exarch of Talmis.[99] Ikhmindi clearly dates long after the end of the Kushite state and

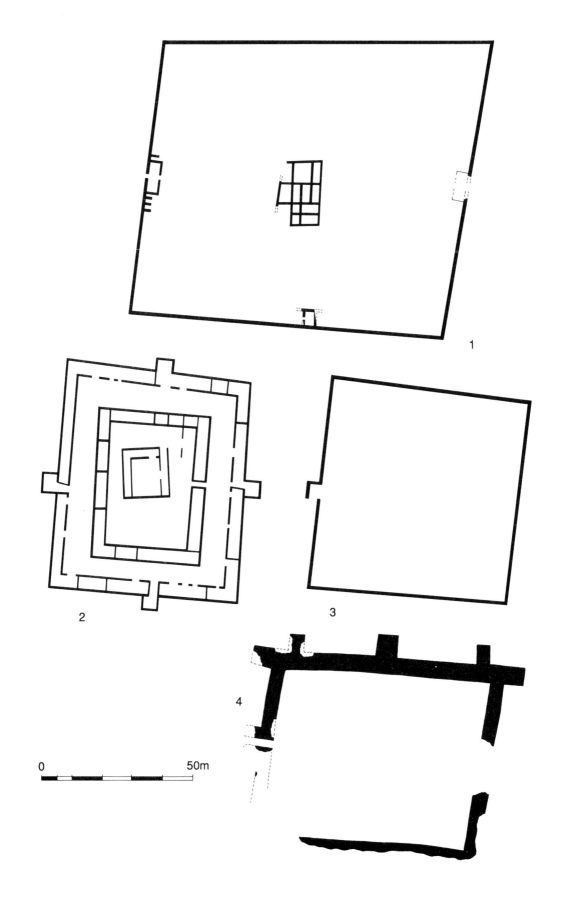

1

2   3

4

0   50m

16 *Umm Ruweim 1 in the Wadi Abu Dom. (D. A. Welsby)*

all these defended sites may have no connection with the Kushite military defence of this area.

To the south, gateways of this type occur on two small square enclosures, at Umm Ruweim 2 (fig. 15.3) and Umm Khafur, and presumably at the nearby site Umm Ruweim 1 in the Wadi Abu Dom.[100] Another site, Umm Kuweib, perhaps to be associated with these, lies 3 km to the east. It has a simple opening on one side of the rectangular enclosure. The plan of Umm Ruweim 1 is the most complex (fig. 15.2). It is a rectangular enclosure with a projecting tower (one containing a gate?) in the middle of each side. Around the inner face of the wall is a continuous range of rooms. Within the enclosure is a small rectangle entered by a simple opening from the south-east and also

Opposite **15** *'Military' installations*
  1 *Hosh el Kafir. (After Lenoble 1992)*
  2 *Umm Ruweim 1. (After Chittick 1955)*
  3 *Umm Ruweim 2. (After Chittick 1955)*
  4 *Fura Wells. (After Crawford 1953a)*

with a range of rooms right around the inside. An isolated building, on a markedly different alignment, occupies the northern part of the inner enclosure (fig. 16).

Whatever the function of these structures, their proximity to each other and the absence of other similar sites in the vicinity indicate that they cannot be military sites associated with the protection of the cross-Bayuda route from Napata to Meroe. Umm Kuweib in particular is unlikely to be a military installation, as it lies very close to high ground from which it could have been dominated. A similar problem is posed by the location of other military installations along the river between the confluence of the Niles and the Dongola Reach. These are too dispersed to suggest any coherent defensive scheme. However, more sites may remain to be discovered. The rectangular stone fort with two opposed entrances and rectangular projecting towers at Fura Wells (fig. 15.4), on the other hand, can be readily understood as defending this important watering point on the cross-Bayuda route. Pottery of late Kushite type is said to have been found within it.[101]

Excavations at these sites have been limited to small-scale work at Hosh el Kafir near el Hobagi[102] and at Jebel Umm Marrahi. The regular layout of Hosh el Kafir (fig. 15.1), with its two opposing gateways flanked by 'guard-chambers' and with a centrally-placed building, brings to mind contemporary Roman military installations.[103] Accommodation and workshop facilities were constructed up against the inner face of the defensive wall. A large number of the functional type of archer's loose were found in these rooms, together with iron arrowheads. There was also evidence for ironworking and domestic activities.

At Jebel Umm Marrahi there are two enclosures, the northernmost of which is defended by a stone wall, 3.4 m thick, enclosing a square area, 83 m a side. At each corner is a projecting tower and there is another tower in the centre of each of the sides.[104] The tower on the river-side houses a gateway of the type seen at Faras and elsewhere. Small-scale excavations here by the University of Khartoum indicated that the structure was of Kushite date.[105] Dangeil, near Berber, has a massive mud brick fortification, faced on the exterior with red brick and associated with much Kushite pottery. The defences, strengthened by at least one large projecting tower, enclose a rectangular area 318 paces by 144 paces.[106] At Jebel Nakharu, across the river from Dangeil, there is a contemporary defended annex.[107]

The people of Kush

The range of representations of the people of Kush in various artistic media gives us a good idea of the physical appearance of a wide spectrum of the population. A large proportion of the individuals depicted are members of the ruling house and a number of their representations are certainly idealised to a greater or lesser extent. What is clear is that many had markedly negroid features and dark skins. Diodorus describes the majority of the 'Ethiopians', particularly those living along the Nile, as being black in colour, with flat noses and woolly hair.[108] By the later Kushite period corpulence among women was obviously a mark of earthly distinction and royal ladies are of considerable size. Goddesses, on the other hand, retained their slim figures.

A limited number of palaeopathological and physical anthropological studies have been undertaken on Kushite human remains. We thus have little data on their general physical well-being and on their life expectancy. Among the rulers, Harsiyotef reigned for at least thirty-five years, while Taharqo reigned for twenty-six, dying at the age of forty-six or forty-seven. King Irike-Amanote was forty-one years old at his accession.[109]

Studies of cemeteries provisionally indicate that life expectancy may have been a few years less than the 20–25 year expectancy in pharaonic Egypt and in the Neolithic period. The peak in adult mortality at Wadi Qitna reached 29 years for males and 28.8 years for females. Females were much more at risk during the child-bearing years but near, or shortly after, their thirtieth year there is a relative increase in male mortality rates. The data derived from cemeteries are complex. Rarely is a whole cemetery excavated and frequently a number of other factors can affect the results, such as the burial of children away from the main cemetery.[110]

The excellent preservation of many of the bodies, where even skin and hair survives, allows the identification of diseases which affect the soft tissues as well as those which leave marks on the bones. It appears that many of the common diseases which afflict the people of the Middle Nile today were already present in Kushite times. In AD 200 the Roman Emperor Septimius Severus visited the Roman-Kushite border 'but he was unable to pass the frontier of Ethiopia because of a pestilence'.[111] Other instances of plague apparently emanating from Kushite territory are noted by Thucydides in 431 BC and in the mid-third century AD.[112]

Kushite fashion

Early Kushite kings are depicted wearing kilts, skirts and shoulder-fastened tunics of traditional Egyptian type, yet combining elements culled from the late Old Kingdom, late XVIIIth Dynasty and Ramesside periods.[113] How closely this reflects the actual clothing they wore in real life is unclear but one may assume that the figural representations, harking back as they do to much earlier Egyptian models, may have little bearing on current fashions. In his tomb Tanwetamani is shown with a long-sleeved white tunic covered in part by a coat, which passes over the right shoulder and has a decorated band of rosettes down its centre (col. pl. 1). This latter garment was one of the insignia of royal power and its fastening formed a part of the coronation rite.[114] In the late third century BC the royal costume was reorganised. Thereafter, kings and queens frequently wear a long gown reaching to the ankles, a finely pleated sash draped across the right shoulder covering the chest, and long tasselled sashes hanging from the shoulder to the level of the calves at front and back.[115]

The upper and middle classes are depicted on their stelae. On a number of these stelae the individuals, both males and females, are shown naked although sometimes bejewelled. Females frequently are bare-breasted but covered from the waist down by a long skirt often finished off with an elaborate openwork fringe.[116]

The *ba*-statue (a part-human, part-bird-like image of the soul of mobility) of the official Malaton wears a long double coat with a broad apron largely covered by a shorter outer garment, draped over the left shoulder, leaving the other shoulder bare.[117] A figure from Shablul is similarly attired but only has a single under-garment.[118]

A number of peasants are depicted on pottery, where they appear to be naked, as Diodorus tells us. He noted that others used sheep-skin loincloths.[119]

Actual remains of clothing are rare but fine collections have been recovered from Qasr Ibrim and the graves at Ballana and Qustul. Among the items are tunics, loin-cloths and wide decorated belts. One complete example of a tunic from a woman's grave, possibly of Kushite date, is a rectangle of cloth with a simple slit for the head. It is decorated with two parallel purple stripes on either side of the neck-hole and with two grain motifs.[120] A fine leather garment, recovered from a grave at Semna South, is decorated with printed motifs relating to the Lion God Apedemak.[121]

Among the many pieces from Qasr Ibrim is part of a pendant apron decorated with embroidered blue cotton thread, thirteen slightly raised discs and a representation of a human face.[122] Such aprons were worn in association with loincloths, the loincloth being placed over the upper part of the apron. At least some of the elaborate decoration of clothing seen on a number of reliefs appears to have been executed in tapestry weave and examples of fabric from Ibrim can be compared closely with the examples depicted on reliefs.[123]

On their feet the Kushites wore shoes or sandals, or they went barefoot. The sandals are secured at the front either by a toe-strap or by a band running across the foot. A strap running behind the heel may also be provided. Royal sandals frequently have a high curving strap, which extends along the foot and joins the sole in front of the toes. The more fancy type of sandal was made of leather, but palm was used for the coarser variety. Many of the sandals found at Karanog were rather elaborate, with the uppers made of coloured leathers, red, yellow, green and white. Stamped decoration was also used. A particularly fine pair from grave G345 had the soles covered with a reticulated pattern with a filling of rosettes, and around the edge of the sole a border of snake pattern. The red leather uppers were stamped with rows of snake pattern.[124]

Jewellery was worn extensively by both males and females and in the early period was distinctly Kushite in style, even when depicted on the very conservative royal statues. Its use does not appear to have been confined to the upper classes and it is a common find in relatively poor graves (fig. 17). A wide range of jewellery was made from all kinds of material, from very fine gold earrings to bead necklaces of ostrich eggshell and massive bangles and anklets of copper-alloy and iron.

As one might expect, closely cropped hair is the most common hairstyle. This is sometimes embellished with a small top knot.[125] In the cemetery at Nag el Arab a number of the adult female bodies had nails and hair stained with henna,[126] a method of personal adornment still used in Sudan today. At Meroe and Naqa royal ladies are depicted on reliefs sporting very long fingernails.

17 *Jewellery recovered by Griffith from the tombs at Faras.*
(Courtesy of The Griffith Institute, Oxford)

Kohl was very commonly used as a cosmetic, and large numbers of often very elaborate tubes of wood and ivory for storing the kohl have been found (fig. 18). It was applied to the face with iron, copper-alloy and wooden sticks.

Evidence for scarification as practised until very recently in northern Sudan is to be found on *ba*-statues, where a number of individuals are depicted with three vertical lines on the cheeks and horizontal lines on the forehead.[127] Similar scars can also be seen on figures used to adorn pottery and on one of the terracotta coffins found at Argin.[128]

Recreation

The evidence both of imported wine amphorae and of wine presses indicates that the Kushites were not averse to imbibing alcohol. The evidence for local wine production

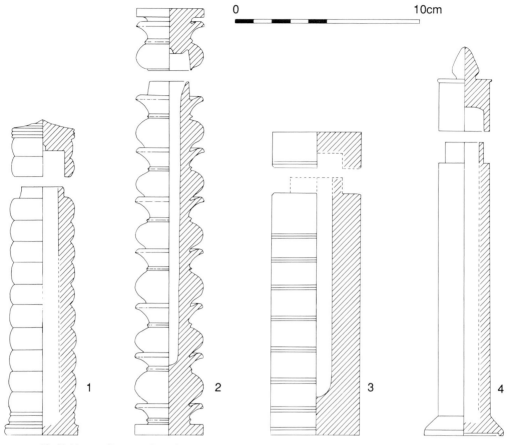

18 *Kohl pots of ivory and wood*
1, 3 and 4 West Cemetery, Meroe. (After Dunham 1963)
2 From Missiminia. (After Vila 1982)

is known only as far south as Kawa, and the availability of imported wine to the less wealthy presumably decreased as one moved away from the production areas. In the far north wine-drinking establishments have been excavated at Sayala and Abd el Qadir but these appear to date after the demise of the Kushite kingdom. The only Kushite 'tavern' is at Qasr Ibrim where a rectangular building of six interconnecting rooms was associated, along with its neighbour, with thousands of fragments of amphorae and goblets. The lower part of two of its external walls is of well dressed stonework, two blocks of which bear carvings of a wine amphora in a stand and of a bunch of grapes. The building retained its function for several centuries thereafter.[129] One of the graffiti at Musawwarat es Sufra shows two people happily drinking through straws from a large pot.[130]

No Kushite musical notation has survived, but a number of representations of musicians and discoveries of actual instruments have been made. In the temple built by

Taharqo at Kawa one wall is decorated with a procession of musicians playing trumpets, horns, double-ended drums (of the type known as a *daluka*, which is suspended around the neck (fig. 19) and six- and seven-string harps with boat-shaped bodies.[131] A bronze object, perhaps to be identified as the mouthpiece of a trumpet, was found on the site.[132] A more complete example from temple IID at Musawwarat es Sufra is made of iron and is 36 cm in length.[133]

During Garstang's excavations at Meroe, he found at least five *auloi* (flutes), and at least four further instruments of this type were found in the tomb of Queen Amanishakheto Beg.N.6 by Reisner. Several pieces of sculpture also from Meroe depict musicians playing this instrument. A study of the physical remains of the instruments indicates that they were of Greek or Graeco-Egyptian manufacture.[134]

A number of royal inscriptions record the dedication of sisters of the king to be sistrum-players for the gods in various temples, and representations of sistra are very common. Music will have been an important feature of religious ritual but its role in a secular context is less well documented.

19 *A daluka-player on a pot from Meroe.*
(Courtesy of the University of Liverpool)

Scenes of dancing are preserved on the east wall of the funerary chapel forecourt of Beg.N.11 at Meroe, but funeral dances hardly come under the heading of recreation. A similar dance, however, is depicted on a pot found at Meroe and suggests that they may not always have been connected with funerary ritual. The dance is accompanied by a man playing a *daluka*.[135]

Among the children's toys known is a doll in terracotta with painted decoration from the grave of a juvenile or a child at Karanog and a wooden mouse from tomb Beg.W.308 at Meroe, the grave of a male child.[136]

Hunting was presumably a popular pastime of the rich. A large number of graffiti on the walls of Musawwarat es Sufra are devoted to this subject. Weapons being used are bows and arrows, throwing sticks and spears. Among the animals hunted are lions and rhinoceroses, while dogs chasing hares are also commonly shown.[137]

CHAPTER THREE

The Kushites on the World Stage

By the later eighth century BC the kings of Kush had assumed the titles of the Pharaoh of Egypt, 'King of Upper and Lower Egypt', and ruled territory stretching from the borders of Palestine to Central Sudan. The rise of Kush and its transformation to a world power is, in its early stages, difficult to document.

The borders of Kush

Frontiers are points of contact between one political, cultural or religious grouping and another, but they can be positioned and defined in a number of ways. They can delineate the furthest point of military conquest, marking a perceived acceptable boundary, the limit to which, given the relative strengths of the combatants, it is possible to go. Alternatively they are the result of a political agreement or compromise between two adjacent powers. However, frontiers can also be very ill-defined, actual control giving way to spheres of influence which can also transcend officially agreed borders. For some periods we may have the confidence to draw the northern frontier of the Kingdom of Kush as a line on the map. This is impossible with the other frontiers of the kingdom, which may well have been the case during the life of the kingdom itself.

The northern frontier

To the north, except during the XXVth Dynasty, the limits of the kingdom were constrained by the political boundary between Kush and Egypt. There were no insurmountable topographical boundaries north of Napata until the Mediterranean coast, while the deserts to the east and west of the Nile provide a logical boundary to the civilisations of the Nile valley.

The southern frontier

To the south, as far as we are aware at least until the early centuries of our era, there were no major political groupings which could have challenged the expansion of the Kushites into central Africa. Furthermore, as one moves south up the Nile valley, conditions for agriculture and hence for human settlement become much more favourable, making this area extremely attractive to a people who, in their heartland, were largely confined to a very narrow strip of arable land alongside the river. At Napata there is very little rainfall and we have no reason to suspect that in the Kushite period there was a significantly different climate. At the confluence of the White and Blue Niles, the site of the present day capital of Sudan at Khartoum, the average annual rainfall is 164 mm. Three hundred kilometres further south, at Kosti on the White Nile, it is 407 mm.[1]

There are, however, topographical limits to expansion to the south. On the White Nile the area of the Sudd, a vast and virtually impenetrable swamp, provides a barrier between the Sahelian lands of central Sudan and the areas further upstream. The most southerly find of Kushite material on the White Nile is at Kosti, where a steatite scarab has been found.[2] Occupation mounds with pottery of Kushite date, although not of typical Kushite type, were also found in the same town. Other occupation mounds are known far to the south at the confluence of the rivers Sobat and White Nile.[3] No archaeological work has been conducted at these sites and their dates of occupation are unknown.

Ease of travel up the valley of the Blue Nile is seriously impeded at the point where the river debouches from the gorge it has cut through the rim of the Ethiopian plateau. Kushite material has been claimed at Rossieres on the Blue Nile. The number of objects is small and does not prove direct Kushite control of those areas. There is no reason to doubt the ability of the Kushites to have conquered to these topographical limits, but the evidence for the extent of their penetration upriver at present available to us suggests that their territorial claims were rather more modest.

At Abu Geili on the Blue Nile a settlement of mud brick houses was associated with pottery and objects of Kushite manufacture along with some material which is not closely paralleled on sites further to the north.[4] Certainly the people living at Abu Geili had access to Kushite goods. The distinctive nature of the many objects, presumably made locally, suggests regional diversity rather than that the area lay beyond the southern frontier of the Kingdom of Kush. One might suggest that the settlement was occupied largely by the indigenous population rather than by settlers from the Kushite heartland to the north.

The major Kushite settlement in the area, and the immediate source of the Kushite objects at Abu Geili, may have lain a few kilometres to the south, opposite the modern town of Sennar which, as the capital of the Funj kingdom, was a place of considerable importance from the sixteenth until the nineteenth centuries AD. In 1921, during works associated with the construction of a new dam, a number of graves were destroyed. No grave was examined archaeologically and, therefore, much data has been lost. Among the objects recovered and brought to the attention of the authorities was a fine collection of copper-alloy vessels, finger rings and beads. The status of the occupants whose graves contained these objects must have been high and this indicates the importance of the adjacent settlement, which has yet to be located. This was clearly not a poor border post on the fringes of the Kushite empire, but a major regional centre, perhaps comparable with those known towards the northern frontier.[5] Other objects relevant to the discussion of the Kushite occupation of the Upper Blue Nile valley, found in the vicinity of Sennar, include a Roman coin of the fourth century AD and a steatite scarab of the Kushite king Shabaqo.[6]

The most southerly monumental pagan structure known to date is the recently excavated temple at Soba East, 22 km up the Blue Nile from its confluence with the White Nile.[7] However, this temple is not associated with any recognisably Kushite material. It may have been constructed by the Alwans[8] following Kushite religious and architectural traditions, but after the political power of the Kushite kings had collapsed. It is highly likely that others remain to be located yet further to the south.[9]

The eastern and western frontiers

In the desert regions of the north the effective limits of the kingdom to east and west of the river will have lain at the edge of the irrigated zone, rarely greater than 1 km from the river banks. However, we should note that a number of the ancient sources state that Kushite control was, at least in parts of the Nile valley, confined to the east (or right) bank of the river. Strabo records:

> As the Libyans occupy the western bank of the Nile, and the Ethiopians the country on the other side of the river, they dispute by turns the possession of the islands and the banks of the river, one party repulsing the other, or yielding to the superiority of its opponent.[10]

Ptolemy, writing in the mid-second century AD, reports that the west bank of the Nile was occupied by the Nubae, who were not subjects of the Kushites.[11] The absence of major Kushite sites on the west bank of the Nile in Upper Nubia is particularly interesting in this context. Upstream from Sanam virtually no Kushite settlement is known on the left bank of the river in contrast to the large numbers of sites in the Island of Meroe, both on the river banks and in its hinterland. One should note that this situation appears to have persisted up to the present. Today the major settlements are still to be found on the right bank of the river. This is not a result of the proximity of the railway; it was also the case prior to the conquest of the Sudan by the Anglo-Egyptian forces in 1896–8. The fact that the major sites are on one side of the river may reflect the presence of the primary lines of communication along one or other bank.

In contrast to the major settlements there are a vast number of burial mounds on the west bank of the river from Khartoum to Abu Hamed, many more than are known on the right bank. If there are ritual reasons for the placing of these tumuli, we are not aware of them. Unfortunately very few of these mounds have been excavated and we have little indication of their dates and the identities of their occupants. To contrast them with the major Kushite settlements on the opposite bank may be invalid. The recent work at el Hobagi, 65 km south-west of Meroe, is particularly interesting in this respect and suggests that at least some of the tumuli date to the very late Meroitic and post-Meroitic periods, when the towns on the opposite bank and in the Butana were in serious decline. This will be further discussed in Chapter 9.

The tribesmen of the Eastern Desert had a long history of preying on the sedentary peoples of the Nile valley and continued to do so into the medieval period. We have epigraphic evidence from Jebel Barkal and from Kawa for conflicts with the deserts nomads. A number of enemies are described, but it is not clear in all cases where these peoples lived. Anlamani sent an army against the Belhe who are thought to have lived to the east of Kawa[12] and these may be the same people who made an incursion into Kushite territory in the reign of Irike-Amanote, when they are called the Meded.[13] The stela of Nastasen also records attacks on Kawa and the looting from the temple of some of its treasures given by King Aspelta.[14] Today this area is very inhospitable.

A number of the Kawa inscriptions records kings donating territories they had captured for the upkeep of the Temple of Amun. We have no idea where these territories were, nor how extensive were the campaigns to capture them. Such offerings may have been largely ritualised and have involved minimal military activity.

Nastasen, as well as fighting against the Meti, who had stolen the treasure of Aspelta, sent his troops against the chiefs of the lands of Mekhenteqnent, Rebarut, Akarkarhent(?) and Mashat. The rebel lands of Arersat, Mekhsherkherthet and Maikhentkhat(?) were also attacked.[15]

The inscription of King Irike-Amanote found at Kawa records that under his predecessor, Talakhamani, the desert dwellers known as the Rhrhs revolted in the area to the north of the nome of Meroe and 'carried off all the cattle, herds, and men that they could find'.[16] These people are also mentioned on the stela of Harsiyotef as infesting the country near Meroe and as having forced their way either into the city or at least into its nome.[17]

A small bronze figure of a bound captive (fig. 20), wearing a 'pill box' cap adorned with long feathers, discovered in excavations at Meroe in 1911, bears an inscription in Meroitic script on its chest. It has been suggested that this reads 'Qo, king of the Nubians'.[18] If this reading and the date suggested for the piece are correct, it indicates warfare against the Nubians during the first century BC and the first century AD. The presence of the Nubians in the Nile valley is noted as early as the second century BC by the Greek writer Eratosthenes. Another small bronze figure, of the same general type but depicted bare-headed, is inscribed 'Edeqe the Nubians'.[19]

The early first century AD ruler King Shorkaror is represented on a rock carving at Jebel Qeili. This is a victory scene, the king being shown standing on bound captives in the same attitude as the 'king of the Nubians' noted above, and, together with the god, holding further captives. Still other unfortunates are shown tumbling down the hillside in disarray. There is no indication as to whom the king had been fighting, but a campaign against the Axumites, who inhabited the Ethiopian plateau, has been suggested on no good evidence.[20]

Close examination of the figures of captives depicted on Kushite monuments does little to assist us with identifying the enemies of Kush. The Kushites throughout their history appear to have used the prisoner iconography developed in pharaonic Egypt, particularly the New Kingdom representations. We thus sometimes observe the bizarre

20 *Bound Nubian captive. (BM, EA 65222)*

situation which has led one modern scholar to comment 'how is this nonsense possible, that the enemies of Kush are copies of the Kushite enemies of Pharaonic Egypt? Did nobody notice the identity of the captives with the image of their humiliated ancestors?'[21]

As one moves south through the empire, increased seasonal activity away from the river is possible and the dependence of people on the waters of the Nile decreases steadily. In these areas, therefore, we would expect that Kushite control extended much further from the river. Conversely these areas could support a much larger nomadic population and, therefore, could potentially support groups who may have posed a significantly greater military threat to the areas under direct Kushite control. As the Kushites pushed further upstream through this productive zone, they were increasing the length of their eastern and western frontiers and it may have been the difficulties of policing these frontiers which curbed their territorial expansion along the Blue and White Niles.

Many scholars, mindful of the long-distance trade across and around the Sahara in the medieval and later periods, have suggested that the Kushites must have had developed contacts with, if not direct control of, areas well to the west of the Nile. One cannot fault the reasoning behind such suggestions, but it must be noted that there is no unambiguous evidence whatsoever for such contact. We are faced with a situation to the west of the Nile where the total absence of evidence for Kushite influence goes hand in hand with an almost total absence of archaeological work. Although the suggestion of contact with Kordofan, Darfur and areas further to the west is attractive, we cannot at present take this discussion further. It may be that the Kushites were actually able to obtain sufficient commodities from the south of their kingdom, where transport along the Nile facilitated movement of goods, as to render the savannah areas to the west less desirable to them. This may have been particularly the case if the hostile Nuba occupied those areas.

In the northern part of the kingdom the only sites away from the river may have been those connected with the cross-desert trade routes. A site possibly of this type has recently been discovered in the Wadi Howar 110 km to the west of the river, but it has not been explored in detail and we are uncertain of its date and function.[22] The sites in the Wadi Abu Dom clearly are situated along the major route from Napata to Meroe. In the Keraba and Butana, Kushite sites are found well to the east of the river, but the most easterly evidence for Kushite penetration is the rock-cut relief and inscription at Jebel Qeili and the hafir with its statuary and stela at Umm Usuda (col. pl. 2). We have no evidence of any Kushite presence on the Red Sea coast; trade along that coast seems to have lain within the control of the rulers of Egypt or with the kingdoms based in the Arabian peninsula and on the Ethiopian plateau.

In the absence of literary evidence, we have to rely on the presence of distinctive artefacts to reconstruct the political and cultural affiliations of an area. Factors such as the cost of transporting pottery or other distinctive artefacts by land may be partly responsible for the absence of evidence for Kushite control. As Adams has put it, 'The absence of wheel-made "Meroitic" pottery on sites away from the Nile is not a priori evidence that the people who lived in them were not civilised, or even that they were not Kushite in a cultural or political sense.'[23]

The Kushites in Egypt

As the Kushites moved across the southern Egyptian frontier at the First Cataract and entered the land of Kemet, their activities are recorded for us by a much wider range of sources than those to be found relating to the heartland of the kingdom. These include epigraphic material written in the language of Egypt and by the Asiatic foes with whom the Kushites came into contact, and also in the records of the ancient historians of the Greek and Roman worlds. The Kushite king of Taharqo (as Tirhakah) even gets a mention in the Bible.[24]

The reasons for the Kushites' Egyptian adventure, however, are nowhere expressly stated. There is clear evidence for strong Egyptian influences on the mortuary practices of the Kushite rulers buried at el Kurru from the time of the second generation of rulers onwards, and this has been connected with an influx of Egyptians into that area. The situation in Egypt at this time is well known to us. There was considerable conflict between the pharaoh Takeloth II, *c.*840 BC, and the priesthood of the Temple of Amun at Thebes, the most important of Egypt's innumerable sanctuaries. It is possible that the Egyptians we have evidence for at the court of the Kushite kings were priests of Amun fleeing before this persecution.[25] The sanctity of the area of Napata to Amun had been established with the building of an Egyptian temple at Jebel Barkal during the XVIIIth Dynasty, and the designation of Jebel Barkal as the home of the *ka* (soul of sustenance) of Amun of Thebes.[26] The stela of Thutmose III set up at Barkal makes it clear that that king considered his divine mandate to rule to come both from Amun of Thebes and Amun of Barkal.

The arrival of the Egyptian priests may have been the catalyst which brought about a renewed veneration of Amun at Napata and made the kings of Kush aware of the political capital to be gained from their championing of the cause of Amun against the 'legitimate' pharaohs of Egypt. Reference to the Thutmose III stela could have been taken as justifying the rulers of Barkal in assuming control of Thebes. However, the apparent lack of interest in maintaining a firm control over their Egyptian conquests by Kashta and Piye suggests that they were motivated more by piety than by territorial ambitions.

It would appear that Kashta was the first of the Kushite kings to enter Egypt. He journeyed to Thebes around 760 BC[27] to receive the divine mandate to rule from Amun and he forced the high priestess of Amun to adopt his daughter as her successor-designate.[28] Our sources do not record a military campaign by Kashta in Egypt, but we can hardly doubt that he was accompanied by a military force and that he established control over the Theban area. The designation of his daughter as the next high priestess of Amun shows that he intended to maintain his influence, if not his direct rule, over Thebes.

A stela,[29] set up at Jebel Barkal in the third year of the reign of his successor Piye, implies some control over, or influence upon, Egyptian affairs. In the twenty-first year of the king's reign it is clear that his troops, or at least troops loyal to him, occupied much of Upper Egypt. At this time Tefnakht, a local dynast at Sais in the Delta, established his control throughout Lower Egypt and began to threaten the river valley to the south. We are extremely fortunate to have preserved for us a very detailed contemporary account of the developing crisis which ensued and of the campaigns to defeat Tefnakht, which it would appear incidentally brought about the Kushite conquest of the whole of Egypt.

In 1862 a large granite stela, inscribed in Egyptian hieroglyphs, was found in the Temple of Amun at Jebel Barkal where it had been set up by Piye. The stela, the upper part of which has a relief showing Piye before Amun and Mut and with the conquered kings and princes of Egypt paying homage to him, tells of the initial requests from Egypt for Piye to intervene and of his instructions to his forces in Egypt to begin operations, while he advanced with his army from the south. Piye did not come as an alien conqueror but as a protector of the ancient gods of Egypt (exactly as his later successors, the Macedonians and Romans, posed as the legitimate successors of the pharaohs of old). On his way north Piye took pains to honour Amun by celebrating the feast of Opet at Thebes, and throughout his campaign he showed great deference to the Egyptian gods and protected their shrines.

Having achieved his aim of thwarting the ambitions of Tefnakht, whom he spared, he appears to have withdrawn to the south, where he remained for the rest of his reign. Gradually Kushite control over Egypt lapsed and there is no indication that Piye did anything to maintain the integrity of his northern conquests. On his death the kingdom passed to his brother Shabaqo, who vigorously reasserted Kushite control and it is he, rather than Piye, who was credited by the Egyptian chronicler, Manetho, with founding the XXVth Dynasty. Shabaqo went far beyond the brief of Piye and carved out for himself a massive empire extending at least 3,379 km along the Nile, which was only surpassed in size on the conquest of Sudan by Mohammed Ali in 1819–20.

Shabaqo established firm control over Egypt, moved the capital of Kush to Thebes, and adopted the titles of the pharaoh. The possession of the territory of Egypt brought to the Kushite rulers an acceptance of Egypt's age-old ambition to meddle in the affairs of the lands to the north-east, and the problems which the frictions in that area brought.

It was the misfortune of the Kushites that their rule in Egypt coincided with the rise and expansion of the armies of Assyria. The Assyrians, in pursuit of their wars of aggression to the west, inevitably came into conflict with the Kushite forces. Initially contacts were of a peaceful nature and there is evidence, in the form of a clay tablet found in the Assyrian royal archives at Nineveh bearing the impressions of seals of Shabaqo and the Assyrian king Sennacherib, of diplomatic contacts between the two 'world' powers. The flashpoint centred on the small kingdom of Judah, which was supported by Shabaqo when the Assyrians invaded it. On this occasion, however, the armies did not engage; plague swept through the Assyrian forces besieging Jerusalem and forced Sennacherib to evacuate Palestine.

There is no record of hostilities during the short reign of Shebitqo, a son of Piye, who was assisted by Taharqo. Taharqo ascended to the throne in 690 BC. At the beginning of his reign an inscription – copies of which were set up at Tanis in the Delta, Quft in Upper Egypt and at Kawa in Upper Nubia – gives the boundaries of his domain as Qebh-Hor in Asia and Retehu-Qabet, an unidentified site presumably somewhere upstream of Napata.

Taharqo appears to have resided at Tanis in the Delta, highlighting the importance of maintaining a close watch on Egypt's north-eastern frontier. We hear of intrigue between Taharqo and the Assyrian vassals in Phoenicia, but of no direct involvement by the Kushites outside Egypt's borders. In 671 BC the inevitable assault came, led by King Esarhaddon.

The formidable Assyrian war machine appears to have had little difficulty, after an initial reverse, in inflicting defeat on the Kushites and advancing as far as Memphis, which was besieged and captured. The Assyrian perception of the might of the Kushite armies had earlier been voiced by Sennacherib, when he spoke to the king of Judah: 'Now, behold, thou trustest on the staff of this bruised reed, even upon Egypt, on which if a man leans, it will go into his hand, and pierce it; so is Pharaoh king of Egypt unto all that trust on him.'[30]

The Assyrian king assumed the title of 'King of Upper and Lower Egypt' and imposed tribute, but then withdrew allowing Taharqo to reoccupy Memphis in 669 BC, as well as the Delta, and to recommence his intrigues with the king of Tyre. Esarhaddon again led his army to Egypt and on his death the command passed to his successor Assurbanipal. This time the Assyrians advanced at least as far south as Thebes, but direct Assyrian control was not established, Egyptian vassal princes being installed. Even this was not the end of Kushite ambitions in Egypt. The rulers of Thebes still appear to have considered themselves vassals of Kush rather than of Assyria and the next Kushite king Tanwetamani was able to reconquer as far north as Memphis. This provoked the last of Assyria's interventions into the Nile valley when in 663 BC they again advanced as far as Thebes and devastated the area. Their vassal Psammetik I[31] then extended his control over Lower Egypt and by 654 BC he had established his daughter as successor-designate of the high priestess of Amun at Thebes, replacing the Kushite incumbent of that post and marking the end of the Kushite domination of Egypt. Intermittently for the next five hundred years the Kushites seem to have fallen prey to aggression by a succession of Egyptian rulers.

Invasions from the north

Psammetik was succeeded by Psammetik II, who invaded Kush in 593 BC, perhaps during the reign of Aspelta, and defeated the Kushites at a battle fought somewhere near the Third Cataract. The Egyptians may have gone on to sack Napata, although there is no good evidence to indicate that they actually did so.[32] The destruction at Napata of royal statues including some of Aspelta, thought in the past to have been the result of this invasion, may reflect the animosity between Aspelta and the priesthood of the Amun temple, or more likely, to be related to internal dynastic upheavals.[33] No permanent territorial gains appear to have been made, but this campaign must have brought home to the Kushites that any thoughts they may have entertained about reasserting their rights to Egypt would be doomed to failure. The invasion and conquest of Nubia by Egypt were the norm; the episode of Kushite domination of Egypt stands out as an unparalleled event in the history of the Nile valley. The animosity felt by Psammetik II towards the Kushites is reflected in the careful erasure of the names of the XXVth Dynasty rulers throughout Egypt and by the erasure of the specifically Kushite elements in the crowns depicted on the heads of Kushite rulers on the temple reliefs.[34]

The Assyrians may have been one of the first invaders to enter Egypt from the north-east, but they were by no means the last. In 525 BC Egypt fell to the Persians and remained under their control until 332 BC, with a brief period of Egyptian independence from 400 to 343 BC. The historian Herodotus records that the Persian king Cambyses also invaded Nubia and that his expedition perished miserably in the desert.[35] Herodotus is our only source for these events. Being a Greek and writing during the fifth century BC in the aftermath of the great wars between the Greek and Persian worlds, he can only be expected to be extremely hostile to the Persians. His reporting of the mishandling of the campaign by Cambyses and its lack of achievement must be seen in the context of his gloating over the misfortunes of the Greeks' main enemy.

The reasons for the campaign – whether the Persians were reacting to a perceived threat from Kush, for example – are unknown, nor are the Persian objectives explained. The kingdoms based on the Middle Nile had a tradition throughout history of meddling in Egyptian affairs when central control there was weak. That the Kushites may have taken advantage of the upheavals caused by the Persian invasion of their northern neighbour to do a bit of raiding and pillaging of their own is entirely possible. Scholars have doubted that this Persian expedition ever took place, but we know so little of Kushite history at this period that the silence of the other sources and the absence of evidence for the campaign on the ground are not sufficient for us to dismiss Herodotus' account out of hand. A recent reconsideration of the archaeological evidence from the fort at Dorginarti at the Second Cataract has suggested that it was occupied in the seventh and sixth centuries, perhaps by the Saite rulers of Egypt, and then by their successors the Persians when it may have marked the southern border of their African empire. Persian inscriptions both in Egypt and Iran include Kush within the bounds of the Persian empire.[36]

The inscription of King Harsiyotef dated to the first third of the fourth century BC[37] records that he extended his control, at least temporarily, as far as Aswan.[38] An inscription of King Nastasen records that he fought against a foreign invader from the north who came with a fleet. This may be understood in the context of an attempt to reinstate Nectanebo II, who had fled to Kush on his defeat by the armies of the Persian 'King of Kings', Artaxerxes, in 343 BC.[39]

Under the Macedonian dynasty founded by Ptolemy I, one of the generals of Alexander, direct Egyptian control was extended to Maharraqa (Hiera Sykaminos), a distance of 12 *schoenoi* (about 120 km) from Aswan, and this area hence came to be known as the Dodekaschoinos. We do not know of the Kushite reaction to these events, but it is thought that at that time there was no occupation in this part of the Nile valley.[40] Why this should have been the case is unknown and one might suspect that the apparent abandonment of this zone is a result of our misinterpretation of the archaeological evidence. Recent work at Qasr Ibrim has suggested that at that site there was continuity of occupation throughout the period.[41]

The expansion of the Ptolemies allowed them to control the routes to the gold mines in the Wadi el Allaqi. There is no record of immediate conflict with the Kushites. Directly following the occupation of the new territory the Ptolemies built new temples at Pselchis (Dakka) and Dabod. Soon after, the Kushite king, Arkamani, constructed a small entrance hall to the temple built by Ptolemy IV at Pselchis and constructed a temple at Philae to which Ptolemy contributed an entrance hall. At some later date King Adkeramon built a small temple near Philae to which Ptolemy VII made additions.[42] This appears to be an amazing situation when one considers the propaganda value inherent in the construction of major monuments in the ancient world. The situation of a ruler of a major power erecting a monument on the sovereign territory of a potentially hostile neighbour is difficult to parallel.

The Ptolemies had assumed the titles of the pharaohs of Upper and Lower Egypt, titles still retained by the Kushite kings as a legacy from the XXVth Dynasty. Throughout the Saite, Persian, Ptolemaic and Roman periods, the Kushite rulers – the descendants of the XXVth Dynasty pharaohs, and the guardians of the Temple of Amun at Jebel Barkal – could have pressed their 'legitimate' claim for the control of Egypt and they thus posed a potential threat to the rulers of Egypt.

This can hardly have been conducive to stability in the frontier zone, particularly when one or other of the protagonists felt capable of establishing firm control over the Dodekaschoinos. In this context the likelihood of one side allowing the other the opportunity of a propaganda coup – such as the construction of a major monument in the disputed area – is not high.[43] One scholar has drawn the obvious conclusion from the juxtaposition of these monuments and has suggested that they reflect alternate periods of Kushite and Ptolemaic domination rather than co-operation.[44] The situation in the Dodekaschoinos must have been complicated by the fact that presumably much of the administrative infrastructure and the inhabitants of the area will have remained the same, while the protagonists disputed the control of the territory at a political and presumably at a military level.

There were disturbances on the frontier during the reigns of Ptolemy v and vi. Ptolemy v caused the name of Arkamani to be defaced from the inscriptions at Philae and it has been suggested that this is to be connected with a serious revolt in Upper Egypt at the end of the reign of Ptolemy iv.[45] If this was the case, presumably the Kushites were attempting to interfere in the internal affairs of Egypt. The presence of Greeks from Cyrene, who cut inscriptions on a pillar of the temple at Buhen,[46] suggests that one result of this conflict was a Ptolemaic occupation at least as far south as the Second Cataract. The ruined Egyptian Middle Kingdom fortress at Mirgissa[47] also seems to have been occupied by Ptolemaic troops. This extended area of control is recorded in an inscription of Ptolemy vi as the Triakontaschoenos, the land of the 30 *schoenoi*.[48]

What Egyptian control there had been of the Triakontaschoenos lapsed after the death of Ptolemy vi, probably partly as a result of the dynastic struggles which dominated the later years of the Macedonian dynasty. Recent excavations at the fortress of Qasr Ibrim, and a re-examination of earlier finds from the site, have highlighted the total absence of Ptolemaic pottery, casting some doubts on the duration and effectiveness of Ptolemaic control of this area.[49] During this period the Kushites reasserted their control. Qasr Ibrim was then certainly occupied and perhaps garrisoned, and it has been suggested that further garrisons may have been placed at Jebel Adda and perhaps at Buhen.

During the first century BC the land of Kush is described in inscriptions at the Temple of Edfu as the country of Seth, indicating a revival of anti-Kushite feeling in Egypt, no doubt the result of the Kushite support offered to those who led revolts against the Ptolemies in Upper Egypt.

The end of the Ptolemaic dynasty came about when the last of the line, Cleopatra, became embroiled in a struggle for control of the Roman empire between Mark Antony and Octavian. The stakes were high. Had Antony won, an entirely possible outcome, Cleopatra might have shared in the rule of an empire stretching from Aswan to the Atlantic Ocean. Backing the loser brought death and direct control of Egypt by the Romans. The Romans rapidly consolidated their power and, following negotiations with the Kushites at Philae, drew the southern border of the province of Egypt at Aswan. The Kingdom of Kush was awarded the status of a client kingdom, standard Roman frontier policy when direct control was not deemed desirable. They appointed a viceroy (*tyrannus*) to control the whole of the Triakontaschoenos and there is some evidence to indicate that they assumed de facto control over the Dodekaschoinos, relegating the Kushites in that area to the status of tributaries.[50] This situation may have been little different to that pertaining under Ptolemaic rule.

That it was apparently unacceptable to the Kushites may reflect their territorial ambitions and their desire to challenge the new power that had appeared on the scene. Alternatively, it has been suggested that the revolt by the inhabitants of the area against the Romans was against excessive taxation. Not dissimilar unrest occurred elsewhere in the Roman empire, in Germany, which culminated in the revolt of Arminus in AD 9, and in Britain in the revolt of Boudicca to name but two. However, the unrest in the area to the south of Aswan does not appear to have been a popular uprising, but to have been supported from the first by the armies of Kush.

As soon as the Roman forces at Aswan were depleted, being withdrawn to fight in the Arabian campaign of 24 BC, the Kushites seized their chance and sacked Aswan with an army of 30,000 men (according to Strabo) and destroyed imperial statues which had been set up at Philae.[51] During the excavations within the city of Meroe in 1910 by a British expedition from Liverpool University, a fine over-life-size bronze head of the emperor Augustus was found buried in front of the threshold of one of the temples. This may have belonged to one of these bronze statues, although Strabo records that the statues were returned to the Romans at an early stage in the fighting.[52]

For the Romans' reaction to these events we have a detailed account not only by Strabo but also by the elder Pliny. We may also have a detailed description of events as seen from the Kushite side on a stela found in a small red-brick temple at Hamadab (fig. 21), several kilometres south of Meroe. Unfortunately our ignorance of the Kushite language allows us to obtain no more than a hint of the inscription's meaning.[53]

With a force of one legion and auxiliaries (10,000 infantry and 800 horse, according to Strabo),[54] the prefect of Egypt, Gaius Petronius, pushed the invaders back to Pselchis (Dakka) where negotiations took place. When these negotiations broke down, the Romans moved south, taking Pselchis and the fortress at Primis (Qasr Ibrim). Two Roman camps have been discovered within the last few years less than 1 km to the north of the latter site and these almost certainly date from this campaign.[55] Although the internal arrangement is unclear, both have the wall on one side of their gateways curved inwards, forming a *clavicula* which can be paralleled at the camp near Philae at Shellal,[56] and which is a diagnostic feature of Roman camps, many examples of which are known in northern Britain and Palestine. The ancient sources go on to

21 *Hamadab temple with the two stelae flanking the entrance.*
(Courtesy of the University of Liverpool)

record that the Roman army marched on to Napata, where it sacked the city.

Over 100 km upstream of Qasr Ibrim there is another Roman camp at Mirgissa overlying the remains of the pharaonic town. Like the camps at Qasr Ibrim, it has *claviculae* at the entrances. Archaeological evidence in support of the Roman penetration beyond the Second Cataract to Napata is tenuous and some have doubted that the Romans advanced south of Saras.[57] However, there are a number of very large defended enclosures in the Batn el Hajar and one near the Dal Cataract which have much in common with Roman camps known from elsewhere in the empire although they lack *claviculae* at the entrances. The date of these remains is uncertain.[58] The identification of the fortified enclosure a few kilometres downstream of Jebel Barkal as a Roman fort has little to recommend it.[59]

After the sack of Napata the army returned to Alexandria with prisoners and plunder. Petronius on his way north installed a garrison of 400 men at Primis, apparently with supplies to last for two years. Among the evidence for the Romans' occupation of Primis is a quantity of military equipment, including a large number of artillery projectiles (stone shot[60] and catapult quarrels with iron heads). Hostilities were renewed when the Kushites attacked Primis, but the situation was saved by the arrival of Petronius and the Kushites were forced to sue for peace, envoys being sent to the emperor

Augustus, who was at that time residing at Samos while he settled the affairs of the eastern Mediterranean. As part of the peace treaty the Roman frontier was extended to Hiera Sykaminos (Maharraqa), where the southern border of Egypt had lain for most of the Ptolemaic period. This arrangement of the frontier appears to have guaranteed peace for most of the next 300 years and we have no definite evidence of further clashes between the Romans and the Kushites.

The Roman writers Seneca and Pliny both record an expedition made during the reign of the emperor Nero south from Aswan. The former writer notes that the expedition met a king of the Kushites, while Pliny records that they met a queen. This has led to the suggestion that there were actually two expeditions, one in around AD 62 and the other in AD 66 or 67.[61] There has been much speculation as to the nature and purpose of these expeditions, which journeyed to immense marshes where the plants were so entangled that they were impenetrable.[62] This sounds very like a description of the Sudd, the vast swamps on the White Nile over 1000 km upstream from Meroe.

Pliny[63] records that the exploratory party was sent by Nero when he was actually contemplating an attack on Ethiopia and this seems a more plausible reason than the desire for scientific knowledge recorded by Seneca. Cambyses had also sent a mission to the Kushite court, the members of which were blatantly spying. Nero's 'explorers' may well have had a similar purpose. Over the eighty years separating the treaty between Rome and the Kushites from the expeditions of Nero's reign, there had been a change in imperial foreign policy. The system of client kingdoms lying immediately beyond many of Rome's frontiers had given way to one of direct control and this process was to continue under Nero's immediate successors. During the early Roman empire expansion was the norm and there is no reason to doubt that the Romans would not have contemplated the conquest and incorporation of the Kushite Empire.

Whatever imperial ambitions Nero may have had on the Middle Nile, these would have been terminated by the Jewish Revolt which broke out in AD 66 and by Nero's death two years later. The Kingdom of Kush may have been saved from Roman domination by events elsewhere in the empire, as was northern Britain in the AD 80s and again in the early third century.

In the next decade Rome's attention switched to the areas west of the Nile valley. A Roman army marched south to the Fezzan and beyond,[64] but no permanent conquests were made in that area. No other emperor seems to have paid any particular attention to the lands beyond Egypt's southern frontier except in so far as their inhabitants affected the security of Egypt itself.

After the accounts of these expeditions there are very few further references to the Kushites in the classical sources. The expeditions under Nero may have convinced the Romans that there was little to be gained from military activity to the south of Egypt and already the major trade route for central African goods had moved from the Nile to the Red Sea.

Among the snippets of information relating to Romano-Kushite contacts is a small papyrus fragment, of unknown provenance, which appears to relate details of an engagement between a Roman cavalry force under a certain Rufus and the Kushites, and is perhaps to be dated to the late first century AD.[65]

The Roman emperor Septimius Severus was on the frontier in AD 200 but a pestilence deterred him from crossing it.[66] Particularly intriguing is a letter sent soon after AD 247, perhaps from Qasr Ibrim, well to the south of the frontier, which records the presence there of a number of senior officers of the *legio II Traiana Fortis*, including the prefect.[67] However, there is some doubt over the correct reading of the words *actum Prem[is]*. If these words have been incorrectly read, then all connection between Qasr Ibrim and the army units is void.[68]

Two third-century kings of the Kushites are recorded at Philae, one in a graffito, the other in an inscription. The earlier of the two may be the graffito[69] recording in demotic the name of King Tqrrm, who has been identified with the Teqerideamani buried in pyramid Beg.N.28 at Meroe. It dates from the third year of the Roman emperor Trebonianus Gallus (AD 253). The other king is 'Yesbokheamani'[70] the name written above the figure of a king who is also named at Qasr Ibrim. It has been suggested that this king reigned from AD 283–300 and that during that period there may have been a Kushite reoccupation of lower Nubia after Diocletian withdrew Roman forces back to Aswan in AD 298.[71] Others noting the activities of Kushites, including officials of the king, in the Dodekaschoinos as far north as the sanctuary of Philae, have envisaged a de facto Kushite control of that area for at least part of the third century.[72] Diocletian is credited with a victory over the Kushites and Blemmyes in AD 297[73] but the whereabouts of the fighting is not clear. Diocletian's withdrawal from the Dodekaschoinos may only have been a formal acceptance of the status quo,[74] in the same way that the emperor Aurelian in AD 270 had been forced to acknowledge officially the loss of Dacia. The sixth-century Roman historian Procopius mentions that Diocletian's agreement was with the Nobatae and not with the Kushites.

By the end of the third century the stability of the northern frontier zone was under threat from other peoples, but this story belongs to that of the decline and fall of the Kushite kingdom.

CHAPTER FOUR

Religion and Funerary Ritual

K ushite religion and the rituals associated with it can be studied using information from a variety of sources. In the very earliest period we rely entirely on the
archaeological remains of the tombs themselves and on the artefacts associated
with the burials. With the adoption of the practice of writing in ancient Egyptian, a
number of Kushite texts relating to religious matters can be read and these provide invaluable first-hand data. However, these inscriptions relate to a comparatively restricted
time span and are mainly concerned with the worship of the Egyptian pantheon. Little
information is provided on indigenous religious beliefs and practices where they differ
from those of Egypt. When the Kushites write their own language, using their own
script, we are unable to understand the inscriptions. We are then forced to again rely
on archaeological evidence. The most useful is the abundant scenes carved on the walls
of temples and offering chapels and painted on the walls of the tomb chambers. This
material can be supplemented by the finds of offering tables, ritual deposits and sacrifices, and by a close study of the Kushite religious monuments themselves. Towards
the end of the Kushite period the evidence becomes rather sparse and we are forced to
look to the tomb monuments and grave offerings as our sole source of data.

One additional source for Kushite religion which has been much used in the past is
the information contained in the writings of a number of ancient authors – Greek and
Roman writers who attempted to explain Kushite religion to their readers by equating
it with the familiar Graeco-Roman pantheon. These writers were often ill-informed
and the information they provide is only of value when it can be supported by evidence
derived from within the Kingdom of Kush.

Under the New Kingdom Egyptian gods became well established in Nubia and were
worshipped in temples as far upstream as Jebel Barkal. As one would expect, the local
élite in the areas under direct Egyptian control will have found it prudent to be seen to
be converts to the religion of their conquerors. How far down the social spectrum the
appeal of Egyptian gods went is not easy to say. With the removal of Egyptian control
at the end of the XXth Dynasty the fate of the Egyptian cult centres left behind is
uncertain. There is evidence which suggests that the cult of Amun, and of the other
Egyptian gods who had temples at Jebel Barkal, did not survive. The Temple of Amun

B500 certainly seems to have been ruined when Piye began to show an interest in it. To which gods the local inhabitants turned after the Egyptians left is uncertain and we know very little of the religious beliefs of the earliest Kushite rulers. It is perhaps pertinent to note that the earliest rulers were not buried in the vicinity of the religious complex at Barkal but 12 km downstream at el Kurru.

It has been suggested recently that it was political and military events in Egypt which may have brought about a sudden influx of Egyptian priestly exiles from Thebes to the court of the rulers in el Kurru during the reign of the second of the Kushite monarchs, whose tomb is known at el Kurru. If this is correct, then one can readily understand the rather sudden Egyptianising of the Kushite funerary ritual at this time. It has further been suggested that the Temple of Amun at Jebel Barkal was also reoccupied at this time and the practice of the state religion of Egypt developed anew. Egyptian priests may have been common in the earlier Kushite period when a knowledge of the Egyptian language was a prerequisite. This is well illustrated by the fact that of the fifteen priests known to us who were attached to the Temple of Amun at Sanam, four have Egyptian names.

Throughout Kushite history there is a dichotomy in religious beliefs and practices. Although in the state religion of the earlier Kushite period the foreign Egyptian gods dominated the scene (a perception enhanced by the use of Egyptian styles of sacral architecture and religious art), the underlying local beliefs were never entirely banished from the scene. Thus Kushite religion and ritual exhibit a number of features distinct from those of pharaonic Egypt and there are several gods, the most important being the lion god Apedemak, who are not members of the Egyptian pantheon at all.

Egyptian gods

The chief god of the Kushite state, at least by the time of the XXVth Dynasty, was Amun, the great god of Egypt, who had ruled supreme, except for a brief period under the pharaoh Akhenaten and his immediate successors, since the beginning of the second millenium BC.[1] Amun was by no means a new arrival to the northern part of the Kingdom of Kush. Temples to him had been constructed south of Aswan during the New Kingdom and one stood on the southern border of Egypt's conquered territories at Jebel Barkal only 12 km upstream from el Kurru. The earliest shrine to Amun at Jebel Barkal was erected in the fortress built by Thutmose III, the first Egyptian ruler to reach the area. The construction of the temple at the foot of Jebel Barkal, which was to develop into the largest of all Kushite temples, was begun by Horemheb or Sety I and completed by Rameses II. Although the original temple was of small size, Jebel Barkal itself seems to have held a special place in Egyptian religious beliefs as the 'Throne of the Two Lands', the chief, and perhaps the original residence of the Theban Amun. The close link between the Theban and Barkal temples probably reflects the function of the Barkal sanctuary as the centre for the collection and stockpiling of Nubian products destined for the temple at Karnak.[2]

The early kings of Kush were quick to pose as the earthly champions of Amun and this policy brought them great success in their attempts to dominate Egypt. Many subsequent rulers of Egypt also deemed it prudent to maintain the religious status quo so as not to antagonise the population and to legitimise their positions as the rightful successors of the pharaohs. However, although the apparently rapid assimilation of the Egyptian gods and of Amun in particular must have been a great advantage to the Kushites when they began to meddle in Egyptian affairs, they had already adopted Egyptian religious ideology and used it for their own ends in Kush. A large part of the attraction of the northern religious ideology was conditioned by political considerations. This is well illustrated by the way the Kushite rulers only accepted certain features of Egyptian religion, particularly those which could be used to legitimise their right to rule.[3]

Amun was pre-eminent in the Kushite pantheon, and his close association with the kingship ideology guaranteed that he remained so throughout Kushite history. A large number of temples, in a purely Egyptian style, were constructed for him. Restoration and enlargement of the pharaonic Temple of Amun at Jebel Barkal was begun under Piye. Taharqo further enlarged the temples at Barkal, built the Temple of Amun at Kawa and perhaps those at Sanam and Tabo. The date of the construction of the extant Temple of Amun at Meroe, which lay immediately outside the 'Royal City', is uncertain but appears to be rather later, but there is evidence for an earlier temple to this god within the area subsequently enclosed by the wall of the Royal City.[4] Inscriptions record that all these temples (apart from those at Meroe and Sanam) were visited as part of the coronation ritual, the new king beginning his journey from his residence at Meroe and progressing to Napata, Krtn (Korti?), Kawa and Pnubs.[5]

Other temples to that god were constructed as late as the beginning of our era when the rulers Natakamani and Amanitore built the temple at Naqa (fig. 22). A temple at Jebel Adda, claimed by its excavator to be the latest to have been built in Lower Nubia, was apparently dedicated to the worship of Amun and indicates that the cult retained its importance to the end of the Kushite period.[6]

Unlike the situation during the New Kingdom when Amun of Thebes was worshipped in a uniform way throughout the area of Egyptian control, under the Kushites the god appears to have been venerated in a number of forms. Amun without any epithet was worshipped in many temples, sometimes alongside the local Amun, or with other gods. The local forms were on occasion worshipped away from their place of origin. Amun of Napata, for example, is found as a guest in a small number of temples, among them the temple at Abu Simbel where he had been venerated during the New Kingdom.

The local forms of Amun can often be recognised in the iconography. The most important of these was Amun of Napata, who is frequently depicted as a ram-headed human figure holding a divine staff in one hand and an ankh (the symbol of life) in the other. He is crowned with the sun disc with tall feathers behind. As early as the New Kingdom Amun was thought to inhabit the mountain of Jebel Barkal and a number of

22 *Temple of Amun at Naqa. (D. A. Welsby)*

representations of Kushite date depict the god within the mountain, which has a large *uraeus* at its front. It has been suggested that the prominent stone pinnacle on the southern face of the mountain was identified as a *uraeus*. An inscription on the pinnacle was set up by Taharqo stressing the importance of this natural feature, and further inscriptions were added by Irike-Amanote and Nastasen.[7] Amun of Kawa wears a similar crown but, whereas Amun of Napata has the ram's head with the forward-curving horns of the species *ovis platyura aegyptiaca*, Amun of Kawa has the straight horns of the older species *ovis longipes palaeoaegyptiaca* (fig. 23). Other representations of Amun of Kawa are crowned only by a sun disc and *uraeus*.[8]

Another particularly important Egyptian deity was Isis (that is, the Isis of Philae rather than the manifestation of the goddess whose worship extended throughout the

23 *Bronze inlay sphinxes, Amun of Gematon, from Kawa. (BM, EA 63590–1)*

Greek and Roman worlds). A number of inscriptions from Philae record the visits made by Kushites to her temple, bringing offerings and participating in the festivals. These were official embassies sent from the royal court and included royal princes among their number.[9] As early as the New Kingdom, Isis is described as 'Mistress of Kush'. An inscription of Harsiyotef found at Jebel Barkal records the creation of festivals to Isis and Osiris throughout the kingdom.[10] A temple probably dedicated to her was identified during Garstang's excavations at Meroe in 1909–10.[11] She appears in almost every major temple relief in the kingdom, often as a counterpart to Apedemak.[12] Together with Osiris she is invariably invoked on the funerary stelae, large numbers of which have been recovered from Lower Nubia, particularly in the cemeteries at Karanog and Shablul.

In the world of the living, Isis was personified in the person of the queen mother, her son the king representing Horus. The interaction of these two mortals closely followed that of the divine duo. The king derived his legitimacy from being the son of the queen mother and for his part his actions as heir confirmed his right to rule. A number of iconographic scenes served to highlight this parallelism and inscriptions clearly make reference to this legitimisation procedure. Thus great importance was attached to the queen mother being present to observe her son performing actions in accordance with *maat* – the cosmic harmony established by the creator-god at the beginning of time – the maintenance of which was the king's most important function. The king is frequently depicted being suckled by Isis and, a uniquely Kushite feature, some scenes show the queen also being suckled, illustrating the different role of the queen in the Kushite monarchy.

Amun, Isis, Horus, and Osiris are the most important of the many Egyptian gods included in the Kushite pantheon. In the northern part of the kingdom, the area most open to influences from Egypt, and also the area which had remained under Egyptian control for the longest period, the gods of the pharaonic and Ptolemaic pantheon dominated the scene.

Once established in Kush the ancient religion of Egypt flourished and was spread to the furthest corners of the kingdom. Indeed, the Kushites remained champions of the old religion long after many Egyptians had succumbed to the allure of Christianity. The final triumph of Christianity over the gods of Egypt was thus delayed until the Byzantine missionaries entered Nubia in the sixth century AD.

Kushite gods

Of the non-Egyptian gods Apedemak was the most important. A number of temples dedicated to him are known, all clustered in the Island of Meroe. Two of these, at Naqa and at Musawwarat es Sufra, where the fallen blocks from the temple have been re-erected, are extremely well preserved and their reliefs and inscriptions provide detailed information on the physical nature of the god and on the rituals associated with him. The temple at Musawwarat has been dated to around 220 BC,[13] that at Naqa to the beginning of our era. Evidence for the worship of Apedemak in the north of the kingdom is sparse, but a priesthood of the god may be mentioned on an inscription from Arminna West[14] and the name of the god is written in hieroglyphs on the shrine at Dabod.[15]

In many representations Apedemak is shown holding a bow and arrows. He holds captives and is depicted in the act of slaying them. This clearly points to his function as a war god, and in a hymn to the god, inscribed on the south wall of the Lion Temple at Musawwarat es Sufra, he is described as 'one who sends forth a flaming breath against his enemies in this his name Great of Power, who slays the rebels with (his) strength(?)'.[16] Apedemak also appears usurping the role of Osiris as the consort of Isis and forming together with Horus a divine triad.[17]

Although Apedemak was pre-eminent among the non-Egyptian gods, at least in the Island of Meroe, the iconography associated with him has a good Egyptian pedigree. Lion gods were common in Egypt and the attributes and functions of one of these in particular, Mahas, were intimately connected with the worship of Apedemak. This is just one of the many examples of syncretism between Egyptian and Kushite gods, reflecting a similar trend in Egypt itself where many of the characteristic features of individual gods were attributed to others who had initially been totally distinct.[18] Even when discussing 'local' Kushite gods, therefore, the influence of Egypt is ever present, an influence manifested both on a theological and iconographic level.

The two gods, Sebiumeker and Arensnuphis (Iryhemesnefer) are usually found together and appear to have had the function of divine guardians. In this role their stone images flank the doorway into Temple 300 at Musawwarat es Sufra[19] and two massive free-standing statues of these gods, 7 m in height and weighing 30 tons each, stood in front of the Temple of Amun at Tabo (fig. 24). On a lintel from 'Temple' 100 at Musawwarat they are shown flanking Amun.[20] One half of the north-west wall of the Lion Temple at Musawwarat is occupied by Sebiumeker in the guise of a creator god and a row of ankhs is carved beneath him. Apedemak occupies the other half of the wall and, by contrast, a row of prisoners and elephants highlight his war-like status.[21] The Kushite origin of Sebiumeker is not in doubt, but there is strong evidence to indicate that, contrary to what is generally assumed to be the case, Arensnuphis was an Egyptian god who was adopted by the Kushites.[22]

Although there is epigraphic evidence for the god Amanap of Meroe he is, at least by the third century AD, associated with Primis (Qasr Ibrim) and is commonly invoked at the nearby site of Karanog. Presumably he is related in some way to Amun and it is

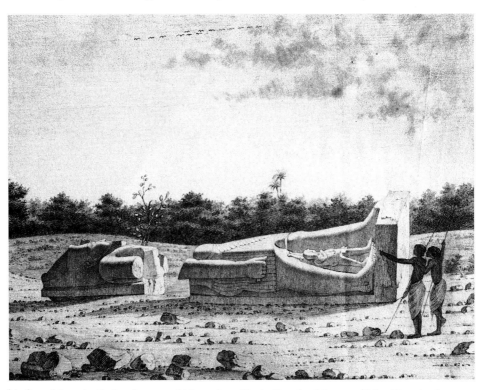

24 *One of the pair of colossal statues which stood outside the Temple of Amun at Tabo. (Drawing by Linant de Bellefonds 1822, courtesy of The Bankes Collection, The National Trust)*

possible that his name may be a shortened version of Amanapate, Amun of Napata. The worship of Mash is closely associated with that of Amanap and they appear to have shared a joint priesthood. Like Amanap, Mash is known mainly from Karanog. He may be a sun god. Other Kushite gods not familiar from the Egyptian pantheon are recorded on an inscription of Haramadeye from Karanog. These include Ariten, Amanete, Harendotes and Makedeke. We know nothing of them beyond their names.[23] The preponderance of local gods in the Karanog area may relate more to the number of inscriptions known from there rather than to the particular piety of the inhabitants. Of the local gods in other areas of the empire we are totally ignorant.

There is no evidence to suggest that the Kushites worshipped their rulers as gods within their own lifetimes. However, the Coronation Stela of Aspelta describes the recently deceased king as a god[24] and the rulers thought of themselves as sons of Amun even when they were female. An inscription, dating from the mid third century AD, suggests that a cult of the deceased ruler was then in existence.[25] Reliefs in the funerary chapels at Meroe indicate that the deceased rulers were equated with the gods Osiris or Sokar.[26]

'Popular religion'

To what extent the ordinary people were involved with their gods on a day-to-day basis is unclear. No household shrines have been discovered,[27] but the importance of the gods to the individual can be gauged to some extent by the numerous invocations to them in the form of graffiti carved on the walls of buildings, particularly temples, and also on rock outcrops. Such graffiti are, in the northern part of the kingdom, frequently accompanied by a small picture of an offering table or of a human foot.[28] This is most graphically illustrated at Qasr Ibrim where the paving slabs on the so-called podium are covered with incised depictions of human feet, often with the name of the owner scratched beside them, usually in Greek but also in Meroitic (fig. 25).[29]

A number of hill-tops seem to have been chosen as sites of special religious importance. One such site was located 2 km to the south of the settlement at Jebel Adda where there were sixteen graffiti in Meroitic and one in demotic. Another manifestation of ritual activity on hills is provided by the deposits of pottery of late Kushite and later dates at their foot, a phenomenon noted both in Lower Nubia and at Meroe.[30] The evidence from Meroe suggests that funerary banquets were conducted on the hill-tops. These involved animal sacrifice and the utilisation of the types of pottery associated with the funerary cult. The vast quantities of residue, consisting mainly of pottery, were then thrown down the hillside.

The laying of foundation deposits was a particularly common feature of early Kushite ritual and followed standard Egyptian practice. The objects included in foundation deposits, which are most frequently placed in pits dug under the corners of buildings or tomb monuments, vary greatly. Objects specifically produced for this function include rectangular plaques, in a variety of materials, either inscribed or plain (col. pl. 3), and model tools of copper-alloy and of iron. Frequently, however, objects

25 *Foot carvings on the paving in the podium at Qasr Ibrim. (D. A. Welsby)*

in general use were buried, including stone mortars and grinders, items of personal ornament, pottery and animal bones.[31]

Mortuary practices

> You shall know these things which the son of Ra, Aspelta did for me: he built for me a pyramid of good white stone of the living rock; he provisioned for me a chapel of millions of years with every good thing; he made my name to grow therein; he made many offerings of gold and silver; he gave me meat offerings; . . .
>
> (Funerary stela of Aspelta's son Piankhy-Khariuwt)[32]

The earliest evidence we have for the existence of the Kingdom of Kush is that provided by the tombs of the rulers buried at el Kurru. The antecedents of these rulers are unknown, but we can immediately appreciate, from observations of their mortuary practices, that they are an indigenous although not necessarily local group. They were each interred in a simple pit beneath a tumulus, the standard mode of burial seen in Nubia since the A-Group.

Burial attitude

The burials of the Kushite rulers and of the other occupants of the royal cemeteries have suffered very badly from the activities of tomb robbers. Most of the bodies have been disturbed so that the original burial attitude is no longer identifiable. The individual buried in tumulus Ku.Tum.1, thought to be that of the earliest ruler of Kush known to us, was laid in a contracted position lying on the right side with the head to the south and looking east while that in Ku.10 may have been laid on the left side, head to the south facing west. This orientation at el Kurru puts the body roughly parallel to the course of the Nile and remained the norm for five generations of rulers.

In the earliest burials at el Kurru, the bodies were usually placed so that the deceased faced east. This orientation may relate to a veneration of the sun in some form and can be compared with the importance of orientation to the east in Egyptian religion. However, a veneration of the sun and adherence to this orientation was by no means confined to Egypt. The early Kushites may have been influenced either directly or indirectly by Egyptian beliefs, but this was not necessarily the case.

Kashta was perhaps the first ruler to be buried in an extended position.[33] In the burials of Kashta and his wife the axis of the burial chamber was rotated through 90 degrees so that the bodies lay perpendicular to the river.[34] By this device the individuals still 'faced' to the east. This east-west orientation with the skeletons dorsally extended thereafter was invariably adhered to at least in royal burials.

In the more humble burials the east–west orientation with the head to the west was the most frequent, although the practice of using river north as opposed to true north does introduce a degree of variation. However, there is no rigid conformity to the east–west orientation. At Sanam, where some 1550 graves dating from the early Kushite period were excavated, many were found to be rather carelessly orientated, but a few were markedly different being 90° to the axis of the bulk of the graves. A considerable number of the east–west burials had the bodies placed with the head to the east.[35]

At Sanam the mummified burials were all extended inhumations with the body usually placed on its back, although in multiple burials – in an attempt to make the most efficient use of the space available – they were occasionally placed on their sides. Of the bodies which were not mummified there were both extended and crouched examples. The extended burials had the hands in the pelvic region or by the sides of the body. The crouched examples frequently had the hands before the face and the heels close to the hips.[36] A number of graves with contemporary grave goods contained extended or crouched inhumations indicating that both burial attitudes were in use at the same period. This was conclusively demonstrated by the burials in grave no. 221 where the male was laid in an extended position with his head to the west and the female in a crouched position on her right side with her head to the east. This has been thought to reflect the adherence of the woman to the local burial custom and of the man to the more fashionable, Egyptianising customs.[37]

Bed burials
Bed burials have been a common feature of Nubian mortuary practice at many periods in history and the presence of burials of this type reflects the prominence of indigenous traditions. A number of the early burials at el Kurru were placed on beds with the legs

either set into individual holes cut in the floor of the burial chamber or set in trenches. Subsequently the bed was placed on a stone bench with recesses to take the legs.[38] The use of a bed was also found in graves of more humble folk and has been recorded in a number of cemeteries as at Meroe but not, surprisingly, at Sanam.

The provision of the stone bench to support the bed allowed a coffin to be placed upon it. This arrangement is first observed in the tomb of Piye, Ku.17, where the Nubian bed becomes equated with the Egyptian embalming bed and neatly ties in with Piye's (or at least his immediate successors') acceptance of the concept of preserving the body after death. Piye was the first to be buried with a set of canopic jars, although these were symbolic. Each jar had been hollowed out by the rim, presumably so that the lid could be accommodated, but the rest of the vessel was solid.[39]

In later tombs the bed was no longer provided, the bench, either free-standing or attached to the wall of the chamber, supporting the coffin unaided.

Coffins and cartonnage
Kashta may have been the first ruler to have been laid within a gilded wooden anthropoid coffin of a type familiar from the graves of later Kushite rulers. From this coffin only fragments of gold foil, coloured glass and lapis lazuli remain in the burial chamber.

Burials mummified in typical Egyptian manner, with the body placed in a coffin or in anthropomorphic cartonnage, are also a feature of certain non-royal cemeteries. The Sanam cemetery had bodies wrapped in bandages, often covered in bead nets.[40]

Coffins of wood, including hollowed-out tree trunks, and occasionally of pottery have been noted in a number of cemeteries. A fine pottery example came from Argin and is decorated with a human head in relief at one end and with moulded feet and hands.[41] From the west cemetery at Meroe came a plain, oval coffin made from pottery containing the body of a child and covered by a lid of grey mud on which was a crudely modelled face.[42]

Stone sarcophagi are uncommon and are confined to the royal burials at Nuri and Meroe. Two of the finest are of the kings Anlamani and his successor Aspelta. Although the sarcophagus of Anlamani is the slightly smaller of the two, their decoration is virtually identical. A close study of these sarcophagi has revealed that the motifs and texts with which they are inscribed are derived from a wide range of sources, from XVIIIth Dynasty royal sarcophagi, priestly sarcophagi of the XXVth and XXVIth Dynasties, passages from Coffin Texts, from the Book of the Dead and from Pyramid Texts. The continuing knowledge of this material into the seventh and sixth centuries BC, some of which was by then two thousand years old, is noteworthy. Presumably at Napata there must have been an extensive 'library' of mortuary texts and a body of scribes, whether Egyptian or Kushite, who had a thorough knowledge of the material.[43] The absence of any non-Egyptian motifs and texts on the sarcophagi reflects the conservatism of royal mortuary practices. This aping of pharaonic iconography can be paralleled in the statuary of this period. Only three stone coffins are known at Meroe. They are each of similar form with a relief on the lid of Osiris with Isis to one side and Nephthys on the other.[44]

Grave goods

Kushite religion, even before its beliefs became assimilated with and largely dominated by those of Egypt, accepted the concept of life after death, a life where the worldly status of the individual would be perpetuated. Such a belief necessitated the inclusion of grave goods with the dead to allow him or her to be well provided for in the afterlife and to have with them those personal items which they had especially appreciated while this side of the grave. Ku.Tum.1, the burial of the first recognisable ruler of Kush, contained a large number of objects, including gold jewellery and pottery.

The provision of grave goods was extremely common, but was by no means a universal feature. The presence or absence of grave goods was perhaps in many cases a reflection of the individual wealth of the occupant or his family. This, however, was presumably not always the case, as in the grave under a substantial tumulus, KE5 at Kawa, where the primary burial was accompanied only by animal bones.[45] At Sanam many of the larger graves and particularly those containing multiple burials were without grave goods.[46]

The full range of artefacts used in the Kushite period can be found in graves but pottery and personal ornaments are the most common (figs 26, 27, 28). At Sanam it was the burials of women, young girls and children which were particularly well provided with jewellery.[47] Although much of the pottery buried with the dead is of the same types as those used by the living, a number bear decorative motifs which appear to have a specifically funerary significance. Among these are pots decorated with representations of offering tables (col. pl. 4, bottom left) together, in some cases, with the symbol of Isis. These latter vessels may have been produced for use as female mortuary goods.[48] Particularly common is the association of vessels used as containers for liquids with cups of bronze or pottery which are often placed over the neck of the jars. This association can be found in graves with the very fine painted wares, but also continued into the very late period and can be observed, for example, in the graves at el Hobagi (fig. 28).

The desire to provide a large number of grave goods in the royal tombs at el Kurru may have influenced the design of tomb chambers. The move away from the side-niche grave to the placing of the burial on the floor of the shaft itself, first seen in Ku.23, allowed much greater space for the grave goods.[49] These simple chambers had developed into triple chambers by around 600 BC. The inner chamber housed the burial and also the grave goods, which sometimes overflowed into the middle chamber.[50]

Even in relatively humble graves the quantity of (albeit low-value) grave goods could be considerable. Some graves had special provision for the placing of grave goods. In a number of side-niche graves two slots cut transversely across the floor of the shaft contained the objects. These slots are very reminiscent of those dug in graves of the Kerma period to house the legs of the funerary bed.[51] At Sanam a few of the large

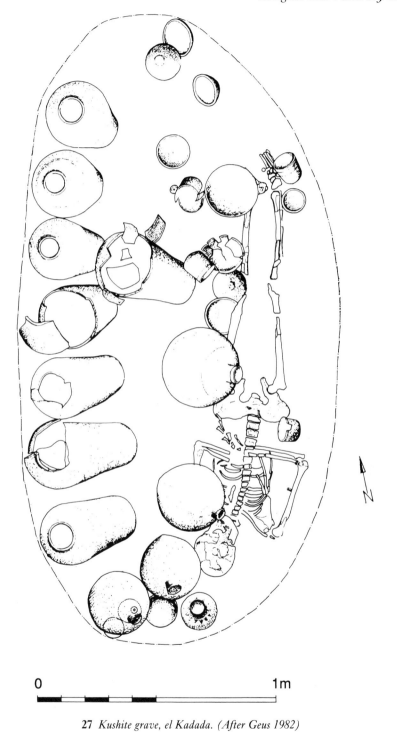

27 *Kushite grave, el Kadada. (After Geus 1982)*

Opposite **26** *Grave 2923 at Faras excavated by Griffith. (Courtesy of the Griffith Institute, Oxford)*

28 *Grave goods consisting of 'beer' jars and bronze cups from the burial beneath tumulus III at el Hobagi.* *(P. Lenoble)*

rectangular brick graves had pits dug in the corners to receive pottery and metal vessels.[52] Equally commonly the pots were placed by the head of the deceased. A tomb beneath a pyramid at Jebel Adda had notched wooden pegs driven into the wall for the suspension of offerings.[53] A bronze camel lamp was found *in situ* still suspended from the vault of a tomb at Qasr Ibrim. The tomb contained a wide range of grave goods of Kushite and classical design and pottery of 'post-Meroitic' types.[54]

All Kushite burials seem to have been placed beneath the ground and where an above-ground tomb monument is provided it is a solid structure with no connection with the grave which it may seal. The royal pyramids of Kush thus differ from a number of the pyramids of the Old Kingdom of Egypt where the burial chamber is within the super-structure. There does, however, appear to have been one notable exception to this rule. An Italian doctor named Ferlini, who had been in the employ of the Egyptian Government, was convinced that the Meroe pyramids contained treasure and in 1834 he proceeded to remove the tops of many of them in his quest for gold. He was richly rewarded for his vandalism during the demolition of the pyramid over the grave of

Queen Amanishakheto. From a chamber located a little below the apex he retrieved a superb hoard of jewellery, and about halfway down the pyramid two metal bowls were found in a hollow.[55] Although we have no record of other treasure being found within the structure of royal pyramids a similar concept of burying objects in tomb monuments has been observed at Karanog.[56] Two fragmentary faience statues and two fragments of offering tables were recovered from the fill of one of the latest pyramids at Meroe, Beg.N.51.[57] Whether they were added to the fill for ritual reasons or whether they had no more significance than the other pieces of rubble is unclear.

Many pyramids have a niche in their eastern face set towards the apex. It has been suggested that these were false entrances into imaginary chambers inhabited by the *ba*, the spirit of the deceased. As far as we know only Amanishakheto's *ba* was given a physical chamber to occupy, where it was surrounded by her jewellery.[58]

Piye was the first ruler to adopt the Egyptian practice of providing himself with *shabti* figures, surrogates who would undertake menial tasks in the afterlife on behalf of Piye. Over sixty mummiform faience figures, including a number of kilted 'foremen', each inscribed with the legend 'King of Upper and Lower Egypt, Piye', were recovered from the tomb and many others were found scattered around the site.[59] Taharqo was accompanied by over 1070 *shabti* of varying sizes and made of granite, green ankerite and alabaster.[60]

Funerary banquets

There seems to have been a ritual meal at the burial of the individual in Ku.Tum.1. A cattle skull was found, and charred dom palm nuts together with sherds from red ceramic food bowls and drinking cups. In later tumuli the quantity of ceramic material is considerably greater, suggesting that the funerary feast had become a more important part of the ritual.

Within and around the chapel at Ku.Tum.6 were hundreds of sherds of red wheel-made pottery, including at least six large amphorae and twenty small bowls as well as other vessels. The amphorae are decorated in Egyptian style with white painted scenes of mourning – processions of mourners, and mummiform figures. All the vessels have been broken into small pieces and are presumably those used in the funerary banquet which were ritually smashed at the end of the ceremony.[61]

The abundant Egyptian pottery decorated with Egyptian funerary scenes, presumably painted by Egyptian artists, may suggest that they were being used to perform the ancient Egyptian ritual of 'breaking the pots'. However, it has recently been stressed that this ritual, being found associated with the very earliest tombs, pre-dates the period of Egyptian influence. It can thus be seen as an indigenous tradition, and certainly the concept of the funerary banquet is well known at an earlier period, for example at Kerma, where large numbers of pots are found by the tumuli.[62] We do not need to postulate major Egyptian influences on the burial rites or that the rituals themselves were organised by Egyptian priests. The presence of Egyptian scribes is suggested by the hieroglyphic name plaques found at a number of the tumuli.[63]

The construction of an offering chapel against the east side of Ku.Tum.6 may be a physical manifestation of the desire to institute a funerary cult for the deceased ruler, a typical Egyptian practice which was to become an essential feature of all subsequent royal Kushite burials down to the fourth century AD.[64] However, even before the provision of an offering chapel a special function for the area immediately to the east of the tomb may have been allocated. It has been suggested that in the earliest generation at el Kurru the funerary ritual feast took place in this area. The wall around the tomb Ku.19 is entered from the east where an open space is enclosed.[65]

Offering chapels were not confined to the graves of rulers and even relatively humble tombs had a small chamber, often only the size of a cupboard, on the east side of the tomb monument (fig. 29). At Karanog the excavators suggested that the *ba* statue was placed in the offering chapel on a shelf.[66] Elsewhere the funerary stela is placed at the western end of the chapel. In some cases, as at Jebel Adda, an offering table was placed on a podium immediately to the east of the chapel.[67]

'Sacrifices'

The deposition of ritual objects from the funerary feast can be paralleled by the ritual killing of humans at some graves. The ritual slaughter of humans to accompany the

29 *Burial at Faras showing the vaulted tomb and the base of the mud brick pyramid with its offering chapel and offering table. (Courtesy of The Griffith Institute, Oxford)*

30 *General view of the north and south royal cemeteries at Meroe. (D. A. Welsby)*

dead ruler is (to modern eyes) a shocking feature of the burials of the later kings of Kerma which date to the period 1750–1550 BC. In one of the largest tumuli (tumulus KX) in the eastern cemetery at Kerma the bodies of 322 victims, perhaps from an original total of 400, were found during the excavations conducted by Reisner.[68] In the north of the Kushite empire during the fifth and sixth centuries AD the kings and queens of the Ballana culture were also accompanied to the grave by substantial numbers of fellow humans, together with dogs, camels, donkeys and horses. The ritual slaughter was also a feature of Kushite mortuary practices.

Reisner, who conducted extensive excavations in the north cemetery at Meroe (fig. 30), reported that virtually all the tombs contained additional human burials, of the harem and servants of the king.[69] The number of individuals is much smaller than in the burials at Kerma and Ballana/Qustul, although a number of the tomb chambers were filled with dead bodies piled one upon the other.[70] A study of the published evidence indicates that Reisner exaggerated the frequency of the phenomenon. Only sixteen of the tombs in the north and west cemeteries certainly contained additional contemporary inhumations. Of these, five were the tombs of kings, one of a queen and one of a prince. The rank of the owners of the other eight tombs is uncertain.[71]

The status of the individuals killed at the time of the primary burial, as servants or close associates of the deceased, has recently been called into question.[72] It has been suggested that to interpret the observed evidence as indicative of human sacrifice is erroneous and what we are actually seeing is evidence of the ritual slaughter of prisoners. Reliefs adorning temple and offering chapel walls suggest the bellicose nature of the rulers of Kush. Lines of bound prisoners are a frequent motif, as are scenes of the kings and queens holding groups of prisoners by the hair, as on the pylon of the small temple at Naqa (fig. 6). However, these stereotyped scenes have more to do with the ideology of kingship, with the ruler defending the state against the forces of evil and chaos. Like the records of campaigns against the desert tribes, supposedly one of the first acts of the new rulers, these reliefs probably bear little relation to historical reality.

Ritual slaughter as an element of triumphal celebration may not have been confined to a funerary context; numerous pots filled with burnt human bones and charcoal have been found in close association with the Sun Temple at Meroe[73] and may indicate that temple ritual also played its part in reducing the problem posed by prisoners of war.

One tumulus recently excavated in the eastern cemetery of Kawa contained three secondary graves. The occupant of the southern grave was a slightly contracted individual with an additional skull, lower jaw and one long bone. The presence of the additional bones may indicate that even well down the social scale individuals were killed to accompany the grave owner. The situation in the central grave was very strange. It contained a neatly arranged pile of two skulls and a number of long bones at the western end of the long, narrow grave.[74]

Horses, camels and dogs were also frequently included in this ritual slaughter.[75] The earliest known animal burials are those of the royal horses interred at el Kurru. Twenty-four graves of horses were found arranged in four parallel rows. Each row appears to have contained the horses of a particular ruler. Two of these rows could be dated to the reigns of Shabaqo and Shebitqo and it is likely that the other two belong to Piye and Tanwetamani. The graves are all designed to take a single standing horse with, in some cases, interior supports for the belly and neck. Recent work has shown that fragments of skulls were found, indicating that the animals had not been decapitated before burial as had previously been thought.[76] Within the horse cemetery there was a single burial of a dog in a small circular grave (Ku.226).[77]

The importance of the horse to the rulers of Kush is illustrated by a passage on the stela of Piye, erected at Jebel Barkal. On the capture of the Egyptian city of Hermopolis after a violent siege '... his Majesty went on to the place where the horses were kept, and into the stalls of the foals, and he perceived that they had been suffering from hunger and he said "I swear by my own life, and by the love which I have for Ra, who reneweth the [breath of] life which is in my nostrils, that to my mind to have allowed my horses to suffer is the worst of all the evil things which thou hast done ..."'[78]

In the later periods the animals were more closely associated with the human victims being located in the tomb chambers, at the foot of the ramp giving access to the chamber, and in the fill of the ramp itself. The function of the dog as the ritual guardian can be clearly paralleled on the reliefs of the tomb chapels, where the dogs are depicted assuming this role. They are also shown guarding prisoners.[79]

Burials of other animals are uncommon. At Meroe there are some examples of the burial of cattle and perhaps sheep.[80] The burials within the cemetery at Sanam of three young lions are rather different and their ritual significance is unclear. Two of these were accompanied by items of jewellery; in burial 1080 a Horus [Udjet] eye at the throat; and in 1449 a blue glaze spherical bead at the throat and a quadruple blue glaze tubular bead at one ankle.[81] A burial of two large fish was also noted.

Graves and tombs generally were only designed to contain a single 'primary' burial and the nature of the tomb monuments will often have precluded subsequent use of the tomb. A rare example of a multiple burial has been discovered at Kerma. The long, narrow, vaulted chamber was probably designed for multiple burials from its inception and contained the skeletons of seven children, one adolescent and five adults.[82] At Sedeinga a second burial was inserted into tomb WT3, which was surmounted by a pyramid, and a second pyramid – presumably to commemorate the inserted individual – was then built over the stairway. A whole series of such 'coupled' pyramids are to be seen in the cemetery.[83]

Tomb monuments

Many of the known Kushite graves have no tomb monuments at ground level, although this may in many cases be the result of later erosion. To perform the funerary ritual, which demanded that offerings and libations be made to the dead, even the poorest graves required a marker on the surface. At Karanog a number of graves of this sort preserved evidence of wooden poles; the extant examples 0.08 m and 0.3 m in diameter. One or two of these may have marked all the graves without any other form of superstructure.[84] In many graves elsewhere the evidence for similar poles may have been overlooked.

The form of tomb monument varies widely and includes both fine masonry pyramids and tumuli of sand and earth. From the eighth century BC until the fourth century AD all royal tombs were marked by pyramids and lesser individuals also made use of this type of monument (fig. 29). Certainly by the late Kushite period tumuli were very commonly employed. It is unclear to what extent social, economic, chronological and regional factors affected the choice of monument. In the eastern cemetery at Kawa tumuli, mastabas and structures built of dressed stone (perhaps pyramids) are found in close juxtaposition. At Emir Abdallah near Abri adult graves were marked by pyramids while children were buried in graves parallel to the sides of the monuments.[85] There is no evidence to indicate that the different types of monument imply differing religious beliefs, and fashion may have been a major determining factor.

In their use of the pyramid it would appear that, mirroring Egyptian religious thought, the Kushites also appreciated the symbolism inherent in that type of monu-

31 *Relief on the north wall of the chapel of Beg.N.28 at Meroe. (After Lepsius 1849–59)*

ment. A ceramic pyramidion found at Kerma, and dating to the early Kushite period, bears an inscription in which the Egyptian name of the great sun sanctuary at Heliopolis occurs. The connection of the pyramid with this sanctuary conforms with the solar symbolism of the pyramid.[86]

In the south of the kingdom the very latest 'royal' burials were marked by tumuli and have been noted at el Hobagi (fig. 30)[87] and perhaps at Meroe and near Jebel Qisi.[88] The Dynasty buried at Ballana and Qustul, which assumed power on the break-up of the Kushite kingdom in the north, were also buried under tumuli.[89] However, a number of very interesting tomb monuments at the nearby site of Jebel Adda, identified by their excavator as pyramids, marked the positions of tombs which contained grave goods of typical post-Meroitic (X-Group) type.[90] The excavator thought that these graves were being reused, but the logical interpretation of the observed evidence is that these pyramids, if that was their original form, are contemporary with the material found within them. If this is the correct interpretation, these are the latest known pyramids in the Nile valley.

The mortuary ritual practised in the graves at el Hobagi demonstrates the survival of Kushite religious ideology into the later fourth century AD at the earliest.[91] In the far north, at Qasr Ibrim, a temple continued to function until its violent and deliberate destruction in the sixth century AD,[92] as did the Temple of Isis at Philae until its closure by the Roman general Narses on the orders of the emperor Justinian around AD 540. By that date the Kingdom of Kush was long gone, but it had successfully acted as a guardian of the gods of ancient Egypt for over 1000 years and passed on that religion to the Blemmyes and Noba in the north and to whomever dominated the southern part of the kingdom. Although it was the arrival of Christianity, perhaps from as early as the fifth century AD, but certainly from the sixth century, which led to the terminal decline of the old religion, how rapid a process that was is difficult to determine.

Funerary beliefs

Our best evidence for the funerary beliefs of the Kushites comes from the scenes and inscriptions painted or incised on the walls of their tomb chambers and on the walls of their offering chapels. These are largely confined to royal tombs and to the tombs of the richer inhabitants. Reliefs and inscriptions on funerary stelae and on offering tables, which have a much wider distribution through the social spectrum, also contribute to our knowledge of this subject.

The earliest decorated tomb is that of the king Tanwetamani at el Kurru (Ku.16). The paintings, executed on the plaster lining of the two chambers, are extremely well preserved and depict scenes showing the royal experience in the afterworld. The style is purely Egyptian, as is the subject matter.[93] Painted tomb chambers survive into the third century BC and those in the southern cemetery at Meroe are reasonably well preserved. The scenes in Beg.S.10 show standing figures of gods with bands of hiero-glyphic inscriptions. Over the doorway is a winged disc and *uraei* and the roof has a representation of Nut. Some of the decoration of Beg.S.503 is very similar, but the inscriptions are very debased and largely illegible. A figure of Nut adorns the roof in one chamber.

In the early burials of kings in triple chambered tombs, that is from the time of King Senkamanisken (later seventh century BC), the two outer rooms were inscribed with set texts, from the 125th chapter of the Book of the Dead in the antechamber, and with the 'Negative Confession', also from the Book of the Dead, in the middle room.[94]

The interiors of offering chapels are often profusely decorated with reliefs, although even in the heyday of the kingdom this is not invariably the case. At Meroe three major decoration types have been identified. The earliest, dated to the third century BC, comprises Egyptian offering scenes with inscriptions in hieroglyphs. The second type, dating from the late third century BC into the early first century AD, has a mixture of offering scenes, Book of the Dead vignettes and ritual scenes of the sort seen in New Kingdom temples. The latest type falls into two sub-groups, the so-called type C(1) confined to the chapels of King Natakamani, his queen, Amanitore and their son Ari-khankharer; and type C(2) found in all later royal funerary chapels. The former sub-group illustrates a renewed passion for Egyptian religious forms and demonstrates a precise and scholarly knowledge of Egyptian sources. Type C(2) is very consistent, with the surviving walls almost invariably showing either a prince with an incense burner fumigating the enthroned ruler (fig. 31) or Nephthys and/or Anubis pouring a libation offering.[95] The ruler is usually depicted sitting on the Lion Throne (fig. 32) under a canopy, often under the protection of a winged figure of Isis who stands behind the throne, as on the north wall of the offering chapel Beg.N.28 at Meroe.

The libation scene is closely comparable with that shown on sixteen offering tables from the north and west cemeteries at Meroe and dating to the first and second centuries AD. Depicted on them are the gods Anubis and Nephthys pouring a libation of milk onto an offering table covered with loaves of bread. This ritual is closely associated with the worship of Isis at Philae and demonstrates the influence of Isisaic ritual at the royal court at this time.[96]

Offering tables are usually of a standard form, a thick rectangular stone slab with a recessed centre and a protruding spout to one side. The centre is frequently decorated with relief and the raised border carries an inscription naming the deceased along with

32 *Relief on the north wall of Beg.N.36 of King Aryesbokhe, early third century* AD. *(D.A.Welsby)*

33 *Offering table of a* pesto *from Faras. (BM, EA 1576)*

the customary Kushite offering formula (fig. 33). Among the rather rare exceptions to this type are a number of examples from Qasr Ibrim. One has nine shallow circular depressions in the upper face of the stone joined by channels to form three rows which communicate by further channels with the spout. Others of pottery and stone are divided into compartments, the pottery examples being painted with snakes, birds and *uraei*.[97]

The scenes on the offering tables frequently depict the offering table itself being used. The projecting horns and disc motif on one of the Qasr Ibrim offering tables, a

motif scratched onto a ceramic example from the same site, make the association of both tables with Isis highly probable and may suggest that the painted motifs are also connected with her worship.[98]

Stelae, frequently of rectangular form with a rounded top, bear inscriptions and often incised decoration, but occasionally the decoration is in relief or is painted. The simpler stelae are inscribed only with the text. The inscriptions take a standard form on tombstones of private individuals. The stela of Tedeqen from Karanog begins with an appeal to the gods of the dead followed by the name of the deceased and the prayer with the plea for water and bread, or benediction. The panel above shows the deceased before the gods Isis and Osiris.[99]

A common feature of a number of later Kushite cemeteries is the presence of *ba*-statues, usually of human form with the addition of folded wings (fig. 34, col. pl. 5). They represent the soul of the deceased and often are sculpted with the facial and other physical characteristics of the tomb owner. *Ba*-statues were set up for both men and women and are abundant in the north of Nubia where important state officials are among those so depicted. In the southern part of the empire they are extremely rare. No examples are published from the royal cemetery at Nuri and only a handful are known from the royal cemeteries at Meroe. Although the concept of the *ba*, the soul of the deceased, is derived from Egyptian religion the form of the Kushite *ba*-statues is an essentially local manifestation.[100]

Respect for the dead

A great deal of effort was taken to ensure that the deceased was well provided for in the afterlife. Royal burials and those of other élite members of society were buried with objects often of great intrinsic value. It is to be hoped that the dead did not actually require these trappings of their worldly status in the afterlife, for few enjoyed the possession of them for long. In Egypt documentary evidence clearly indicates that even the most elaborate precautions and the direst punishments for offenders did little to curb this rough and ready redistribution system, the robbing of tombs. That a similar, although less well-documented, situation existed in the Kingdom of Kush is very likely, although it is often very difficult to ascertain the date of the robbing of a tomb. At el Kurru in the late Kushite period, the body of the tomb owner of Ku.11 had been unceremoniously dragged out through the plunderer's hole.[101] A number of the tombs at that site were reused in the later Kushite period and had presumably already been robbed. Among these Ku.15 contained at least ten secondary burials.[102] Within the royal tombs at Nuri there is a profusion of medieval objects but the tombs had probably been robbed long before.

The most graphic evidence for the robbing of a royal tomb comes from the northern cemetery at Meroe. During the construction of tomb Beg.N.12 the workmen appear to

Opposite **34** *Ba-statue. (Courtesy of the Ashmolean Museum, Oxford)*

have dug a narrow passage from its outer chamber into the adjacent tomb Beg.N.11, presumably to remove its contents. The illegal nature of their work is illustrated by the very careful way in which they blocked the entrance to their tunnel. They may well have escaped detection, as the tunnel was still sealed when excavated by Reisner.

The overwhelming impression that one gets from the study of Kushite religion is of the survival of Egyptian religion and mortuary beliefs, although the indigenous traditions such as human and animal sacrifices noted above are also a significant feature and serve to highlight the fusion of the foreign and local beliefs. The variations in religious practices which can be observed both chronologically and spatially throughout Kushite history reflect the relative strengths of these two differing traditions at any one place and time.

CHAPTER FIVE

Architecture

In the far north of Nubia the almost total absence of rainfall has allowed even the relatively vulnerable mud brick structures to survive for thousands of years, often in a remarkably good state of preservation. The most dramatic examples of these were the Middle Kingdom pharaonic fortresses on the Second Cataract which now, alas, have been dissolved by the waters of Lake Nasser. To the south the western *deffufa* (a Nubian term for an upstanding brick ruin) at Kerma, a mud brick structure of slightly later date, still stands to a height of 18 m. The relative isolation and sparse population of Nubia have also assisted the considerable degree of survival of ancient buildings. Mud bricks in particular are not easy to reuse, so there has been little pillaging of mud brick walls to provide construction materials. Buildings made of more solid materials, red (fired) bricks and stone, have attracted the attentions of later builders and many structures have been very severely damaged by these activities. Wind-blown sand has also assisted in the preservation of monuments, covering and thereby protecting walls from damage by erosion and human activities. The buildings that have suffered most are those constructed of timber. Timber has always been a sparse commodity in Nubia and thus was reused time and again. It was also destroyed by termites or used for fuel. Timber structures are, therefore, very under-represented in the archaeological record and this needs to be borne in mind when discussing architecture and town planning at any period in Nubia's history.

The earliest evidence we have for the emergence of the Kushite state is the presence of the burials of important personages at el Kurru. The architecture of their tomb monuments is the earliest Kushite architecture that we can recognise. Throughout the history of Kush the royal tomb monuments continue to be one of the most characteristic architectural expressions of the centralised state and they survive as one of the latest expressions of Kushite power. The Kushites constructed a wide range of buildings, from grandiose masonry temples to circular timber huts. They also embarked on civil engineering projects to harness and direct the scanty water resources of the semi-desert to assist animal husbandry and agriculture in marginal areas.

As in most other facets of Kushite life the influence of Egypt on Kushite architecture dominates our perception. However, in the first burials at el Kurru, and in a few buildings at a later date, we get a rare glimpse of the indigenous traditions.

Funerary architecture

Royal burials

The first important personage to be buried at el Kurru was placed in a small chamber or alcove hewn into the side of a shallow rock-cut pit. Over the tomb chamber, which was filled before the superstructure was constructed, was a circular tumulus, which was revetted with a vertical or near vertical wall of rough drystone masonry of uncertain height. The tumulus was about 7.3 m in diameter.[1] Two other burials of similar type are thought to be associated with this tumulus.[2]

The antecedents of these burials can be traced in the distant past. They represent the traditional burial type on the Middle Nile, burials under tumuli reappearing throughout Nubian history from the A-Group until the arrival of Christianity in the sixth century AD, a time span of over 3000 years. For some of this time new fashions found favour and supplanted the traditional burial type but the tradition persisted. The revetting wall is a feature of tombs of the C-Group, but not of the later tumuli of the Kerma culture. However, the revetted tumuli at el Kurru are more substantial than the earlier revetted type, though extremely small compared with those of the rulers of Kerma.

At el Kurru the development of the tomb and superstructure types is well documented from the work of the excavator George Reisner. From the earliest tumuli there is some degree of elaboration. The two tumuli of the second generation are of similar design but the revetting wall was set in a shallow foundation trench. Attached to the east face of Ku.Tum.6 was a room constructed of mud brick which is identified as a tomb chapel and is the earliest Kushite building known to us (fig. 35). It can be assumed that the revetting wall, at least of Ku.Tum.6, was as high as the roof of the chapel. The tumuli were surrounded by low stone walls with a rounded coping delimiting a horseshoe shaped enclosure opening to the east. The enclosure wall of Ku.Tum.6 was built of irregular blocks, while the other enclosure wall was of blocks about one Egyptian cubit (523 mm) in width. In both cases the blocks were well cut and mark a distinctive advance in the skill of the builders over their predecessors. The tomb chambers continued to be a simple pit dug into the ground with the body placed in a niche cut into one side. The grave pit beneath Ku.Tum.2 was covered by transverse stone slabs.

The grave Ku.14, thought to be that of the ruler of the next generation, was initially provided with a small stone revetted tumulus with a stone offering chapel to the east. However, the design was soon modified, presumably during the construction, but after at least the lower courses of the chapel and circular revetment had been built, and the whole was encased in a square monument. The enclosure wall around the tomb respects the square monument. The change from a circular to a square tomb monument has been seen as a logical adjunct to the provision of an offering chapel which sits much more comfortably against the flat wall provided by the new monument type. In all subsequent royal burials for the next 1000 years and more the square tomb monument was to remain in fashion, only to be replaced once more by the circular tumulus during the terminal decline of the kingdom in the fourth century AD.

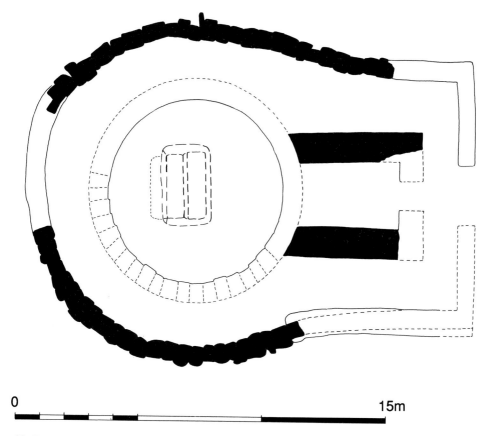

35 *Tumulus Ku.Tum.6 and enclosure wall at el Kurru. (After Dunham 1950)*

The superstructures of most of the tomb monuments at el Kurru have been very badly damaged by people searching for reusable stone and their original form is uncertain. The monument over grave Ku.13, which is thought to be slightly later than the transitional type Ku.14, survived to a height of several courses and has a slightly battered face suggesting that it formed part of a mastaba type superstructure. However, during its excavation a pyramidal 'cap-stone' was recovered, which has led to the suggestion that the mastaba supported a small pyramid. Other examples perhaps of similar type are discussed below.

During the fifth generation, in Ku.23, the provision of a side niche was abandoned and the body was placed at the bottom of the rectangular pit. The pits of this type were roofed, in the earlier examples by stone slabs, as had been the case in graves of generation D (Ku.10 and 11).

The tomb chamber in Ku.8, 3.5 m wide, was dug to a depth of only 2.5 m and was roofed with a corbelled vault constructed of dressed stone. The vault was built well above ground level, being subsequently incorporated into the superstructure. The chamber of Ku.8, thought to have been the tomb of King Kashta, was larger than any of its predecessors. It has been suggested that this was related to the elaboration of the burial rites where more space in the tomb was needed. The roof span was thus too great to be covered by slabs, so an alternative means of roofing had to be employed.

The superstructure of this tomb was originally built of the same grey stone used for the earlier constructions. However, it seems to have been later reconstructed using yellow stone, perhaps in the middle of the XXVth Dynasty when the chapel was furnished with a pair of doors giving access into the room decorated with reliefs and painted plaster. The contemporary tomb, Ku.7, had its chapel extended until it consisted of two rooms or of an inner room with a columned portico.

At el Kurru the next development in the tomb chamber type was to place the cham-

36 *The corbel-roofed tomb chamber of Ku.18, the tomb of King Shebitqo at el Kurru. (D. A. Welsby)*

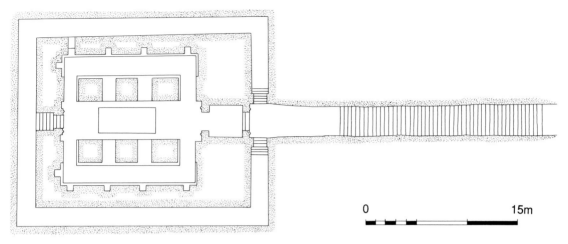

37 *Tomb of Taharqo at Nuri. (After Dunham 1955)*

ber in a deep pit; Piye's tomb (Ku.17) was set in a pit 5.5 m deep. It was again roofed with a corbelled vault, but access to the completed chamber was still possible, being provided down a long flight of stone-cut steps and through a doorway with an arched head, hewn from the living rock (for the type see fig. 36). This made it possible to construct the tomb chamber and to build the superstructure before the burial was introduced into the tomb. Only the sealing of the tomb chamber with a rough wall of stone or mud brick, the back-filling of the entrance ramp and the construction of the chapel had to be completed after the burial. A major advantage of this may have been that the occupant of the tomb was able to appreciate the grandeur of his or her final resting place rather than having to trust to the piety of those remaining in the world of the living. The use of corbelled roofed tombs was confined to the richest burials and was soon rendered redundant when the chambers became entirely rock-cut.

The variation in the form of the rock-cut tombs is considerable. The most elaborate example was that built by Taharqo for himself at Nuri (Nu.1). Taharqo effectively created underground a rectangular building approximately 21 m by 16.5 m in size and with 'walls' between 2 and 3 m thick (fig. 37). The 'structure' was separated from the parent rock on all four sides by a narrow passageway. It was entered from the external stairway through a centrally-placed doorway leading to a small vestibule within the thickness of the 'pylon'. A narrow, centrally placed doorway in the opposite wall allowed access into the surrounding passage. Inside the structure the area was divided into three aisles by two rows of massive square piers set on a low stylobate (plinth), the whole being cut from the living rock. Along the sides and back of the room were small niches. The ceilings of the rooms were cut to the shape of semi-circular barrel vaults.

No later ruler attempted to construct a tomb similar to this. However, a number of tombs had up to three chambers, sometimes with two rows of stone piers being left to support the roof and occasionally with masonry piers being constructed to perform the

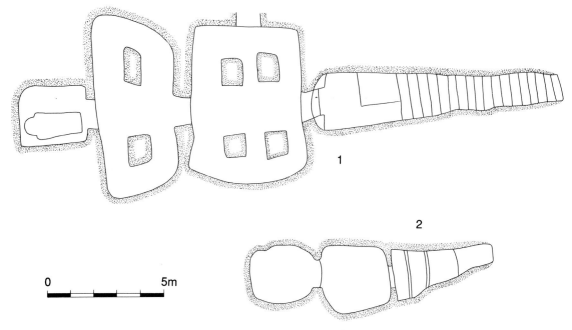

38 *Tombs in the northern cemetery, Meroe. (After Dunham 1957)*
   1 Beg.N.11
   2 Beg.N.25

same function (fig. 38). Roofs were cut to form high vaults, either of semi-circular section or almost flat. Sometimes the 'springing' of the vault was accentuated by a small inset. Doorways were usually entirely rock-cut and arched, although there are examples with flat heads. Occasionally the outer doorway was formed from masonry and given a leaning slab or monolithic arcuate lintel.

   Some of the most elaborate tombs were those of King Aspelta and his family. In these tombs the chambers were lined with sandstone blocks and the floors were paved in stone slabs. These tombs are generally very regular in their layout and the tomb of the king in particular (Nu.8) is noteworthy for the accuracy in the alignment maintained between the below- and above-ground features. The structural independence of the tomb and stairway on the one hand and of the pyramid and chapel on the other has frequently resulted in the two elements following widely diverging alignments. On occasion the tomb and stairway are so far apart as to nowhere impinge one upon the other. The workmen labouring on the excavation of the tomb Beg.N.12 hit a seam of hard stone explaining why, in this particular case, the stairway and tomb chambers lie well to one side of the superstructure.

   In later burials this trend was reversed and the pyramid and chapel came to be built directly over the filling of the stairway, perhaps in a vain attempt to dissuade the tomb robbers from their destructive activities.

   There was frequently considerable architectural embellishment in the tombs, using mouldings and decorated niches carved in the living rock. The walls and ceilings of many of them were plastered and painted with elaborate scenes, while the masonry-lined tombs of Aspelta and his family were covered with inscriptions.

After the burial of the deceased in those tombs which were entered down a stairway, the outer door was sealed before the stairway trench was filled. The method of sealing varied greatly. A wall of well-dressed masonry could be built in the doorway and carefully cut to fit the available space. However, frequently the quality of the sealing wall was rather poor, being constructed from roughly dressed stone blocks, from rubble or of mud brick. The blocking was on occasion built across the front of the doorway rather than within it.

It is thought that Kashta's successor, Piye, was the first person at el Kurru to have had his tomb marked by a true pyramid, which measured 8 m a side at its base. No trace of the superstructure survived at the time of excavation so the identification of its original form is uncertain. The pyramid was the archetypal tomb monument of the Kushite royal family and its close associates. Pyramids are found at the royal cemeteries at el Kurru, Nuri, Jebel Barkal and at Meroe. They are very different from the famous Egyptian examples of the Old and Middle Kingdom pharaohs, which are of colossal

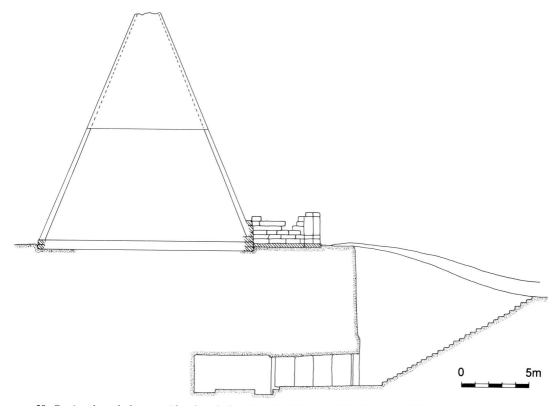

39 *Section through the pyramid and tomb, Bar.4 at Jebel Barkal. (After Dunham 1957)*

size, have sides sloping at an angle of around 52°, and often have the burial chamber within or entered by a passage through the pyramid. It appears that the Kushites were not copying the Old Kingdom royal tomb monuments but the pyramids of the New Kingdom Egyptian and Nubian élites in the cemeteries adjacent to their cities south of Aswan, which must have been a familiar feature of the early Kushite landscape. Kushite pyramids have much in common with these. In all cases the tomb chambers lie beneath and are structurally independent of the pyramid (fig. 39).

Kushite pyramids are characterised by their steep sides, frequently at an angle between 60° and 65°, sometimes as steep as 73°, which gives them a tall, slender appearance. There are, however, one or two exceptions to the norm. At Nuri the angle of the faces of the lower part of Nu.7 are at 60° but the upper part appears to be at an angle of about 45° and thus has a similar profile to the famous bent pyramid at Dashur in Egypt. A lack of confidence in the stability of the structure may have led the builders to modify the plan during construction. The possibility that a number of the early tombs at el Kurru were covered by small pyramids on top of a mastaba has already been noted and the late brick and rubble pyramids at Meroe are of this type. The Meroe pyramid, Beg.N.1, built over the tomb of Queen Amanitore, has a tall stepped base, higher than the chapel roof, on which is set the small, very steep pyramid with a slope angle of 77° (fig. 40.1). Eight courses now survive, but in drawings by early travellers such as Linant de Bellefonds and Cailliaud, it is shown standing to a much greater height. Whether it was further drastically reduced in size before its apex is unknown. If not, its very slender appearance will have been markedly different to that of many of the other pyramids, although Beg.N.17 is similarly steep-sided. Bar.8, constructed on a prominent slope, has a large podium of truncated pyramidal form on which sits the pyramid and probably the chapel. This pyramid is likewise truncated and supports a smaller pyramid above (fig. 40.2). The reason for this curious arrangement is unknown.

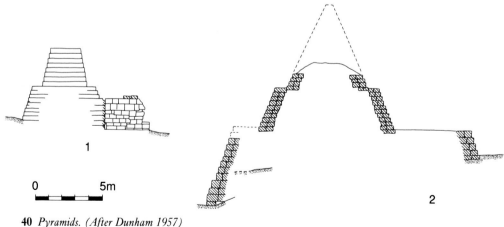

40 *Pyramids. (After Dunham 1957)*
  1 Beg.N.1 at Meroe
  2 Bar.8 at Jebel Barkal

41 *General view of the pyramids at Nuri. (D. A. Welsby)*

Bar.8 dates to the second century BC and Beg.N.1 to around the beginning of our era.

The royal pyramids range considerably in size and vary considerably in detail. The earliest type, used to mark the tombs of all the kings from Piye (or his successor) to Taharqo, have the facing stones dressed at the same angle as the face to give a smooth slope over the whole of the pyramid. These pyramids are solid masonry structures. Taharqo was the first Kushite ruler to forsake the ancestral burial site at el Kurru. His tomb was constructed at Nuri on the left bank of the Nile a little upstream of Jebel Barkal, which is clearly visible from the site. As originally designed, Taharqo's pyramid was of the same type, but of considerably greater dimensions than those at el Kurru.[3] Its estimated size at the base is 28.5 m square. It appears that the pyramid was completed before the decision was taken to provide a much more imposing monument. The new plan called for a pyramid 51.75 m square at the base, which totally encased the earlier structure (fig. 42). The new pyramid had slightly steeper sides and will have attained a height of about twice that of the first phase monument. In contrast to the smooth faces of the earlier pyramid, the larger version had the face of each course cut at a slightly different angle from that of the pyramid, which produced a stepped

42 *The pyramid of Taharqo (N.1) at Nuri with the two phases of construction clearly visible. (Drawing by Linant de Bellefonds 1822, courtesy of the Bankes Collection, The National Trust)*

appearance. This was thereafter the norm at Nuri and is to be found also on a number of the pyramids at Jebel Barkal and Meroe. The same sequence can also be observed at Nu.36, the tomb of Atakhebasken, the wife of Taharqo, where it is clear that the original pyramid had been provided with its chapel before the larger monument was constructed.

The only other example of an increase in pyramid size, from 26.45 m to 32.3 m, is at Nu.12 belonging to Irike-Amanote. Does this reflect the changing perceptions by Taharqo and Irike-Amanote of their own importance as their reigns progressed? Taharqo's second phase pyramid is by far the largest of any ruler of Kush. None of his successors sought to rival his pretensions to grandeur. One of the later kings, Talakhamani, who was buried in the large tomb Nu.16, was commemorated by what appears to be a disproportionately small pyramid. We may perhaps surmise that the ruler met an untimely death and the pyramid was erected in haste by his successor.

The best preserved Kushite pyramids are to be found at Jebel Barkal. Pyramid Bar.3 survives to its full height of 12.9 m above the plinth. The lower parts of each face are stepped for the first twenty-nine courses with the corner blocks being dressed to form a smooth border slightly tapering towards the apex of the pyramid. The upper twelve courses were dressed smooth and delimited by a continuation of the raised border at the corner and across the top. Bar.2 has the same raised border but is stepped to its full height. At Bar.5 there is the same combination of smooth and stepped face as at Bar.3 but where the face is smooth the border changed from being of square section to round.

The simplest form of masonry pyramid was constructed of squared blocks, each course set in a little from that below to form the pyramid. As these were not the earliest type known, the choice of this method of construction probably reflects financial rather than technical considerations. The better quality pyramids were of solid masonry. However, great savings could be made by building a stone revetment and filling the interior with rubble. This option was utilised as early as the burials at el Kurru and was the technique employed by the builders of the revetted stone tumuli of the earliest rulers. Nu.16, which has been already mentioned as a monument perhaps constructed in some haste, is a rubble-filled pyramid with a revetment two to three courses thick. Rubble-filled pyramids are inherently unstable and the pressure of the fill has frequently caused the revetment to buckle outwards and collapse. However, it was a solid masonry pyramid at Meroe, Beg.N.6, which required the construction of a reinforcing wall along its south and part of its west side.

At Meroe rubble-filled pyramids are common and a further economy was achieved by the construction of pyramids of red brick, of stone rubble, or a combination of the two. The red brick pyramids in the north cemetery at Meroe are all set on a tall stone rubble plinth and are late in date.

The attention to detail in the surface treatment of a number of the Barkal pyramids may suggest that the stonework was designed to be seen and appreciated. However, it is clear that at least among the later Kushite pyramids the whole of the exterior surface of the monument was covered in a lime mortar rendering. As early as the pyramid of Irike-Amanote, Nu.12, there may have been an all-over rendering, although the preserved section[4] may represent no more than a liberal pointing of the joints between the blocks, which will have emphasised the block construction of the pyramid's face. The masonry pyramid Beg.N.19 at Meroe, a smooth-faced pyramid, has recently been restored to its original form and provided with rendering. The presence of rendering would have resulted in the crude red brick and rubble pyramids of the late Kushite period being indistinguishable from masonry structures when completed. One of these, Beg.N.25, still retains some of its original rendering. Evidence survives at Meroe to indicate that the rendering, at least in some cases, was painted in red and yellow with a band of stars being added around the base of the pyramid.[5]

The surfaces of a number of pyramids were further embellished by circular faience plaques set into them. In the smooth upper face of Bar.3 three circular plaques were set one above the other. In the rendered pyramid Beg.N.19, a single plaque was set above a small square niche with a moulded cornice. On the east face at the corner of the seventh course of pyramid Beg.N.7 is an incised Udjat eye, which would have been invisible were the pyramid rendered.

The top of the pyramid Bar.3 is flat and approximately 1 m square. Bar.2 is very similar at approximately 0.9 m square. It is not clear whether there are any sockets or other features on the top of these pyramids. Elsewhere pyramidal blocks have been found which have been claimed as pyramid capstones. One from tomb Ku.8 at el Kurru has a substantial square socket cut in the top and others from Nuri and Meroe have two small holes cut in the top. It has been suggested that these were to hold statues and part of one of these has been tentatively identified at el Kurru. Little of this piece remains, but it can be identified as a leg of a bird terminating in a talon. It came from a crudely cast bronze statue 0.5–0.6 m high.[6] Recent finds from Sedeinga suggest that single square sockets may have been designed to support elaborately decorated stone finials.[7] Several capstones of pyramidal form with a short vertical cylindrical projection have been found at Meroe, Jebel Adda[8] and Sai.

Pyramidia reused in the door-blockings in the post-Meroitic cemetery at Meroe are surmounted by two slightly squat spheres.[9] A ceramic example bearing painted decoration and an inscription was found at Kerma.[10] Stone columns and piers with similar moulded tops have been found at Faras among other sites.[11] These may have been designed to be set at the apex of mud brick pyramids, the lower part of the stone being embedded into the structure. Two of these are of particular interest as they preserve the lower part of a bird statue on the squared top of the column.[12] This offers support to the suggestion noted above that bronze bird statues may have adorned the apex of the pyramids at el Kurru.

Offering chapels, attached to the east face of the tomb monuments, are a standard feature of Kushite royal burials from the time of the generation B rulers at el Kurru until the construction of the last pyramids in the north cemetery at Meroe. The earliest example was of mud brick, but they were thereafter most commonly made of dressed sandstone blocks. In basic form they were rectangular, with the long axis extending away from the monument, and were entered by a centrally placed doorway in the east wall (fig. 43). There is evidence from a number of chapels for the presence of double doors pivoting in the lintel and threshold stones and opening inwards where they were sometimes accommodated in a recess in the door jamb. At the other end of the chapel there was either a plain vertical wall or the wall was pierced by a niche often containing a stela. The gap between the vertical end wall of the chapel and the sloping face of the adjacent mastaba or pyramid was filled solid with masonry or rubble. A few of the late pyramids in the north cemetery at Meroe had the chapel abutting onto the vertical face of the rubble podium on which they stand. The stepped pyramid at Jebel Barkal (Bar.8) probably had the chapel on the first 'step', although no means of access visibly led up to it on the axis of the chamber. Some of the late chapels at Meroe North cemetery, which as a result of lack of space were built on a terrace, had flights of steps leading up to them (e.g. Beg.N.28).

The east face of the chapel was sometimes given a monumental aspect by the provision of a pylon of the same form as seen on Kushite temples. The angles of the pylons have, on occasion, a rectangular or circular moulding and the doorways are crowned with a cavetto-moulded lintel. Rectangular faience plaques were inserted into the face of the pylon of Beg.N.17.

Most frequently the chapel consists of a single chamber, but there are more elaborate

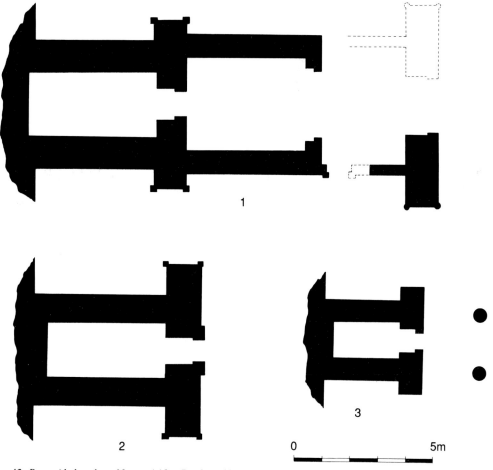

43 *Pyramid chapels at Meroe. (After Dunham 1957)*
  1 Beg.N.11
  2 Beg.N.13
  3 Beg.N.26

forms. Beg.N.11 at Meroe is one of the best preserved and largest examples (fig. 43.1). The eastern chamber with its pylon is fronted by an open court bounded to each side by a wall about 1.7m in height with cavetto-moulded coping. This leads through into another chamber with a pylon of slightly larger size than that into the inner chamber. It was entered from outside the building by a centrally placed door on the long axis in the usual manner and by a small door in the south wall. The outer chamber, with its thin side walls, may have been unroofed.

In the mud brick chapels, roofs were presumably supported on timbers and were of lightweight materials. Of the masonry chapels, where evidence survives, only one had a roof supported by timbers, the chapel of Queen Amanitore (Beg.N.1). The simplest form of stone roof utilised slabs laid transversely across the chamber. More elaborate were those with slabs leaning against each other forming a pitched roof. The most tech-nically demanding arrangement was the provision of a shallow segmental vault with a span, at Beg.N.6, formed by three long voussoirs, the ends of the side voussoirs being supported on a shelf in the side walls of the chamber.

A number of the late pyramids at Meroe, those constructed of fired brick and of rubble, have chapels built of fired brick. The chapels are of the same form as those of stone and some have pylons and porticoes. In order to allow for the necessary relief carving in the chapels, they were lined with sandstone slabs on which this could be executed.

The most unusual chapel is that of King Aryesbekhe[13] at Meroe (Beg.N.16). The position where the original chapel should have been is now partly occupied by pyramid Beg.N.36, which covers a burial thought to date to over a century and a half later. As there is clear evidence that at least later royal families, if no-one else, respected the tombs of their predecessors, it might be suggested that the builder of Beg.N.36 did not demolish the earlier chapel to make room for his monument, but that the earlier chapel was already destroyed. It would appear that, either contemporary with or later than the construction of Beg.N.36, a new chapel was built for King Aryesbekhe by partly demolishing his pyramid and inserting the chapel within it. This is one of only two Kushite royal pyramids known to contain a chamber. The new chapel was provided with a corbelled roof, and presumably the superstructure of the pyramid was rein-stated.

From the time of the burial of the second generation ruler at el Kurru the royal tombs were frequently provided with an enclosure wall. Originally these were of horse-shoe form to enclose the circular tumuli and the rectangular offering chapel. With the changeover to a square tomb monument, a mastaba and thereafter a pyramid, the shape of the enclosure was modified to suit. The enclosure was either rectangular and slightly wider than the monument or had a re-entrant to allow it to follow closely the line of the walls of the chapel, always a narrower structure. An entrance was provided into the enclosure from the east. Because of the projection of the enclosure well beyond the chapel it was frequently constructed over the fill of the stairway trench and was thus the last structural feature associated with a tomb to be built.

A few pyramids have enclosures of different forms. Some have the enclosure wall returning to the pyramid in line with its east face. Rare examples have the wall abutting the base of the pyramid on three sides and projecting to the east where it is open-ended. A further variation is where the enclosure is purely nominal and is indicated by two walls running east for a short distance from the east face of the pyramid.

In the el Kurru cemetery the enclosure was an important feature of the mortuary complex and when overcrowding of the most desirable parts of the cemetery became a serious problem the enclosure occasionally had to deviate from its regular plan so as to fit into the available space. In the main burial field only one burial, Ku.21, does not have an enclosure. At Nuri they are again an important feature. There are only two at Jebel Barkal, and no certain examples in the south and north cemeteries at

Meroe until the vestigial type at the two latest royal burials in the northern cemetery.

These enclosure walls were only ever symbolic, as remains at el Kurru indicate that they only stood a few courses high and were provided with a rounded coping.[14] There is no evidence that their entrances were provided with gates or doors.

At the end of the line of development of the Kushite royal tomb we see a return to a tomb and superstructure type which is similar to that used by the first few kings of Kush who were buried at el Kurru. The arrival of the pyramidal superstructure and the embellishment of the tomb chambers was presumably influenced by Egyptian models. With the relaxation of central control based on Meroe during the fourth century AD, the centre of power in the heartlands of the old Empire appears to have been transferred to the region around el Hobagi and Sururab, on the left bank of the Nile close to the Sixth Cataract, where the highest status burials in the area have been found. That the individuals buried there were totally *au fait* with Kushite mortuary practices is clear from their grave goods. However, they proclaimed their status in the time-honoured way by burial in a pit beneath a tumulus.

These are much more massive structures than the graves of the first rulers of Kush (fig. 44). The largest tumulus at el Hobagi, Tumulus VI, is approximately 40 m in diameter and survives to a height of 3.75 m. It is surrounded by an egg-shaped enclosure delimited by a wall built of rough stone 2–2.5 m thick and at least 1 m high.[15] The mound itself was built in stages and has a stone kerb approximately 30 m in diameter with an opening through it on the east side which is overlain by additional spoil. The burial is in the lowest of three chambers of roughly oval form and is placed beneath an overhang. The quality of construction of the grave chambers and the monument is poor and it is the scale of the undertaking, rather than its architectural pretensions, which amazes.[16]

Transitional forms between the latest pyramids of brick and rubble at Meroe and the tumuli at el Hobagi (and Jebel Qisi) may lie in the Meroe area where a tumulus within an oval enclosure was recorded by the German archaeologist Lepsius in the middle of last century. Unfortunately this monument cannot now be located.[17]

Non-royal tombs

Much of the population of Kush was buried in simple graves with little or no architectural embellishment. Typical niche graves have the niche either at the end or along one or both sides of the shaft, divided off from the shaft by a wall of mud brick, red-brick, rough stone blocks or stone slabs set on edge. On occasion the chamber was roofed with a mud or red-brick barrel vault.

Pyramids and mastabas are not confined to the royal cemeteries. Non-royal pyramids are generally rather small and can be extremely so. At Qustul burial Q363 has a pyramid approximately 2.4 m square at the base with a miniature chapel attached to one face.[18] Other pyramids at the cemetery may be even smaller. In the west cemetery at Meroe some of the pyramids are constructed of dressed stone and are indistinguishable in form from the royal examples. The desire for greater economy in the cost of con-

44 *Tumulus II at el Hobagi. (D.A. Welsby)*

struction is, as one might expect, of greater concern and the use of rubble revetments (which were presumably plastered) is common. One of the most interesting of these, at Sedeinga, has yielded a number of relief blocks, with the lower part of two cartouches of Taharqo, derived from its chapel. The rough stone revetment, measuring 9.8 m square at the base, has a gravel core and the external faces are painted in red. Presumably all the rubble revetted pyramids were painted, or plastered and painted. In the north the virtual absence of rainfall allowed the construction of pyramids with mud brick revetments and large numbers are known at Sedeinga. One of these was covered in red ochre.[19] Mud was used at Meroe as a core material (Beg.W.5) but had to be protected from the elements by an impermeable revetment of stone. Pyramids with a rubble, gravel or mud core were inherently unstable. In a few cases internal walls of rubble (Meroe Beg.W.106) or mud brick (Sedeinga WT3,[20] Qustul Q246[21]) were provided to help contain and, therefore, strengthen the structure.

One of the most unusual pyramids lies in the west cemetery at Meroe (Beg.W.2). The lowest two courses are of dressed stone while the rest of the superstructure was of red-brick. Within the core is a circular chamber with red-brick walls and presumably a red-brick dome. There is a normal tomb chamber below the pyramid. It has been suggested that the red-brick chamber and superstructure date from a reconstruction of the monument, although this still does not explain the function of the chamber.

Enclosures are rare in the royal cemeteries at Meroe, but were much more frequently provided in the western cemetery. They have also been noted at Sedeinga. The date of the tumuli within square stone enclosures noted north of Meroe are uncertain.[22] The tombs associated with the more elaborate non-royal pyramids are similar to those used for the Kushite rulers, while more humble examples are associated with the smaller pyramids. The pyramid of Taharqo at Sedeinga has two chambers, the outer one of which had a corbelled vault and was entered down a flight of steps in the usual manner. Part of the stairway was originally roofed by mud bricks supported on timber beams.

Religious architecture

Temples

No structural evidence for Kushite temples is known from the period preceding their advance into Egypt. In religious, as in funerary architecture, the influence of Egypt was paramount and there was little innovation. The earliest building activities known to us relate to the construction of a mud brick temple at Jebel Barkal by Kashta or possibly by his predecessor Alara. Later, kings of the XXVth Dynasty repaired and embellished Egyptian temples both in Egypt and in the land of Kush. Piye rebuilt the Temple of Amun at Jebel Barkal, which was adopted by the Kushites as their most important religious institution. Archaeological evidence suggests that immediately before this restoration work at least one hall in the temple had lost its roof. The adjacent pharaonic Temple of Mut may also have been in a state of collapse.[23]

The greatest builder of this period appears to have been Taharqo. One of his most famous buildings was a six-columned kiosk constructed in the forecourt of the Temple of Amun at Karnak. His activities, however, were not confined to Egypt. When Taharqo visited Kawa early in his reign at least one temple, built of brick, was buried up to its roof in sand and covered with earth. Taharqo ordered that this situation be rectified and he constructed a new Temple to Amun (Temple T), the architect and builders being brought from Memphis to undertake the work which took four years to complete.[24] At Sanam across the river and a little downstream from Jebel Barkal Taharqo built another temple to Amun, Bull of Bow-land (Nubia), and a third was constructed on Argo Island at Tabo a little to the north of Kawa. These three temples are so similar in design and dimensions as to suggest that they were built by the same design and construction team. There is little that is distinctly Kushite in these buildings apart perhaps from the conscious attempt to revive long outmoded styles of decoration derived from Old Kingdom structures. The temple at Kawa (fig. 45.3), measuring

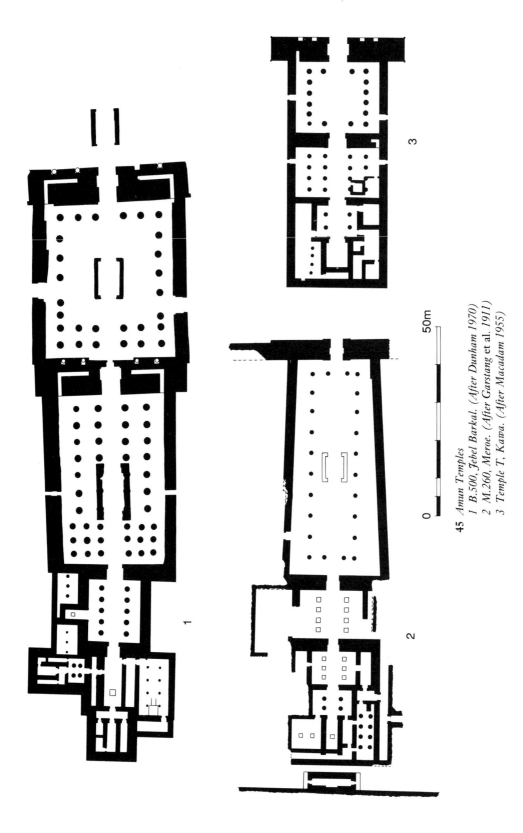

45 *Amun Temples*
1 *B.500, Jebel Barkal. (After Dunham 1970)*
2 *M.260, Meroe. (After Garstang et al. 1911)*
3 *Temple T, Kawa. (After Macadam 1955)*

0   50m

46 *Temple of Amun (B.500), from the top of Jebel Barkal. (D. A. Welsby)*

68.5 m by 38.7 m was constructed throughout from sandstone blocks. It consisted of an outer court with colonnade entered between two pylons. Beyond the court a hypostyle hall led through a pronaos (vestibule) into the sanctuary chamber, which was flanked by a number of ancillary rooms.

Kushite Amun temples are constructed to this basic plan wherever in the kingdom they may be. The two exceptions are the two largest Amun temples, at Jebel Barkal and at Meroe. That at Barkal was anomalous as a result of the long process of building work on the site which was to transform the rather small New Kingdom temple into the largest temple in the Kingdom of Kush. Indeed, in its final form the temple, with a length of approximately 150 m, was by far the largest 'Egyptian' temple ever built in Nubia (figs 45.1, 46). The Amun Temple at Meroe is set within a *temenos* (sacred precinct), the front wall of the temple and the *temenos* wall being one. Whether the superstructure was in the form of a pylon in the traditional manner is unknown but the ground plan gives no support to this suggestion. The first court in its final phase is exceptionally long and narrow. There is no hypostyle hall beyond it but three progressively smaller vestibules with eight, six and four columns respectively (fig. 45.2).[25]

Other temples show much more variety in their plans. Temple B.300 at Jebel Barkal, built by Taharqo, had columns carved in the form of Bes (a god depicted as a dwarf wearing a plumed crown) and other columns with Hathor head capitals (fig. 47). It and

47 *Temple B.300 at Jebel Barkal. (Drawing by Linant de Bellefonds 1822, courtesy of the Bankes Collection, The National Trust)*

its neighbour to the west are built up against the cliff face of the Jebel and the sanctu-ary chambers are rock-cut.

A small temple was built by Taharqo within the hilltop fortress at Qasr Ibrim which at the time of the temple's construction lay far from any potential military threat. The site may have had a purely religious importance at that date although the defences remained in good repair. This temple was built out of mud brick with stone columns reused from a structure of New Kingdom date.[26]

One of the most unusual temples was the so-called Sun Temple at Meroe, which lies on the gravel plain mid-way between the city and the royal pyramid cemeteries. The temple stood on a podium reached by a sloping ramp and with a colonnade running around its edge. It was entered up a flight of shallow steps through a pylon and enclosed a free-standing sanctuary chamber (fig. 48). A relief on the rear wall of the podium shows the building as it appeared when standing. The wall at the front of the podium is carried up to form a tall pylon, while the side wall with rounded crenellations is much lower, allowing a view of the colonnade and the temple within it (fig. 49).[27]

Temples of indigenous Kushite gods, especially the lion-headed god Apedemak, were all single or two-roomed structures. The best preserved is at Naqa and dates to

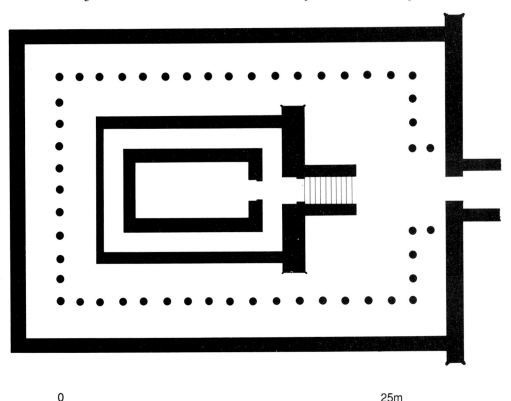

0   25m

48 *M.250, the Sun Temple, Meroe. (After Garstang et al. 1911)*

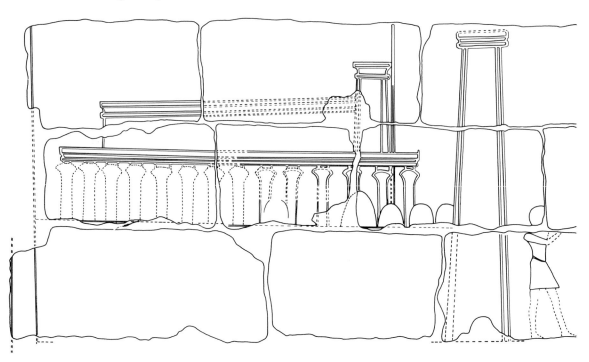

49 *Relief from the rear wall of the Sun Temple podium. (After Hakem 1988)*

the reigns of Natakamani and Amanitore (fig. 6). Large sections of the walls of the Lion Temple at Musawwarat es Sufra collapsed outwards in the distant past allowing the excavators to re-erect the walls (fig. 5). This temple, which was built by Arnekhamani between *c.*235 and 221 BC, is a little larger than the Naqa example with internal dimensions of 12 m by 6.2 m, and the pylon is 7.49 m high. The roof was supported on two rows of three columns (fig. 50.2).[28] A two-roomed Lion Temple, set on a podium, was excavated by Garstang at Meroe. Each of the two rooms had the roof supported on two columns (fig. 50.3).[29] The presence of a colonnade around the outside of temples is a feature seen at a number of sites. At Basa the angles of the colonnade are marked by heart-shaped piers, an architectural device common at Alexandria, and this is one of many instances of the adoption of Alexandrian architectural styles in the Meroe region.[30]

The diversity of temple plans is well illustrated at Meroe among the several temples lining the processional way to the Temple of Amun. The entrance through the pylon of KC.100 gives access to a columnar room beyond which the sanctuary is flanked by a room to either side. M.720 has three narrow rooms running across the building, the rearmost being the sanctuary (fig. 50.1). KC.104 is a double temple, the two elements being mirror images of each other (fig. 50.6). A fourth type represented by KC.101 is a single-roomed structure set on a podium reached by a ramp.[31]

At Meinarti the foundations of a rectangular structure identified as a temple were

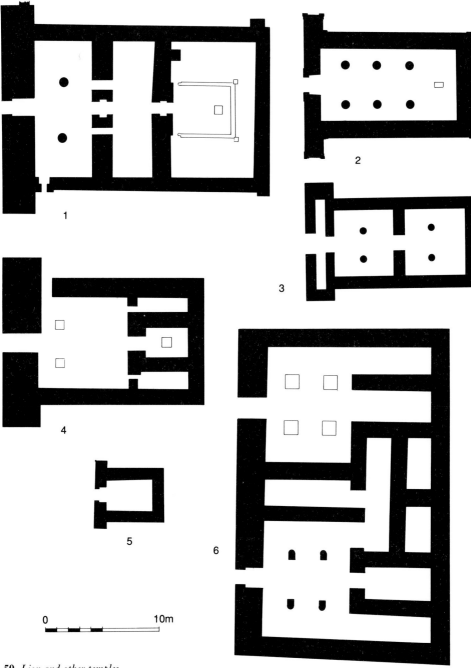

50 *Lion and other temples*
  1 M.720, Meroe. (After Shinnie 1984)
  2 The Lion Temple, Musawwarat es Sufra. (After Hintze 1962a)
  3 M.6, The Lion Temple, Meroe. (After Garstang et al. *1911)*
  4 KC.100, Meroe. (After Shinnie 1984)
  5 Temple IIA, Musawwarat es Sufra. (After Hintze 1962a)
  6 KC.104, Meroe. (After Shinnie 1984)

found. This appeared to consist of a podium presumably formed of timbers supported on rough sandstone piers arranged in rows and each set 1 m from its neighbours. The podium, delimited by a wall of mud brick, had a short flight of stone steps leading up onto it on its short axis, and was surrounded on all sides by narrow mud brick rooms.[32] The form of the building is so far unique and its function must remain in doubt. The possibility of a raised floor suggests comparison with magazines, but the form of the building differs markedly from the adjacent building which has also been identified as a magazine.

Kiosks are a feature of Egyptian temple architecture and a number were constructed to the south of Aswan by the Kushites. Those built by Taharqo at Kawa and Sanam differ a little from the norm as the lower part of the sides of the kiosk are formed from solid walls, the columns being set upon these walls rather than the walls filling the gaps between the columns as was the usual manner. The Kiosk at Naqa, perhaps the most famous example of Kushite architecture, is of the same general form but is unique in its remarkable combination of Egyptian forms and motifs with those derived from the repertoire of Greek and Roman architects (col. pl. 6).

Kushite temples, like their Egyptian predecessors, were often enclosed by a *temenos* wall. That built probably by Taharqo at Kawa was constructed of mud brick and was almost 4 m thick at the base, the outer face showing a pronounced batter.[33] The red-brick *temenos* wall at the Sun Temple at Meroe was much less substantial at 2.25–2.5 m thick and this was the more common type. Kushite *temenoi* are usually rectangular and cover around five times the area of the temple with which they are associated. The Lion Temple at Musawwarat has an oval *temenos*. This *temenos*, which covers a very considerable area, is bounded by a stone wall between 0.5 and 0.8 m high and beehive shaped in section, built of rough blocks. The adjacent Temple IIA also appears to have an oval *temenos*.[34] The form and style of construction of the Lion Temple *temenos* and its wall has much more in common with *hafirs*, such as that at Basa, than with *temenoi* elsewhere.

Water sanctuary

On the discovery of what was immediately christened the Royal Baths at Meroe in 1912, Garstang equated its various parts with the anatomy of a Roman bath suite and used the Latin technical terms to describe it.[35] The undoubted classical inspiration for much of the sculpture found in the building was seen as supporting the Classical inspiration for the structure itself, although on reflection Garstang admitted that it had as much in common with a Greek gymnasium as a Roman bathing establishment. Recently it has been suggested that rather than being a bathing establishment it is a water sanctuary connected with the festivals associated with the rise of the Nile floodwaters.[36]

The central feature of the building is a large pool, 7 m square and a little under 3 m deep, into which access could be gained by a flight of steps along its east side (fig. 51). The edge of the basin on the south side is decorated with a number of lion head spouts, inlaid faience roundels and panels, and by statuary including the famous harpist. The lion head spouts are connected to a system of water channels which will have brought the first flood waters from the Nile into the installation. To the north lay a small exedra with apsidal alcoves around it. Modifications appear to be associated with the necessity to redesign the water intake channels. The whole structure was abandoned and over-built before the end of the Kushite period.

To the south of the palace at Wad ben Naqa is a curious circular building for which no satisfactory function has been suggested. It has an external diameter of 20 m with walls of red brick 3.7 m thick rendered in white plaster on the exterior. The walls still survive to a height of 5 m. Entry is gained up a ramp on the west side and internally down two flights of steps.[37]

51 *Cache of statuary in the water sanctuary, Meroe. (Courtesy of the University of Liverpool)*

Secular architecture

Palaces

The earliest palace known to us is that built by Piye at Jebel Barkal. This building (B1200) was extensively modified by later rulers, making its original plan obscure. Perhaps among these was Harsiyotef whose stela records that he rebuilt the House of the King which had fallen down.[38] It included palatial apartments on the ground floor and two staircases, presumably giving access to an upper storey or to the roof.[39]

The best understood palace is that at Wad ben Naqa, excavated between 1959 and 1960. This building was exactly square, 61 m to a side, with the main entrance from the south giving access to a columned hall and a small suite of rooms (fig. 52). The rest of the ground floor was filled with corridors and long narrow rooms used to store a variety of goods, including elephant tusks, timber and produce contained in jars. The existence of at least one upper storey is confirmed by the presence of a number of fine architectural elements, which have no place in the rooms discovered at ground level. Stairs gave access to this level. Clearly the palatial apartments lay on this upper floor. An inscription found in the building records the name of Queen Amanishakheto, for whom the edifice may have been built.[40]

The palace of Natakamani at Jebel Barkal is a little larger at 63 m square. Although only partly excavated, it appears to have a greater number of palatial rooms on its ground floor than at Wad ben Naqa. The ground floor is raised on a podium 1.8 m high. Access to the podium is gained by a flight of shallow steps which lead through two pillared rooms into a central colonnaded courtyard.[41] Similar central courtyards, which acted as light wells, are to be found in B100 at Barkal and in a number of the palatial buildings within the Royal City at Meroe.

Houses

The earliest dwellings found at Meroe are circular timber huts.[42] At Kerma huts, 4.2 m in diameter, were built to replace mud brick structures which had probably been destroyed by floods.[43] Recent excavations at Soba East have located buildings of this type dating from the period immediately after the demise of the Kushite state. We may assume that timber huts were a commonplace in Kush. A hut of this type, perhaps with an ostrich egg in the centre of its roof, is depicted on a fine bronze cup from Karanog which appears to portray a rural scene.[44] Such buildings presumably coexisted with those constructed of more durable materials.

On the Island of Meili in Northern Nubia two houses of late Kushite date each have one large 'L'-shaped and one small rectangular room.[45] These houses are very small, with an internal area of approximately 8.5 m² and 5.5 m² (fig. 53.5). Isolated houses with two rooms of roughly equal size are known in a number of settlements in Lower Nubia (fig. 51.2). Rather more complex structures have been found on the islands of Gaminarti, Meili and at Abu Geili (figs 53.1 and 4). The Gaminarti houses consist of a series of two-roomed apartments within one building. Hearths were found in the

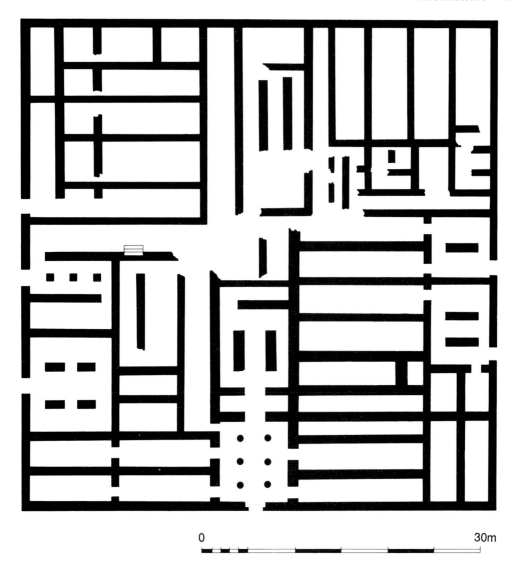

52 *Wad ben Naqa, the palace. (After Vercoutter 1962)*

larger room while the smaller was used for storage. Each unit had an internal area of approximately 18 m². The excavator suggested that these dwellings developed as a result of the need to accommodate 'additional wives in a polygamous household or the building of additional quarters to accommodate married children of the original family'.[46] The house in Meili is less regularly organised and consisted of a much larger unit. It overlay the two small houses noted above.

Although a number of domestic areas have been excavated at Meroe, no complete house plans were uncovered. The plans of the Abu Geili houses are the only ones

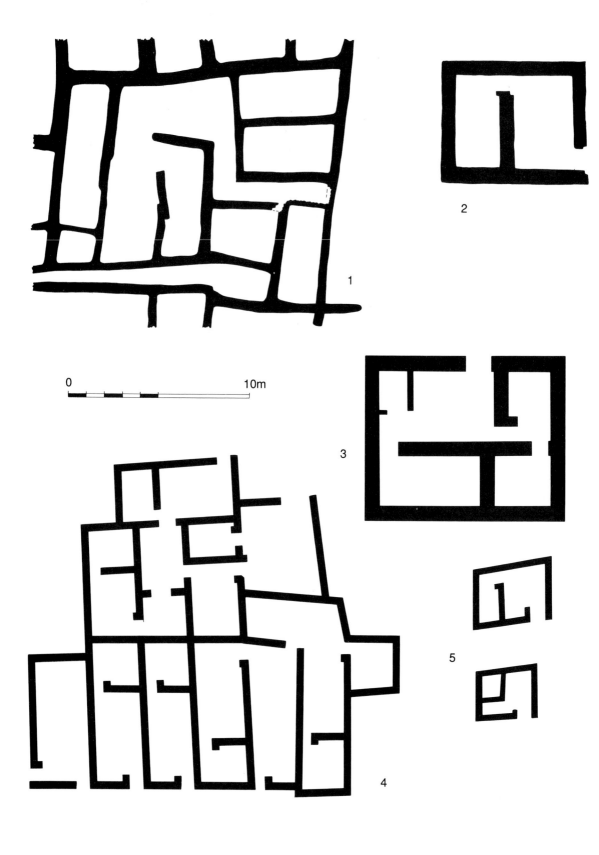

0   10m

known from the southern part of the kingdom. The village is a mass of interconnected rooms, many apparently without doorways, indicating that the dwellings must have been of at least two storeys. The arrangement of individual dwellings is unclear.[47] The nature of the structures suggests a high level of social integration as in the Gaminarti houses, but involving much larger numbers of people.

Houses as Ash Shaukan a little to the north of Abu Simbel were particularly well preserved when excavated. These vaulted structures had a profusion of alcoves and niches, some clearly for utilitarian use, others perhaps connected with domestic cults. Stairways were either external single flights or internal staircases turning around a newel. Fitments included jars, mud storage bins and cooking and bread ovens.[48]

There are also a number of buildings known which are not royal palaces and yet are on such a scale as to suggest that they are not ordinary houses. The most impressive of these is the so-called castle at Karanog, which survived to a height of three storeys until early this century. It was of rectangular plan, constructed throughout of mud brick and consisted of ranges of rooms around a central courtyard. As in many Kushite houses the roofs were vaulted. It has an area of 635 m². Only the ground floor of the nearby house 2 survived but, with a ground area of 660 m² (excluding the two projecting rooms flanking the doorway), it may well have originally been larger.[49]

It has been suggested that the residential building dating from the XXVth Dynasty at Kerma may have been the residence of many generations of administrators.[50] The house in the *temenos* of the Sun Temple at Meroe may have been occupied by priests, although its use by the ruler on the occasion of festivals in the temple has been suggested.[51] The former building, which was totally rebuilt three times to the same basic plan, is perhaps noteworthy for the absence of an internal court, a prominent feature of the priest's house.

In a number of temples there may be evidence for squatter occupation. In the Amun temples at Kawa, Sanam and Jebel Barkal rude mud brick partition walls were constructed.[52] However, at Sanam the temple floors were clean and free from rubbish when these structures were built. One room in the south-east corner of the hypostyle hall contained a pile of bronze statuettes of Osiris and the excavator suggested that these were for sale in the temple. The main axis of the temples remained free from obstructions, offering further evidence that these structures were in someway connected with the still-functioning religious structures.

Opposite **53** *Houses*
1 *Abu Geili. (After Crawford and Addison 1951)*
2 *Arminna. (After Trigger 1967)*
3 *Wadi el Arab. (After Emery and Kirwan 1935)*
4 *Gaminarti. (After Adams 1963)*
5 *Meili Island. (After Adams 1963)*

Civil engineering works

Roads

Only one made road is known in Kush, at Jebel Barkal. This stone paved road, varying in width from 1.65 m to 2.55 m and bounded by high kerbs, runs for only a short distance from near B1200 towards the Temple B700.[53] Vast tracts of the northern Sudan even today do not have made roads and overland transport will have been adequately served by tracks.

Harbours

Harbours or at least quays are perhaps to be expected at a number of sites. No definite Kushite examples are known, although a structure built of massive squared masonry blocks, extending into the river a little to the south of the main town site at Kawa, has been claimed as the remains of a pier.[54]

Wells, hafirs and dams

Wells were, as one might expect, a common feature. The most elaborate known, and perhaps one of the earliest, has been partly excavated at el Kurru. It consisted of a large rectangular pit, 6 m by 4.5 m in size, and was cleared by the archaeologists to a depth of 5 m where the water-table was reached and work was abandoned. A rock-cut stair descended along one side of the well and turned along the adjacent side.[55]

Hafirs, many of them associated with evidence for Kushite occupation, are a common feature of the Keraba and Butana, the areas to the east and south-east of Meroe. Hafirs are also a common feature of the Sahel region of the Sudan and are still constructed and extensively used today. Their importance in the economy of the area is thus highlighted. Very few Kushite hafirs have been excavated. The most extensive work has been undertaken at Musawwarat es Sufra, where a number of trenches were dug in the eastern of the two hafirs. This circular structure, which measures 240–250 m in diameter, had been excavated to a depth of about 6.3 m below the level of the surrounding plain and the upcast used to form a mound which varied considerably in thickness and height. The mound was constructed of alternating layers of gravel, sand and blocks of stone. Leading from the hafir were two parallel earth banks delimiting a ditch which was regularly cleaned out. After it fell into disuse it was replaced by a water channel revetted in stone and capped by stone slabs which penetrated the bank around the hafir and extended for 300 m.[56]

Hafirs with earthen mounds are by far the most common type, the bank sometimes being revetted in stone. The hafir at Basa, although of the same size as that at Musawwarat, Umm Usuda and elsewhere, is of entirely different construction (fig. 54). Today there are no indications of a mound, the hafir being delimited by a narrow wall of rough stone blocks with, at least in one place, an inner face of dressed sandstone. This hafir, like a number of others, has catchment walls designed to funnel surface water into it. The hafir is totally silted up but was originally at least 'five or six feet' deep.[57]

1 *Wall painting of the King in the tomb of Tanwetamani at el Kurru. (T. Kendall)*
2 *The hafir with seated lion at Umm Usuda in the Butana. (D. A. Welsby)*

3 *Foundation deposit of Aspelta from his pyramid at Nuri. (BM, EA 55564)*

4 *Handmade pottery from Meroe and Faras. (BM, EA 49384, 51502, 51631, 51243, 51676)*

5 *Ba-statue head from Faras
with remains of paint. (Courtesy
Ashmolean Museum, Oxford,
A.796)*

6 *The Kiosk, Naqa. (D. A. Welsby)*

7 *The dam at Shaq el Ahmar. (D. A. Welsby)*
8 *'Temple' 100 at Musawwarat es Sufra. (D. A. Welsby)*

9 *Painted pot, from Faras, cemetery 1, grave 2006. (BM, EA 51561)*

10 *Interior of one of the quarries to the east of the north cemetery, Meroe. (D. A. Welsby)*

11 *Unfinished granite statue in the quarry at Tumbus. (D. A. Welsby)*

12 *Tapestry decorated with seated figures of Amun from Qasr Ibrim. (BM, EA 71854)*

54 *Wall of the hafir at Basa. (D. A. Welsby)*

That the hafirs were used for irrigation may be doubted. Installations certainly connected with irrigation have rarely been noted. At Kawa special provision was made to irrigate trees by planting them in specially constructed pits surrounded by rough walls of stone and brick. One of these had a drain leading through the enclosing wall. At the head of the drain was a large bowl with a hole pierced by the base. Water from the bowl flowed along the drain into the pit onto a surface strewn with large pottery sherds which, according to the excavator, was designed to allow the water to seep gently into the soil. The remains of two trees in this pit were identified, one of the family *Sapotaceae* and the other very like *Butyrospermum Parkii*, the shea-butter tree. Elsewhere the pits yielded timber from *Mimusops* sp. (Persea).[58]

Only one dam is known which may be of Kushite date. It lies in a narrow valley at Shaq el Ahmar a little to the north-east of Meroe (see col. pl. 7). It was originally 16–18 m long and was constructed with two battered faces of coursed rubble masonry with a rubble core forming a structure around 8 m thick at the base and 5.4 m at the top 4.5 m above. No associated features were noted.[59]

Miscellaneous structures

Magazines

In the north-east corner of the *temenos* of the temple (Temple T) built by Taharqo at Kawa is a mud brick building, part of which has been identified as a granary and store-house on account of the presence of mud storage bins at ground level and of a timber platform above, a feature claimed by the excavator to be characteristic of Egyptian granaries.[60] These storage facilities are small and may only have served the needs of the occupants of the adjacent domestic building.

The magazine at Sanam consisted of two rows of seventeen equal-sized rooms ranged on either side of a central dividing wall.[61] It was of considerable size, 256 m long by 45 m wide. Originally the roof of each room was supported on twelve stone columns but later sixty-three small stone columns were added, perhaps to support a raised floor rather than as additional roof supports as the excavator suggested. The main floor timbers will have been laid along the long axis of the room, explaining the curious placing of the supports by the central row of original columns.

At Meinarti the magazine is a rectangular building with a central courtyard off which open four rectangular rooms to either side (fig. 55.3). It was constructed with walls much thicker, at 0.8 m, than those of any other contemporary structure in the settle-ment. The storerooms had floors raised 0.8 m above the level of the courtyard on two very low vaulted basements per room. These cellars each had an arched opening into the courtyard.[62] The cellars were too low to have been used for storage and presumably were a product of the desire to elevate the floors of the rooms, much as in the manner of the well-known Roman military granary type. Two bronze scales were found in this building.

The so-called western palace at Faras, a rectangular building 38 m by 36 m, had a range of small rectangular rooms (thirty-five in total) on three sides of a pillared court-yard. The fourth side was occupied by four larger rooms. In the centre was an isolated seven-roomed building (fig. 55.2).[63] At Meroe, overlying the remains of the water sanctuary and the west wall of the Royal City is another building with a range of seven long rectangular rooms opening off a narrow corridor (fig. 55.1).[64] These buildings were also probably magazines. From the Faras building were recovered a number of *ostraca* (pottery sherds) which bear both numbers and words and may be receipts for produce of some sort.[65]

A much smaller magazine within the village of Ash Shaukan consists of three rooms, two of which had no access at ground level. These are vaulted chambers, floored with granite slabs, on which remains of grain were found.[66]

Building construction

During the Kushite period buildings were constructed of timber, mud brick, red-brick and stone, or a combination of two or more of these. The type of material chosen was

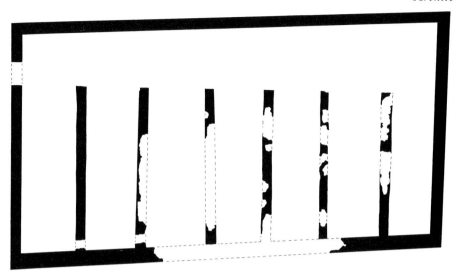

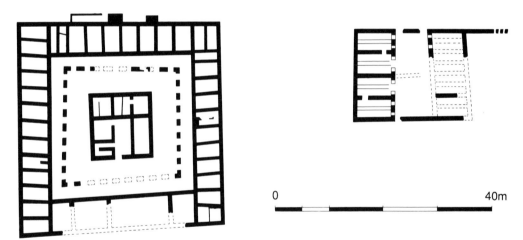

0   40m

55 *Magazines*
   1 M.191, Meroe. (After Garstang 1913)
   2 The 'Western Palace', Faras. (After Griffith 1926)
   3 Meinarti. (After Adams 1965)

dictated to some extent by financial considerations but also by the climate, the desire for prestige and the type of wall decoration to be applied. In the very dry conditions in the north, buildings of mud brick were ideal, while further south the red-brick and stone buildings required much less maintenance. Where relief decoration was to be applied, walls faced in good-quality stone were desirable. Frequently the buildings were constructed largely of stone, although in the late pyramid chapels at Meroe they were constructed of red-brick, the inner face lined with sandstone slabs to take the relief decoration. In many temples door jambs and columns were of stone, the rest of the structure being of the much cheaper mud brick. Stone quoins and socles are also a feature found in a number of mud brick domestic buildings, designed to strengthen the most vulnerable parts of the structure. Most Kushite buildings were rendered and this effectively masked whatever building material had been used. This rendering, which was often painted, was not just for aesthetic appeal: it served to protect mud brick from water damage and the soft mud brick and Nubian sandstone from wind erosion.

Doors were constructed of timber and were pivoted, pivot holes being provided in the lintels and thresholds where these were of stone or in stone pivot blocks. In the Temple of Amun built by Taharqo at Kawa, an upper door shoe of bronze with an iron pivot 90 mm in diameter has been found. The lower door shoe, with the pivot completely worn away, was also recovered.[67] The large temple doorways will have been closed by double doors. Much narrower doorways into the offering chapels of pyramids were closed either by single or double doors. At Kawa the doors were locked with a timber bar set into recesses in the door jambs.

The larger windows were usually rectangular openings with brick arched or flat timber and stone lintels and were perhaps provided with wooden shutters. A number of stone window grilles are also known. An example at Kawa is rectangular with two square holes cut through it.[68] Others are much more elaborate. From Faras comes a fine window grille with a sculptured representation of a female Thoth forming part of the openwork decoration. Another from Qasr Ibrim has a naked man carrying a small elephant on his shoulders.[69] Other windows were tall narrow slits set high in the walls, a common type seen in many periods of Nubian architecture.

Timber was used extensively in domestic buildings for door sills and lintels. Timber really came into its own, however, for roofing. We have already noted the construction of roofs of stone formed of slabs, and of corbelled and true vaults in the tomb chambers and offering chapels. Flat roofs of stone slabs are found in temples but the spans attainable were small and the slabs, being of considerable thickness, required substantial walls or columns to support them. Timber beams could support a light but quite strong roof of greater span, although the most readily available timber, palm, has limited load-bearing capabilities. In the Temple of Amun at Tabo the beams carried a roof of thatch.[70] For the more prestigious building enterprises stronger timbers could be imported. Taharqo had access to the cedars of Lebanon for the construction of his temple at Kawa.[71] The fragments of roof beams found in Temple M.720 at Meroe had been covered in gold leaf and must have had a magnificent appearance.[72] This may be compared with the use of gold leaf to clad the lower parts of the columns within the Lion Temple at Musawwarat es Sufra.[73]

Vaulted roofs of mud brick were another possibility and were used for small tombs (fig. 29) and for domestic architecture. The 'castle' at Karanog makes extensive use of mud brick vaults with spans of up to 4.2 m. The typical 'skew' vault used in Kushite times, and much more extensively in the medieval period, could be erected without the need for timber centring, as each ring of the vault rests against its neighbour. In the houses at Ash Shaukan doorways had segmental relieving arches above the timber and stone lintels.[74]

The use of cramps to assist with binding masonry blocks together has been noted in a number of buildings but is by no means universal. The earliest example is in the temple constructed by Taharqo at Kawa. The cramp holes are of dove-tail form, but no cramps were found *in situ* suggesting that, as was the Egyptian practice, the cramps were designed to hold the blocks while their neighbours were laid and were then removed as the construction work progressed. The cramp holes in the shrine within the temple were filled with mortar.[75] At Qasr Ibrim, however, large numbers were found *in situ*.[76] In the western cemetery at Meroe dove-tailed clamp sockets are visible in the upper course of the stone socle for the red-brick pyramid Beg.W.2. Whether they were an original feature of the pyramid's construction, or whether they relate to the construction of the red-brick superstructure after the partial demolition of a masonry pyramid is not clear. A wooden dove-tailed clamp was found in the north cemetery at Meroe but was thought to be modern by the excavator.[77]

Floors, at least in more humble dwellings, will have been of earth or sand, sometimes coated in a layer of white plaster. Stone slabs were used in more important buildings, as were glazed tiles, but even a number of temples only had earthen floors.

Kushite builders will have used a wide range of tools and equipment to assist with their building activities. During his demolition of the pyramid Beg.N.6 at Meroe, Ferlini found a wooden mallet and sections of rope presumably inadvertently buried during the construction of the monument.[78] The construction of the pyramids and presumably of other tall structures was assisted by the use of a crane based on the *shaduf*, which was widely used for irrigation. Within several pyramids at Meroe and in a pyramid at Karanog timbers set vertically in the centre of the monuments have been found. These were presumably the uprights of the *shaduf* that was used to raise the stone blocks into position. A similar technique was employed recently in the reconstruction of pyramid Beg.N.19 at Meroe to good effect (fig. 56).[79]

Metrology

From a study of the ground plans of Kushite buildings it is sometimes possible to determine what unit of measurement was used to lay them out and how this was actually achieved. Egyptian monuments in Nubia had been constructed using the Egyptian cubit or ell of 523 mm as the basis of measurement. The actual proportions of the buildings were based on the system of internal harmonic proportions where space was designed as one or more rectangles each with sides in the ratio of 8:5. By the combination of a number of different rectangles some diversity of plan could be achieved. This module was used exclusively by the Kushites for temples constructed for the major Egyptian deities. Other Kushite monumental buildings used a similar system, but the module was based on the lower diameter of the columns in the contemporary Greek

56 *The restored pyramid Beg.N.19 in the north cemetery at Meroe. (D. A. Welsby)*

and Roman manner. The area of the building was again determined by the harmonic proportions of 8:5, the space being delimited either by external or internal harmony, but the use of a module unique to each building produced a much greater range of diversity.

A small number of Kushite buildings survive to their full heights. From these it is possible to determine that their elevations were also related to the same module and harmonic proportions as the ground plan. Hence in the Lion Temple at Musawwarat es Sufra, for example, the width of the pylons is 16 modules, the height 10 modules, a ratio of 8:5.[80] Our only internal evidence for the way the Kushite architect went about the process of designing a building comes from Meroe, where on the north wall of the chapel for pyramid Beg.N.8 is the elevation of a pyramid laid out on a rectangular grid

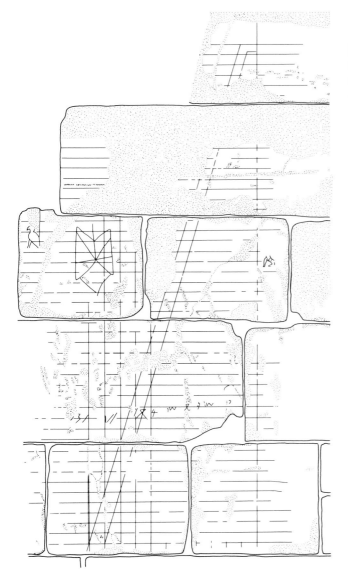

57 *Architect's elevation of a pyramid, Meroe north cemetery. (After Hinkel 1982)*

(fig. 57). The elevation appears to be an exact 1:10 scale representation, with each vertical division representing one ell and each horizontal division the average height of the stone blocks used in each course. The pyramid depicted on the elevation has an inclination of about 72°45′, a base length of 11.6 m, and has moulded corner decoration. Pyramid Beg.N.2. is the only one in the cemetery to meet almost exactly these criteria and there can be no doubt that the elevation was produced for the architect of that structure.

Six *ostraca* from the village of Ash Shaukan have house plans incised or drawn on them in charcoal. It has been suggested that these were connected not with their construction, but with transactions relating to the division of the properties.[81]

Associated with the layout of buildings is their orientation. Amun temples tend to be orientated at 90° to the adjacent river. In the Keraba, temples to the lion god Apedemak are aligned between 135° and 120°, suggesting that they were orientated on a star or planet whose position in the heavens changed markedly over the two centuries or so separating the construction of these buildings.[82]

There will have been little attempt to construct the vast majority of buildings to exact proportions or on exact alignments. However, some consistency will have been the result of the limitations imposed by the building techniques and materials available and the functions of the structures.

CHAPTER SIX

Urban and
Rural Settlement

The environment of Kush was very diverse and must have stimulated the people into practising a number of very different lifestyles. Part of the population was sedentary and occupied permanent dwellings. A significant proportion of the population, however, were transhumers or true nomads. To these peoples permanent dwellings would have been of little use and they presumably lived largely in tents or in simple huts which could be erected and dismantled as and when the need arose.

The lifestyle adopted in any given area depended to a large extent on the water resources and the amount of farming land and/or fodder available. The Nile was an inexhaustible source of water, but many areas along its banks were less than ideal for agricultural use. A few areas, as in the Batn el Hajar, were so inhospitable that any sort of sedentary occupation was difficult. Away from the river the seasonal rainfall in the south could support animal and human populations for at least part of the year and the natural water resources could be augmented by wells and hafirs.

With the relatively primitive technology available to the Kushites the climate, rainfall and geomorphology were the major determining factors affecting settlement patterns. Where the banks of the Nile were suitable for extensive agricultural exploitation, this allowed the growth of large population centres where the people could be fed from locally-grown produce.

Such areas today exist at a number of localities, for example immediately to the south of Shendi, at the downstream end of the Fourth Cataract and in the Kerma Basin. However, much of the prosperity in these areas is based on large-scale irrigation using techniques not available to the Kushites. Although major Kushite settlements are known in these areas, one must be wary in assuming that they were as suitable for agriculture in the period under discussion. The Nile is a dynamic river and its behaviour can fluctuate widely over time. A series of low Niles may render a hitherto productive area uninhabitable within a short period of time. The formation and destruction of islands, which is today a very rapid process, also can have a marked effect on the suitability of an area for sedentary occupation.

Except at the cataracts, the river provided an efficient means of transport and even low-value high-bulk materials such as foodstuffs could have been moved considerable

58 *Jebel Barkal seen from across the river at Merowe. (D. A. Welsby)*

distances. This allowed the demography to be influenced to some extent by other than environmental factors, among them political and economic considerations. The kingdom was divided into a number of regions, each with its own administrative centre and religious institutions. Two of these were of more than local importance. From an early date Jebel Barkal was the major cult centre of the state, while Meroe was the principal residence of the ruler. These two sites in particular, but also the nome capitals to a lesser extent, will have supported a large number of non-food producers: among them administrators, soldiers, priests and artisans. The need for copious quantities of drinking water and the much greater efficiency of transporting food by water rather than by land resulted in all these towns being confined to the river banks. Indeed, apart from one possible exception all major Kushite settlements are immediately adjacent to the river.

We know relatively little of settlement patterns during the life of the Kerma kingdom, largely as a result of the rather ephemeral materials used for most buildings. The Egyptians, on the other hand, built on a massive scale at a number of sites and their monuments appear to have survived long enough to have influenced the location of urban and religious centres in the first millennium BC. One of these was the religious centre at Jebel Barkal (fig. 58), located by this unique natural feature in the Middle Nile valley. Other major Kushite centres, such as Faras, Soleb, Sedeinga, Kerma and Kawa had been important towns in the New Kingdom, although whether they retained their importance in the intervening period between XXth and XXVth Dynasties is uncertain. The New Kingdom sites at Sesebi and Amara West do not appear to have been important centres under the Kushites nor do the Second Cataract fortresses.

The early history of el Kurru – the site of the first royal cemetery of Kush – is obscure, although there is slight evidence for a defended site here. Its early prominence may be due to its having been the home town of the group who rose to prominence during the ninth century BC. It appears to have lost its religious significance to the Napata area with the abandonment of the royal cemeteries. Its secular importance also appears to have waned, although our ignorance of the archaeology of the site may be partly to blame for this. Today the area is fertile, with extensive palm groves. It certainly seems to have regained its importance as a regional centre towards the end of the Kushite state, when major tumuli cemeteries were used immediately across the river at Tanqasi and a little downstream on the right bank at Zuma.

At Meroe the earliest evidence for a settlement dates to the tenth century BC.[1] Today the area around Meroe is not especially productive. The Shendi basin, some 35 km upstream, is a much more fertile area.

One of the determining factors held to account for the location of a number of Kushite settlements is their suitability for trade. The importance of Kawa, in a rather inhospitable location which was plagued by wind-blown sand throughout its history, has been attributed to its position at the north-western end of the Sikkat el Maheila, the cross-desert route which rejoins the river at Jebel Barkal. Although today this is an important route traversed by a twice-weekly bus and by lorries, we have no direct evidence that it was so used by the Kushites. The importance of the route has been adduced from the apparent absence of pharaonic and Kushite sites along the river upstream from Kawa to Barkal. Whether this is the result of the lack of archaeological work in the area or whether it reflects the situation in these periods remains to be seen. At least one major urban centre, recorded on a number of inscriptions and named Krt, has eluded the archaeologists so far.

The importance of Meroe has similarly been ascribed to its favourable location on a number of trade routes. It certainly lay at the south-eastern end of the cross-desert route from Napata, but this route may have been principally developed to facilitate communications between Meroe and Napata rather than being the cause of the growth of Meroe. There is no evidence that it was at a point where trade routes from elsewhere met the river. At a later date Berber, over 100 km downstream, and Shendi, 35 km upstream, were the major trading centres in the area. Shendi has the additional advantage of proximity to the productive Shendi basin and Berber is opposite an extensive area of cultivation. Nor is Meroe particularly well-placed to benefit from trade along the Korosko Road, as that trade route follows the river bank after joining the river in the region of Abu Hamed.

The rise to importance of Meroe may have been a similar phenomenon to the rise of el Kurru, in that it was the home territory of a powerful family who came to dominate the Kushite state.[2] Once the importance of the site was established, the monarchy would have had the power and prestige to maintain it. This 'personal' explanation for its importance is further supported when one considers that, after the demise of the dynasty based at Meroe during the fourth century AD, the centre of power in the area shifted to el Hobagi. Thereafter Meroe lapsed into an obscurity from which it never recovered.

Throughout most of the Kushite period all the major sites in the Shendi reach lie on the east side of the river. Very few are known on the other bank[3] in contrast to the situation in the later fourth and fifth centuries AD when the burial ground at el Hobagi and fortified sites such as Hosh el Kafir were located to the west of the river (fig. 59). A satisfactory explanation for this distribution has yet to be advanced, but to suggest that it is the result of differential archaeological research is becoming less tenable.

As one moves south from Meroe the potential for sedentary occupation away from the river grows with the increase in rainfall. However, the lack of archaeological work both along the river and in its hinterland leaves us largely ignorant of these sites.

A number of sites on the White Nile are known from chance finds. Near the town of el Kawa, the site of Hilat Said has recently yielded objects of gold, probably of Kushite date. At el Kawa itself and at Kosti scarabs of Napatan date have been found. A similar situation exists on the Blue Nile and only the site at Abu Geili has seen extensive excavation.

In the Gezira, the area between the White and Blue Niles, a small farming community has been located at Jebel Tomat. Another settlement lay at Jebel Moya 34 km west of Sennar. There are some Kushite objects amongst the very large amounts of material recovered from this site, but the percentage is small.[4] This need not indicate that Jebel Moya lay beyond the area controlled by Kush. It is not difficult to accept that a settlement set in an isolated position within the Jebel Moya massif could have co-existed with the Kushite settlements in the vicinity of Sennar and elsewhere and yet show little material trace of contact. There is some pottery at Jebel Moya which is of the same type as seen at Abu Geili and similar to types seen at Soba East,[5] both sites where characteristic Kushite material, as defined from the excavations of sites in the Island of Meroe and further to the north, is rare or non-existent.

In the far north downstream of the Second Cataract, sites of the later Kushite Period appear to be common and testify to an extensive exploitation of the area partly influenced by its proximity to Egypt. However, Kushite sites of earlier date are rarer. Although the location of the area close to the frontier in times of unrest will not have encouraged settlement, this was certainly not the situation pertaining during the XXVth Dynasty. In the light of the large amount of detailed archaeological work

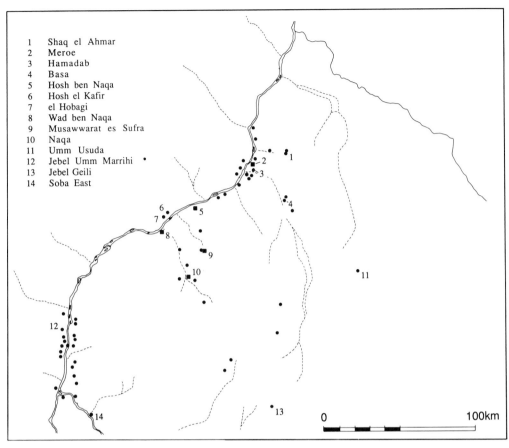

1	Shaq el Ahmar
2	Meroe
3	Hamadab
4	Basa
5	Hosh ben Naqa
6	Hosh el Kafir
7	el Hobagi
8	Wad ben Naqa
9	Musawwarat es Sufra
10	Naqa
11	Umm Usuda
12	Jebel Umm Marrihi
13	Jebel Geili
14	Soba East

59 *Kushite sites in the Nile Valley between Soba East and Atbara, and in the Keraba and Butana.*

undertaken in the area in connection with the Aswan dams, this rarity of early sites does appear to be a real phenomenon. No satisfactory explanation has been advanced to explain the observed data. It is thought that the reoccupation of the area was stimulated by the introduction of a new irrigation device, the *saqia*, allowing an expansion of agriculture.

Kushite occupation sites

Very little archaeological work has been conducted on settlement archaeology of the Kushite period. Individual structures have been excavated and there has been considerable work on cemeteries, but few settlements have been extensively excavated. The greatest concentration of major sites is in the area around Jebel Barkal. At the foot of the Jebel is the major religious centre of the state with many temples and palaces. To the west of the Jebel are two small pyramid cemeteries. Nine km upstream and across the river is the royal burial ground at Nuri, while 6 km downstream on the left bank is a large temple and an extensive early Kushite non-royal cemetery. There seems to have been a deliberate attempt to separate religious, funerary and secular areas. At a later date the development of Meroe with its royal palaces, extensive settlement, religious monuments and royal and plebeian cemeteries may have marked a change in policy.

Religious complexes

The origins of the Barkal religious complex date to the time of the New Kingdom pharaohs. Thutmose III built a fortified enclosure on the site and a small temple to Amun was built by Horemheb or Sety I right up to the base of the Jebel.

Throughout the Kushite period temples were built, refurbished and maintained at Barkal. The orientation of the temples was determined by the course of the river, their long axes being aligned at 90° to it. At Barkal this gave an alignment north-west to

60 *Granite sphinx of Amenophis III from Soleb re-sited before the Temple of Amun at Jebel Barkal. (D. A. Welsby)*

south-east. As had been the standard practice in New Kingdom Egypt, palaces were constructed on the right side of the temples, with their central axes perpendicular to that of the temple and in line with the front of the pylon. This is only demonstrably the case at Barkal where the large building B1200, thought to have been initially constructed by Piye, lies in the expected position relative to temple B800.[6]

Unfortunately excavations have not been undertaken at Sanam, Kawa or Tabo in the relevant areas to prove this hypothesis. The presence of a palace at Sanam is, however, suggested by the Stela of Queen Matisen, which mentions officials of the 'House of the King' being present to witness her endowments to the Amun temple there.[7] At Tabo and Meroe the temples of Amun face away from the present river channel, that at Meroe turning its back on the palace enclosure. Tabo now stands on the island of Argo, the western channel being perennial, the eastern being dry for much of the year. There is clear evidence that there has been considerable changes in the hydrography of this area since the Kerma period. The alignment of the temple may indicate that at the time it was built the major river channel lay to the east of the island. The situation at Meroe is more complex and will be discussed below. No temple has yet been found associated with the palace of Natakamani (B1500) at Barkal.

Little evidence for a settlement has been found at Barkal[8] which thus appears to have been solely a religious complex. Notwithstanding this, the priests and the large number of people engaged in serving the gods must have lived on or close to the site. Other major complexes have been noted at Qasr Ibrim and at Musawwarat es Sufra.

The first defences at Ibrim date from the late eleventh or early tenth century BC and therefore pre-date the arrival of the Kushites in the area. The earliest temple so far located dates to the reign of Taharqo, but by the end of the Kushite period there were seven temples on the site as well as the so-called podium. Recent work has suggested that the layout of the temples was interrelated, with the temples aligned either on the axis of the Taharqo temple or perpendicular to it, or with a similar relationship to the axis of temple 4.[9] Apart from the Taharqo temple, most of the others appear to date to the earlier centuries of the present era at a time when the military importance of the site may have lapsed. During this period the site may have been a pilgrimage centre.[10]

Leading to the south of Ibrim onto the desert plateau and extending for a few kilometres into the desert is a cleared track along the course of which are numerous outlines of feet carved onto the outcropping bed-rock. Among these are some containing inscriptions in Greek and Meroitic and also representations of offering tables. A large number of stone structures, cairns, cleared areas and linear mounds are also to be found in this area. Most of these features appear to date to the later Kushite period. Some are grave monuments and all may be connected with funerary ritual.[11]

Musawwarat es Sufra, which lies 28 km to the south-east of the Nile, is one of the most puzzling of Kushite sites. Very little evidence of dwellings and cemeteries has been found; the graves located so far are of post-Meroitic and medieval date. At Musawwarat there are two hafirs, several isolated temples and other buildings and the Great Enclosure. There has been much discussion of the function of the site in general

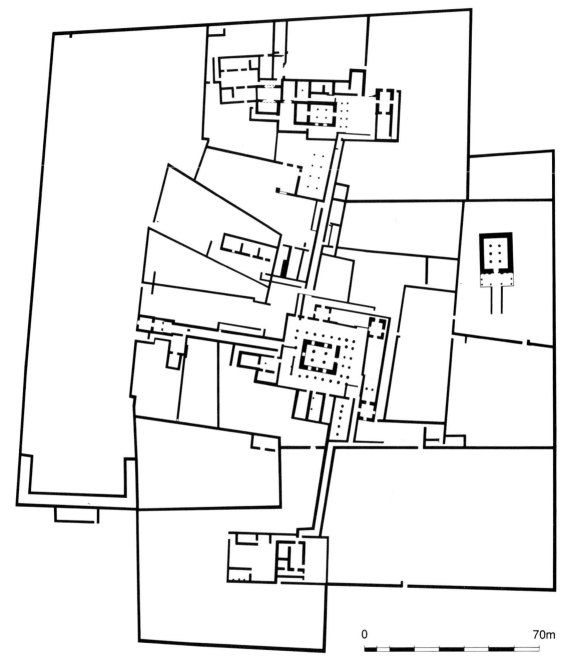

0   70m

61 *Musawwarat es Sufra, the Great Enclosure. (After Wenig 1978)*

Opposite **62** *'Temple' 100, Musawwarat es Sufra. (After Garstang 1910)*

and of specific structures within it in particular. The Great Enclosure is the largest Kushite structure known.

The Great Enclosure (fig. 61) was occupied over a considerable period of time and underwent a number of modifications and additions. As visible today, it consists of three major buildings, traditionally known as temples, surrounded by enclosures, corridors and small rooms. The most important structure is clearly 'Temple' 100, a rectangular room with a portico to the front, surrounded by a colonnade (col. pl. 8) and by a range of rooms on all sides. Beyond the colonnade to the front the range of rooms terminates at either end in what may have been tower-like structures. The roof of the central room is supported on four columns; it is entered through a centrally placed doorway in the east wall and by a further doorway at the east end of the north wall (fig. 62). There are also four large openings in the north and south walls extending from a little above floor level. A square niche occupies the central position in the west wall and there is a smaller one in the south wall. There is little to recommend the identification of this structure as a temple and 'Temple' 200 has many features in common with it.

The identification of Temple 300 as a temple is not in doubt. The other two 'temples' are each connected with a suite of rooms and they have been interpreted as throne rooms, part of a temple-palace complex. The columns in front of 'Temple' 100 are decorated with episodes from the ruler's enthronement cycle[12] and confirm the close association of the structure with the ruler. In this context the long corridor extending from the back wall of 'Temple' 100 and terminating in an elevated room or balcony overlooking the largest of the enclosures is particularly interesting. This has been compared with the 'Window of Appearance', where the Egyptian pharaohs showed themselves to the populace on state occasions, and related to the ceremonial function of the site.[13]

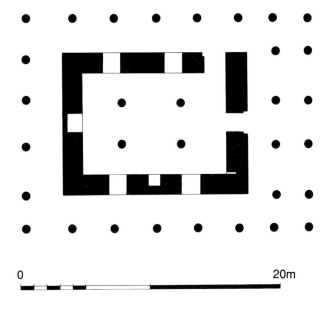

0   20m

63 *View across the Great Enclosure, Musawwarat es Sufra. (D. A. Welsby)*

The function of the enclosures (fig. 63) and of the ramps which are an unusual feature of the complex has led to much debate. If one assumes that this is a cult centre then the enclosures are for the accommodation of pilgrims. The large number of graffiti carved on their walls, many of them of altars and of gods, supports this view. Among these are also invocations to the lion god Apedemak.[14] A wall terminating in an elephant form and the large number of representations of elephants has suggested to some that this was a centre for the training of war and ceremonial elephants, the ramps allowing the movement of these beasts through the complex. A graffito (fig. 64) on the south wall of 'Temple' 200 does appear to show an elephant ascending a ramp.[15] Another theory is that the enclosures were used to house the animals required for the cult ceremonies. Large numbers of animals, among them elephants and cattle, are depicted in procession in reliefs, particularly those on the walls of the Lion Temple which stands 600 m to the south-east of the Great Enclosure.[16]

Across the Keraba and into the Butana several of the hafirs are associated with

64 *Graffito of an elephant on a ramp, Musawwarat es Sufra. (After Hintze 1979)*

65 *Temple and temenos at Jebel Hardan near Naqa. (D. A. Welsby)*

temples or sculpture, or both. Evidence for permanent habitation is rarely present. Presumably the hafirs were constructed to provide water for the nomadic and semi-nomadic pastoralists of the region. The juxtaposition of the temples and statuary to the hafirs served to highlight the fact that it was the gods, through the good offices of the Kushite state, by whose gift the water was made available. Basa is one of the most complex of these rural sanctuaries, with its large hafir, temple and another building as yet unexcavated. Lion statues, a number of them with the lions devouring captives (fig. 10), and two large stone frogs were set up around the hafir and on an island in its midst, and by the temple.[17] The most easterly hafir where there is evidence for a Kushite presence is at Umm Usuda (col. pl. 2). There the banks of the large hafir are surmounted by a number of pieces of statuary and a stela in Meroitic cursive. This hafir lies in the vast grasslands of the Butana, today an area of rich pasture. The hafirs that are certainly of Kushite origin have a much more restricted distribution than the area served by hafirs today,[18] although whether their distribution can be taken as reflecting the areas under direct Kushite control is unclear.

Major settlements

We know virtually nothing of the town at el Kurru apart from a note by Reisner concerning a defensive wall and a temple. No dating evidence for these features is known.

The main settlement at Napata may have lain at Sanam, the term Napata relating to the region around Barkal rather than to the Barkal religious complex itself. The very large early Kushite cemetery at Sanam is the only evidence we have for a major urban settlement within which the Temple of Amun, the 'Treasury' and presumably a royal palace stood.

The town at Meroe consists of three main districts, the so-called Royal City, the Temple of Amun and associated structures, and the town itself (fig. 66). The former has been largely excavated by John Garstang between 1909 and 1914 but the work is only now approaching publication. The standard of the work is not high and our knowledge of the layout of the Royal City is sketchy. Garstang also excavated the Temple of Amun and much more recently Shinnie has excavated a number of associated small temples. This work all remains unpublished in detail. Only very limited excavations have been undertaken in the rest of the town.

The earliest structural evidence for occupation, found at the bottom of one of Shinnie's deep trenches, consisted of circular timber huts. Thereafter there was a long sequence of occupation during which people lived in mud brick buildings. The overall layout of this part of the town is unclear but we may assume that as in most organically developing settlements there was no adherence to a master plan and that expansion developed in a random manner. Habitations and industrial complexes lie cheek by jowl.

The Royal City was a much more planned complex, although it is by no means regular. The enclosure wall, which post-dates a number of monumental structures associ-

Opposite 66 *Meroe, plan of the city. (After Shinnie and Bradley 1984, Adams 1977)*

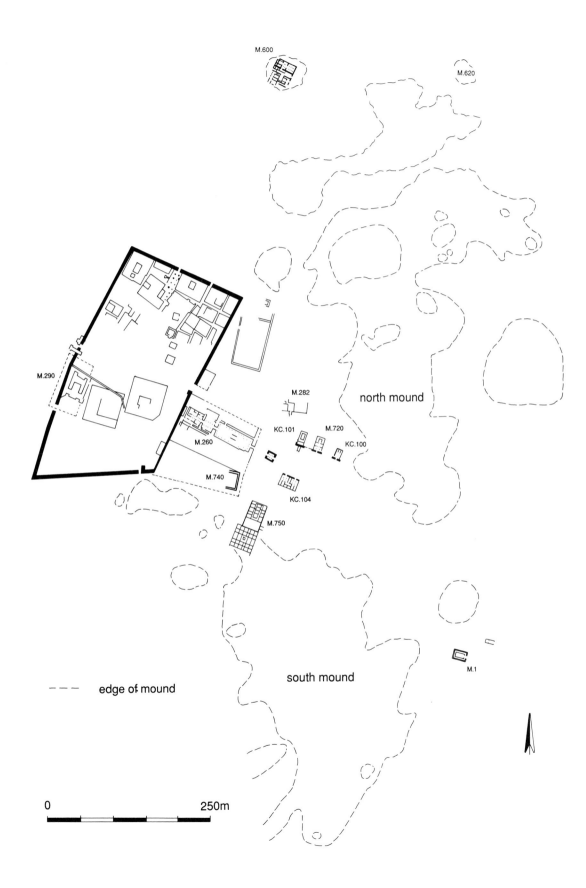

M.600

M.620

north mound

M.282

M.290

KC.101   M.720
              KC.100

M.260

M.740

KC.104

M.750

south mound

M.1

- - - edge of mound

0   250m

ated with various Kushite kings, describes an irregular trapezium and is pierced by five openings. Two of these are approximately in the centre of the long walls and roughly opposite each other, suggesting a main axis in the internal arrangement at that time. One of these, a wide thoroughfare, probably a processional way, was lined on both sides with trees set in walled tree pits.[19] The Royal City had a long and dynamic history with considerable modifications to the original layout, which is little known. Many of the later buildings are on markedly different orientations from the enclosure wall and this culminated in the first and second centuries AD in the construction of structures across the line of the wall itself. The structures within the enclosure include temples, palatial dwellings and a water sanctuary, the so-called Royal Bath.

As noted above, the Amun Temple faces away from the river and appears to be aligned, as are many of the other temples, on the sunrise at the winter solstice.[20] As such it also faces towards the royal burial ground leading to the suggestion that it may have been connected to the royal funerary cult. Alternatively the temple may be aligned as are the other Amun temples, i.e. towards the river if the suggestion is correct that Meroe originally stood on an island and was only united with the east bank around 300 BC.[21] Whatever the true reason for its orientation, it set the scene for the other religious monuments in the area. A number of temples were arranged on both sides of the avenue leading to the temple and these were aligned perpendicular to it. One of the structures on the right-hand side of the avenue, M.750, has been claimed as a palace.[22] When this processional way was laid out a number of domestic buildings had to be demolished along its line.[23]

At Kawa the settlement covers an area of approximately 36 hectares. This was one of the nome capitals and was the site of an Amun temple built by Taharqo. The temple, together with two earlier and smaller temples, stood within a *temenos* surrounded by a substantial mud brick wall. Within this complex were ancillary buildings, a granary, wine-press and gardens. A number of other buildings are visible on the surface of the site, but their functions are unclear and an assessment of the town plan is premature. Further north Faras was for a time the headquarters of the *pesto*. The walled enclosure, thought to be of Kushite date by Griffith, is probably later. Although a few Kushite buildings are known, again we have no idea of the nature of the settlement.

At Wad ben Naqa there is a large palace and a number of other official buildings including temples. The status of the settlement here is unknown, although one may suppose that a sizeable population would have been required simply to service the official buildings.

The only major Kushite settlement away from the river is at Naqa. Although 29 km from the Nile, the town stands alongside the large Wadi Awatib and hence has access to a considerable area of productive farmland, the agriculture supported by rainfall. Adjacent to the town are two hafirs and also two cemeteries.

Naqa is famous for its surviving religious buildings and these have been intensively studied. Elsewhere in the town there has been no excavation and only one grave in the south cemetery has been investigated.[24] Although many of the buildings are temples, others appear to be of a different character. Whether there are any ordinary dwellings among them remains to be seen, but the surface remains suggest that all the buildings visible are of monumental character. In the present climatic regime the nomadic population and their herds have to obtain all their water from a deep well in the dry season. Unless the climate was markedly wetter in the Kushite period it is difficult to see how a large sedentary population could have been maintained at Naqa. It is unlikely that the hafir could have catered for the needs of the population all the year round and no other water storage facilities have been observed. We must reserve judgement as to the status of the settlement at Naqa until excavations are conducted on the site.

Rural settlement

Most of the population of Kush, particularly in the north, was engaged in farming activities, which were confined to the banks of the Nile. Then, as today, settlements were to be found along the river valley in close proximity to the fields. A number of these were excavated in connection with the heightening of the Aswan Dam and the construction of the High Dam. The village at Wadi el Arab, which was partly excavated between 1929 and 1930 consisted of a ribbon development – substantial nucleated dwellings interspersed with more flimsy structures. The only specialised structure in the village was a wine-press set within a rectangular building at the north end of the settlement.[25] A little upstream at Karanog ten dwellings within the settlement, some of considerable size, set on the sloping ground running up from the river and on the top of the bluffs above, have been excavated. The size and complexity of the so-called castle and house 2 suggests that they were not ordinary dwellings, although their function is uncertain.[26]

The settlement on the Island of Meinarti consisted of a complex of substantial official buildings with traces of domestic structures in the immediate vicinity. As at Wadi el Arab one of these contained a wine-press. This lay adjacent to a large store building and a possible temple.[27] It has been suggested that settlements in this area may have developed from military camps or caravan stops[28] and this may go some way towards explaining the high proportion of 'official' buildings within them. The difficulty of locating sites was highlighted at Gaminarti, where the presence of a few Kushite sherds on the surface was the only indication of the two substantial houses revealed by excavation. No other buildings were found in association with these structures. Similarly on Meili Island two small houses, later covered by a larger structure of the Gaminarti type, were isolated.[29]

Towards the southern edge of the Kushite kingdom on the Blue Nile lay the settlement of Abu Geili. The presence of Kushite objects from the site, and the recovery of fine Kushite objects a little to the south, suggests that this site should be considered Kushite. Whether it is typical of rural settlements in the southern part of the kingdom is uncertain. In the 2000 m² of the site uncovered there is a solid mass of roughly rectangular rooms delimited by walls of mud brick (fig. 53.1). Alleys giving access to individual properties are extremely uncommon and it is difficult to see how one pro-gressed through the village. Scant remains of an earlier settlement suggest that it may have consisted of larger units. No 'official' structures can be recognised.[30]

The likelihood of there being settlements consisting largely or entirely of timber huts, which can only be discovered through excavation, may account for the apparent scarcity of settlement, particularly in the southern part of the kingdom.

Population

Attempts to estimate population from archaeological data are fraught with difficulties. One can either look at the number of dwellings in a settlement as a basis for the calcu-lation of population size or look to the cemeteries. In both cases the approach is only valid if all the dwellings and graves have been located and if the contemporaneity of those used to establish the population size is known. Rarely can any of these criteria be satisfied. This has made archaeologists wary of attempting to suggest population size.

Notwithstanding these difficulties the population of Lower Nubia in the later Kushite period, which includes the part of the area under Roman control, has been put at 60,000.[31] Of more significance is the fact that this is higher than the suggested popu-lation for this area at any other time from prehistory until the end of the medieval period.[32] Assuming a given area required for each inhabitant of a settlement and then assuming that two-thirds of the settlement was given over to dwellings, it has been suggested that in their heydays Meroe had a population in the order of 20,000 to 25,000 and Kawa of 6200 to 7800 people.[33]

CHAPTER SEVEN

The Economy

As with the other major civilisations of Antiquity, agriculture and animal husbandry were the mainstays of the Kushite economy. We may be confident in suggesting that the vast bulk of the population will have worked on, and earned its living from, the land.

This having been said, we know very little of these activities and any discussion of them has to rely heavily on an appreciation of the potential of the land derived from early modern and present day observations. Most of northern and central Sudan is marginal and hence is very susceptible to even relatively minor fluctuations in climate and rainfall. These factors, as has been highlighted by the recent years of drought and the very high Nile floods of 1988, are not constant even over a short period of time. Kushite history extends over 1000 years. Within that period there were presumably fluctuations of the climate which resulted in the agricultural and pastoral potential of the kingdom varying to a degree. The relevance of modern data for the Kushite period is hence fraught with uncertainty, but it forms the bulk of the information that we at present have available.

The Kushite state for much of its history extended into a number of very diverse climatic zones which offered vastly different potential for agricultural activities. Some degree of homogeneity in the lifestyle of the peoples inhabiting its banks, however, was provided by the river Nile which traversed these zones. In the northern part of the kingdom, in the almost totally arid zone, permanent human settlement away from the river was impossible and there is very limited potential for a nomadic lifestyle. However, it would appear that the deserts of the north were not uninhabited wastelands and could support nomadic groups, which were on occasion sizeable enough to threaten the security of the settlements along the Nile. A number of raids by these nomads are recorded on Kushite inscriptions. Further south the nomadic lifestyle away from the river became progressively more viable and the vast grasslands of the Sahel offer an ideal habitat for nomadic groups.

These peoples are by the nature of their lifestyle very difficult to recognise archaeologically. Their dwellings are of an ephemeral nature and their artefacts tend to be few in number and to be made of organic materials which only survive in the most favourable conditions. Their relationship to the Kushite administration may well have been a fraught one. Throughout history nomads and farmers have not tended to co-exist peacefully, the former eschewing all constraints on movement, the latter demanding security of land tenure to allow for long-term agricultural development. However, nomadism and settled agriculture are not necessarily mutually exclusive and they can usefully contribute one to another. Farmers at harvest time need a considerable short-term increase in their labour force which has in many areas of the world been furnished by nomadic groups. Also, after the harvest of cereal crops in particular, there is much edible material left which can be utilised by the animals of the nomads which in turn assist by returning digested humic material to the land.[1]

This division, however, into sedentary agriculturalists and nomadic pastoralists is probably an oversimplification. The practice of animal husbandry by the sedentary population is highly likely, as is the limited planting of crops in the desert wadis when-ever the conditions were favourable. Immediately prior to the final flooding of Lower Nubia in the 1960s, in an area where pastoralism away from the river is not feasible, the sedentary population of 50,000 people owned an animal population which included 2831 cattle, 19,335 sheep and 34,146 goats.[2] Clearly a symbiotic relationship between agriculture and animal husbandry was the most efficient method of utilisation of limited land resources.

In the arid environment of Nubia the nomads today, presumably as in the past, are only able to range over a large area during the rainy season. Within the rain belt, partic-ularly in the Keraba, the construction of hafirs in the Kushite period will have provided a source of drinking water for animals long after the seasonal watercourses had dried up. This will have allowed the utilisation of the areas away from the river for a much greater proportion of the year.[3] Thereafter their activities must have been concentrated closer to a perennial water source which in much of the Kushite kingdom will have resulted in their being confined to the Nile or, to a lesser extent, to the vicinity of reli-able wells. A few wells, lined with dressed blocks of stone, are known in the Keraba which may date from this time. By one of these is a fragment from a Kushite stone lion.[4]

Cattle require a relatively high and frequent water intake and are not well adapted to arid zones. Sheep and goats are much more hardy and can exist on a wider range of foodstuffs. That caprines were herded extensively in the Kushite period cannot be doubted. The only evidence available for the relative importance of these three species comes from Meroe. Here skeletal material from excavation has indicated an increase in the proportion of cattle to caprines during the Kushite period. It was suggested that this was the result of overgrazing by caprines leading to the decline of their preferred food supply in the environs of the city. This proportionately will have favoured cattle.[5] However, this data, recovered from one small area within the city may have little rele-vance to the general situation in the region around Meroe, and even less to that of other areas in the kingdom. The ritual importance of cattle is clear from their frequent in-clusion on reliefs where they are shown in processions. Some of these cattle have one horn trained downwards, a tradition seen in Egypt in the Old Kingdom, during the C-Group, and still practised by Nilotic tribes of southern Sudan.[6]

Of all the domesticated animals the camel is the best adapted to desert conditions, but its role in the Kushite period is unclear. The camel was present in Egypt and else-where in North Africa before the beginning of the Dynastic period.[7] It may, however, have become extinct in that area being reintroduced from Asia to Egypt at a much later date.[8]

The earliest evidence for the presence of camels in Kush, in a context where it was presumably domesticated, comes from Qasr Ibrim. Radiocarbon dating of camel dung suggests that the dung was deposited in the early first millennium BC.[9] The potential of the camel for cross-desert travel was demonstrated to the Kushites by the Assyrian foes of Taharqo, who used a camel train to cross the Sinai in 671 BC.[10] Camel bones have been recovered from the royal tombs at Meroe, along with a camel saddle.[11] Represen-tations of the camel in Kushite art are rare. A camel is depicted on a wall of the chapel of Beg.N.15 at Meroe, where it was drawn by Lepsius.[12] It was destroyed by Budge in 1905 during his 'archaeological' work. The relief was fragmentary and the context of the beast is unknown. It was not depicted carrying any burden. Another is to be found on a fragmentary relief from the chapel of Beg.N.17. Also from the Royal cemetery at Meroe is a small copper-alloy figurine.[13] These all date from around the beginning of our era or a little later.

Recent studies have highlighted the importance of the horse in the Kushite econ-omy, at least in the early period.[14] The famous passage in the great stela of Piye has already been noted (see p. 90) as have the horse burials at el Kurru, a tradition begun by Piye. Assyrian texts appear to make numerous references to the prowess of Kushite horses and indicate that large numbers were being imported into the Middle East. The evidence is, however, not certain and although it remains an interesting possibility further proof is required. Horsemen as a major component of the Kushite army are noted on Kushite inscriptions and they appear on reliefs. However, many of these riders shown on reliefs appear to be mounted on donkeys.

Agriculture

In ancient Egypt large-scale agricultural activities were confined to the flood plain of the river and to the Fayyum depression, which was watered by the Bahr el Yusuf, an offshoot of the river. The Nile flood plain in Egypt was – prior to the construction and reconstruction of the dams at Aswan – flooded each year, and the water and the deposited silt from the river resulted in the legendary fertility of the land. The flood plain is a virtually continuous strip of land up to several kilometres in width from Aswan to the apex of the Delta, north of which the whole Delta was available.

Only rarely is a similar agricultural potential realised to the south of the First Cataract. There the Nile generally flows between high banks above which it does not usually flood. The areas which are inundated in a good year, referred to today as *seluka* land, are generally few and of limited extent, although the agricultural potential of the low lying islands must not be underestimated. Only in the Letti and Kerma basins are there substantial areas which may have been watered directly by the river in a good year. It is interesting to observe that the potential of these two areas presumably led to their being chosen as the site of the capital of the Kerma culture in the third and second millennia BC and of the medieval kingdom of Makuria.

The variability in the level of the Nile flood, however, renders much of the basin land unsuitable for agriculture. In the recent past figures for a very good year (1938) indicated that the Nile in the Shendi and Dongola reaches flooded an area of 109,280 feddans (45,898 hectares), while in a bad year (1949) only 10,730 feddans (4507 hectares) were flooded.[15] We have little idea of flood levels in the Kushite period, although there were some exceptionally high Nile floods which eroded early Kushite cemeteries at Sanam, at Kerma and presumably at Kawa. One exceptionally high Nile flood is recorded by Taharqo as having occurred in the sixth year of his reign (684 BC), together with rain in Nubia.[16] The basins will have been more reliable as pasture and this potential of the Kerma basin may be reflected in the large numbers of cattle available for slaughter at funerary feasts in the Kerma period.

The high banks of the river renders the use of its water for agriculture difficult. Throughout the Kushite period the primitive *shaduf*, a counterweighted lifting device, was available, but this could only effectively raise water a maximum of 3 m and in limited amounts. It has been estimated that it is only suitable for the irrigation of areas of one-half or two-thirds of a feddan (0.21–0.28 hectares).[17]

A more efficient device for raising water, the *saqia*, spread to Egypt from Mesopotamia in the Hellenistic period and thence into Nubia.[18] The *saqia* is a vertical wooden wheel which carries two parallel loops of rope to which pots are attached. It is rotated through a series of gears by a draught animal, usually an ox. The pots fill with water as they are submerged and empty the water at a higher level into an aqueduct.[19] The pots used on the *saqia*, called *qadus* in Arabic, are of a special design with a cordon below the neck and a small button base to assist with their attachment to the ropes. It is the presence or absence of the distinctive pots which has fuelled the debate on the date of the introduction of the *saqia*.

Some scholars consider the arrival of the *saqia* on the Middle Nile during the early centuries AD as having a fundamental effect on the agricultural potential, particularly of Lower Nubia. This increased potential has been seen as the catalyst which brought about the repopulation of a large tract of the river valley following a period of almost total desertion.[20] Others have doubted whether the *saqia* was introduced into the area before the break-up of the Kushite state in the fourth and fifth centuries AD. At Tabo a *saqia* pit and *qadus* have been found sealed beneath a pagan temple, while another *saqia* pit, thought to be of Kushite date, has been excavated at Meinarti.[21] In the southern areas of the empire *qadus* have not been recovered presumably because there was sufficient agricultural land available, watered by the Nile flood and by rainfall, to render the use of the *saqia* unnecessary.[22]

Modern estimates of the relative efficiency of the *saqia* over the *shaduf* as an irrigation device suggest a substantial increase in the amount of land which could be utilised for agricultural activities. Such an increase might be expected to have had a marked effect on demography. No such changes are visible in the mid-first millennium AD.

Although the *saqia*, with a lift of between 3 m and 8 m, does allow more land to be brought into cultivation, it is still a relatively inefficient machine and the increase in crops grown is partly offset by the fodder required to feed the oxen which power the wheel. In the recent past one *saqia* driven by two oxen rarely irrigated an area in excess of three feddans (1.26 hectares), although the actual amount of irrigated land varies dramatically depending on the height of the river and hence the magnitude of the lift. The agricultural importance of *seluka* land, however, remained and, immediately prior to the introduction of modern pumps, nearly 50 per cent of the cultivated land in the Dongola Reach was *seluka* land.[23]

In the Island of Meroe and further south there is sufficient rainfall in a normal to good year to allow rain-fed agriculture. Some areas are more favourable than others. Where the rainfall is low the run-off from a considerable area needs to be channelled into a restricted zone so that the water moistens the soil sufficiently to allow the crops to grow to maturity. In the Island of Meroe such a situation exists, thanks to extensive wadi systems which drain a large catchment area. Where they debouch onto the plain the wide wadi floors are suitable for agriculture and sizeable areas can be farmed for several months of the year. The Wadi Awatib adjacent to the Kushite site at Naqa is one such wadi which has been extensively farmed in the recent past, although a period of aridity in the last decade has not been conducive to this activity. It is unlikely that the hafirs could have been used as part of an irrigation system, as the volume of water even the largest could hold would not have been sufficient to irrigate substantial areas of farming land.[24]

There is little evidence, apart from the hafirs, for attempts to actively manage the water supply away from the river. For the potential for agricultural exploitation of this area we can compare the utilisation of similar pre-desert environments on the northern edge of the Sahara. Contemporary with the Kushite settlements and structures in the Keraba are the very extensive artificial water catchment systems employed by the Romans in Tripolitania and in the Negev.[25]

In Tripolitania rainwater was collected in plaster-lined cisterns, for the use of men and animals, an equivalent function to that of the Kushite hafirs. The advantage of the cistern over the hafir was that the former was a covered and largely sealed container and thus little water would be lost to evaporation and seepage. To provide the necessary water for agriculture a system of transverse walls was built across the wadi floor. These were designed to slow down the water both to reduce its erosive force and to allow it time to soak into the ground. The efficiency of these installations can be judged from the frequency of farmsteads up to the 25 mm isohyet (the limit of the area receiving an average annual rainfall of 25 mm or more). In the sub-Saharan Nile valley this amount of annual rainfall today falls as far north as the Fourth Cataract.[26] Virtually no similar installations have been observed within the Kingdom of Kush. However, a little up-stream of the hafir at Basa one cross-wadi wall has been noted and further research may reveal that this is part of a coherent system of water management.[27]

Dams share many of the disadvantages of hafirs, the resulting reservoirs suffering greatly from silting, evaporation and seepage. They are an uncommon feature in the pre-desert areas of the Roman empire, but were presumably suited to specific situations as for example where the volume of water flowing along a given wadi greatly exceeded that which could be managed by the wadi wall systems. The only Kushite dam known, at Shaq el Ahmar (see col. pl. 7), was presumably associated with a system of water channels, although these have not been noted on the ground.[28]

It should be borne in mind that to make investment in complex water catchment systems in marginal areas worthwhile, a ready market for the produce must be available. In the Roman world there was a vast demand for olive oil and wheat and the progressive extension of agriculture into the pre-desert was fuelled by this demand. It is unlikely that there was the same demand in the Kushite state, which was less urbanised than the Roman empire. The absence of the commercial incentive to produce a surplus would not have favoured agricultural investment in marginal areas.

Crops

The Kingdom of Kush extended over an area lying wholly within the Tropics and its climatic regime differs markedly from that found around the Mediterranean. A number of Mediterranean plant species are adapted to the hot dry summers, but require cold wet winters to thrive. In Kushite territory what rains there are fall in the middle of the summer, and the winters – although not always hot by any means – are invariably dry. Thus the olive tree, which was one of the agricultural mainstays of the pre-desert zone of Roman North Africa, cannot be grown.[29]

The climate is not ideal for vines, although limited local production did occur. In the early seventh century BC Taharqo boasts that the wine produced in the city of Kawa 'is more abundant than that of Djesdjes', the famous wine growing area of the Oasis Bahriyah.[30] A possible wine-pressing installation was found at that site.[31] This consists of a D-shaped pit, presumably the lower basin of a press, with a flight of steps in one corner and a stone channel leading into it. The installations associated with the pressing floor, apart from its stone flags, have been totally removed during a later modification of the building. The function of the lower basin is to allow the positioning of jars below the spout so that they could be filled directly from the press. At the time of excavation no such jar was present, but two amphorae stood in the basin. This is consistent with other presses of this type where the lower basin was often used to store the amphorae. The type of amphorae suggest a date for the structure in the second or first half of the third century AD.[32]

Twelve structures identified as wine-presses have been located between Ikhmindi and Meinarti in the north of the kingdom.[33] Two of these have been dated to the early fourth century AD and the similarity of form suggests that the others are contemporary. A description of the press found at Meinarti will serve to illustrate the type.[34]

The installation was set within a small rectangular mud brick room (fig. 67). At the north-east end was a basin raised above the general floor level and sloping towards the

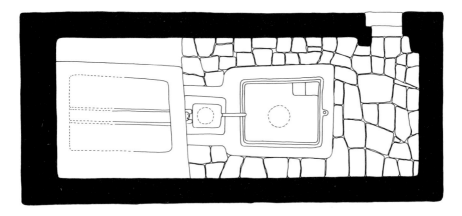

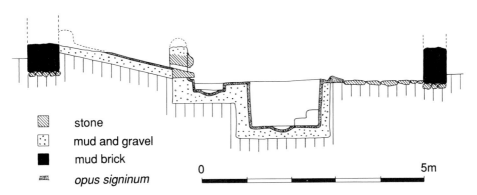

	stone
	mud and gravel
	mud brick
	opus signinum

0   5m

67 *Wine press at Meinarti. (After Adams 1966)*

south-west with a deep central channel. This communicated through the wall of the basin via a stone spout decorated with a lion's head into a small and shallow basin and then via a shallow groove cut in the brim into a basin 1.3 m deep, which has two steps in one corner. The grapes, placed in the upper basin, were presumably pressed by human feet as is shown on a number of Egyptian reliefs. The juice and debris flowed along the channel into the small central basin, which acted as a settling tank. The juice then flowed on into the lowest basin. The absence of a spout suggests that the juice was not put directly into containers but collected in the basin.

A shallow depression in the centre of the basin will have assisted in the collection of the last drop of juice while a similar depression in the central basin assisted in its cleaning. The two lower basins were surrounded by a splash gutter. All three basins are lined with a waterproof plaster, which was painted a deep maroon colour in the lower basins. No amphorae have been found in association with the northern presses; this has led to the suggestion that the juice was fermented in the basin, which was presumably covered by a wooden cover, and was then distributed in skins. It should be noted, however, that it is at the consumption end of the chain that we would expect the discarded containers to be found and not at the wine producing site.

The use of these presses appears to have been short-lived and has been related to the period immediately after the Roman withdrawal from the Dodekaschoinos. At this time the trade network between Kush and Egypt may have been disrupted, favouring the attempt to practice viticulture in the hostile environment of Lower Nubia. A resumption of the wine trade would have rapidly brought about the demise of the undertaking.[35]

A number of ancient writers record that cotton was grown in Nubia. Pliny notes that it was the material preferred by the Egyptian priests for their garments and so was presumably accorded a high status. Cotton cloth may have been the only manufactured material to have been exported by the Kushites. It was also used extensively for the home market. Cotton fabric has been recovered from the tombs beneath the royal pyramids at Meroe and is a common find in the north, where the dry conditions favour the preservation of organic material. Textiles recovered from the Kushite tombs at Ballana and Qustul excavated in the 1960s were largely of cotton, in marked contrast to those of the succeeding period where cotton was very rare indeed.[36]

In the recent past dates were the major cash crop, at least in the northern part of Nubia, and large quantities were exported to Egypt each year. The potential for such a trade presumably existed in the Kushite period, although we have no evidence that it actually took place. The planting of six date palm groves at Meroe and Napata, on behalf of the god Amun, is recorded on a stela of Harsiyotef.[37]

The growth of sorghum (Arabic *dhura*), which was in later times the principal staple grain in Nubia, is recorded by Strabo.[38] At Qasr Ibrim only the wild sorghum (*S. bicolor verticilliflorum*) is known from early levels, primitive cultivated sorghum only arriving in the post-Meroitic period.[39] At Tanqasi a number of beehive-shaped storage pits were found pre-dating the construction of the post-Meroitic tumuli. These contained small quantities of sorghum, also certainly of the wild type, together with Kushite pottery sherds.[40] Sorghum was also grown by the villagers at Jebel Tomat in the Gezira, the economy being mixed with cattle and caprine herding.[41] A large sample of sorghum, from a context dating to the first few centuries AD, was found in Temple KC.100 at Meroe and another, possibly of similar date, came from Naqa.[42] The importance of sorghum is indicated by the relief at Jebel Qeili where a god offers a bundle of sorghum to King Shorkaror. Apedemak, on the west wall of the temple at Naqa, does the same (figs 68, 69). A bouquet of sorghum of this type was found at Qasr Ibrim placed upside-down in the bottom of a pit.[43]

At Gezira Dabarosa in the far north evidence from domestic deposits dated to the first century AD suggest that the population grew date palms and wheat and raised sheep, goats and a few cattle.[44] On analogy with ancient Egypt and modern Sudan one can suggest that barley, beans and lentils provided additional protein and onions and other green vegetables were probably grown.[45]

68 *Relief of King Shorkaror at Jebel Qeili. (After Hintze 1959)*

69 *Relief of Apedemak on the west wall of the Lion Temple, Naqa. (After Lepsius 1849–59)*

Hunting and fishing

Hunting, on the limited evidence from Meroe, does not appear to have formed an important supplement to the diet of the Kushites. The Nile is rich in fish which could have provided a useful food resource. Fish bones were present in most of the deposits excavated during the 1960s at Meroe, but the proportions of fish bones to those of other phyla was small. Among the fish bones were those of mud fish and Nile perch.[46] An artisan's house at Kerma, dating to the later half of the sixth and the fifth century BC, had a number of jars set into the ground which had contained fish sauce.[47] An inscription of Piye suggests that there was a religious taboo against eating fish: 'and they were eaters of fish, which is an abomination to the House of the king'.[48]

Manufacturing

The most common of the manufactured goods, recovered from sites dating throughout the Kushite period, is pottery. This is in part the result of the virtually indestructible nature of the material and to the very limited opportunities for reuse and recycling. It is only on sites such as Qasr Ibrim, where there is also total preservation of organic material, that the importance of wooden containers and other artefacts can be appreciated. The amount of pottery available during the Kushite period is nonetheless considerable, as it was at many other periods of history on the Middle Nile.

The Kushite wares varied considerably over time and reflect external influences on the repertoire of the pottery both with regard to form and to decoration. Throughout, the influence of Egypt has had a considerable effect on the most 'modern' wares. The traditional pots, which had changed little since the Neolithic, and were destined to change little up until the very recent past, continued to be made in the time-honoured way with traditional forms and decoration. A distinction has been made between the wheel-made wares, thought to have been produced by male professional potters, and which were often traded, and the hand-made wares made by the women for local use. However, this appears too simplistic. Much of the hand-made pottery is very well made and finely decorated. It is not necessarily inferior to the wheel-made wares.

In the early Kushite period pottery was on the whole rather drab and is comparable with the low level of artistic merit of much of pharaonic ceramics, from which some are

70 *Painted bowls from the tombs excavated by Griffith at Faras. (Courtesy of the Griffith Institute, Oxford)*

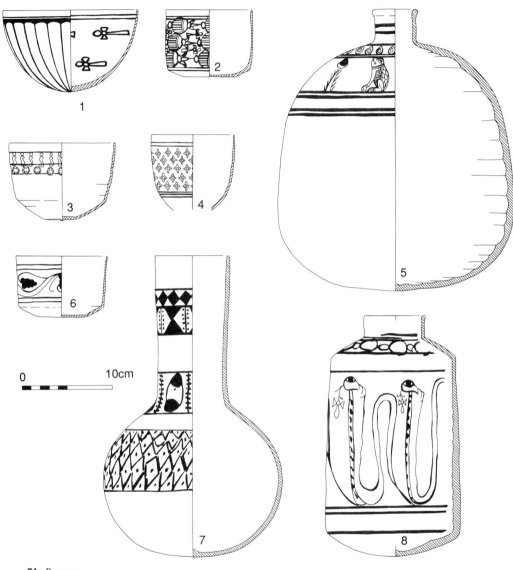

71 *Pottery*
1–5, 8 from Ballana. (After Williams 1991)
6, 7 from Missiminia. (After Vila 1982)

virtually indistinguishable. At that time, presumably, pottery was not seen as a vehicle for artistic expression and had little value. The wares were utilitarian in design.[49]

Under the influence of the Hellenisation of Egypt the perception of pottery changed. It became a recognised art form, although sometimes clearly copying in a cheaper material objects of metal or glass. Kushite fine white wares and egg-shell wares are amongst the most competent products of potters of any age in the Nile Valley.

72 *Painted decoration types on pottery*
1–6 from Ballana and Qustul. (After Williams 1991)
7 from Nag Gamus. (After Almagro 1965)

These pots are profusely decorated either in polychromatic paint or by stamping (figs 70, 71, 72; col. pl. 8). Technically and aesthetically they are superb examples of the potter's art and they are extremely common, particularly in Lower Nubia where even

rather humble sites display a quantity of this material. Their rarity in Upper Nubia may
be more apparent than real, the result of the limited archaeological work conducted in
that area. In this context a recent reappraisal of the ceramic material recovered by John
Garstang from Meroe in 1909–14, and not yet published, is particularly interesting. It
was noted that the earliest examples of fine wares and the widest range of forms and
decoration types has been found there.[50] A source of the fine white clay, kaolin, used in
their manufacture has been noted in the quarries immediately to the east of the northern cemetery at Meroe.[51] At Hamadab, a few kilometres to the south, a vast amount of
fine ware sherds is visible on the surface.[52] The motifs most commonly employed are
either derived from pharaonic or Hellenistic models or drawn from nature. A wide
range of animals is depicted, from snakes to frogs and scorpions. Human figures are
also employed. The diversity of this fine late Kushite pottery may reflect that it was
made at a number of different centres by many different potters, although Meroe
certainly seems to have played a significant role as a centre of manufacture.[53]

Other, more traditional Nubian ceramics were hand-made. Those of the later Kushite
period, which are found throughout the kingdom, are often finely black burnished and
decorated with intricate incised decoration often filled with white pigment, a tradition
dating back to the C-Group (fig. 73; col. pl. 4). The motifs employed are either geo-
metric or floral with the occasional human or animal figure. The forms found are
mainly jars and goblets.

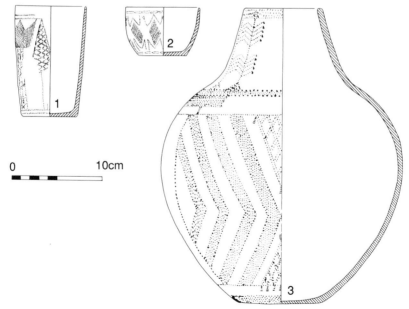

73 *Pottery with incised decoration*
1 and 2 from Nag Gamus. (After Almagro 1965)
3 from Jebel Moya. (After Addison 1949)

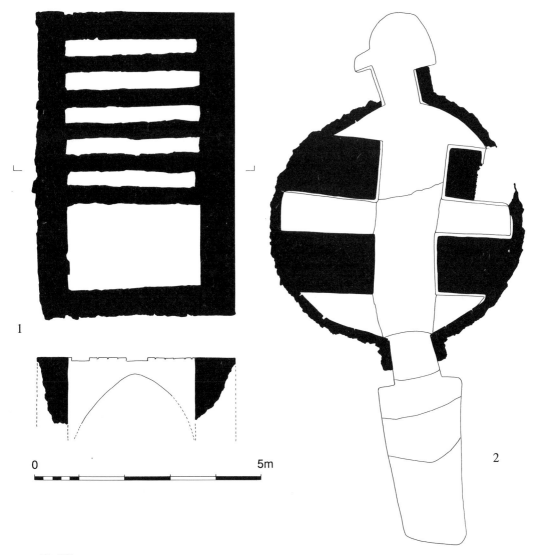

74 *Kilns*
  1 K2, Kawa
  2 Kerma. (After Bonnet and Mohammed Ahmed 1991)

Direct evidence for pottery production is very scarce. At Kerma a potter's workshop, dating from the second half of the sixth to the end of the fifth century BC, has been partly excavated. It consisted of a kiln, pits for the preparation of the clay and a workman's shelter. The kiln (fig. 74.2), cut 0.6 cm into the ground, is circular and measures 2.4 m in diameter. The pit was lined with – and the four piers which supported the firing floor were constructed of – mud brick covered in a layer of mud plaster. There was a single stoke-hole and opposite it an additional opening interpreted by the excavators as a chimney. The kiln had been fired with wood.[54] A structure, perhaps to be identified as a kiln, has been investigated at Argin in the far north[55] and circular kilns have been observed at Kedurma near the Third Cataract.[56] One of these measures 2.02 m in diameter and the floor of the firing chamber was supported on arches resting on two groups of three engaged piers. Towards the northern edge of the city of Meroe a group of well-preserved kilns was excavated in the winter of 1910–11 but full details have yet to be published.[57]

A large number of well-preserved kilns of 'post-Meroitic' and medieval date are known and it is likely that the Kushite kilns were very similar structures. The later kilns are all of the updraught type, with the floor of the firing chamber supported on arches, the chamber being open to the sky. Presumably this opening was covered during firing.[58]

At least some of the hand-made wares were presumably fired in bonfire kilns, a simple pit into which the pots were packed and covered with combustible material, which was then set alight. This method of firing is still employed with some degree of sophistication in western Sudan, but is usually confined to small-scale production. This need not always have been the case and there is evidence from elsewhere for major industries with extensive trading networks relying entirely on pots fired in this way.[59] Who owned the potteries and what mechanisms were used to market the products are unknown.

At Kawa and Tabo there is evidence that the bread cones used to bake bread for temple offerings were manufactured on the site.[60] From within the Temple of Amun at Sanam a number of moulds for making *shabtis* and amulets were recovered. Among the material was one *shabti* mould and one *shabti* of two different queens.[61] This manufacturing activity may have been directly connected with royal burials.

Textiles were presumably largely manufactured in the home. In the houses at Ash Shaukan a very large number of loom weights and bone needles testify to this activity.[62] Textiles were used to decorate temples and perhaps other official buildings, and the very fine clothing depicted on reliefs of royalty may have been manufactured in more specialist workshops of which we are entirely ignorant.

There is little evidence for the production of glass by the Kushites. Much of the extremely fine glassware recovered from royal and other burials is certainly imported from the north and the bulk of the glass found in Kush may have come from the same source.[63] However, a few globular vessels, in a deep red translucent glass, may be of local production as they appear to copy distinctly Kushite pottery forms.[64]

Building materials

A large rectangular kiln at Kawa (fig. 74.1) is so far unique in the Nile valley and its form suggests influence from kilns of the Roman period. Kilns of this type, used for the production of brick, tile and pottery, are well known in the western Mediterranean and north-western provinces of the Roman Empire.[65] We have no details of the brick kiln found at Meroe overlying the Roman bath.[66] In pharaonic Egypt bricks were fired in clamps and this technique is still used extensively today. The technique leaves little trace in the archaeological record. One can assume that the Kushites also made use of this basic technology, the raw material being the readily available Nile silt.

The dwellings used by the vast bulk of the population were constructed from timber and mud brick, both of which were available locally, although the amount and types of timber depended on the locality. In the north, palm would have been used extensively, an important by-product of the cultivation of dates and dom nuts.

Although there is evidence for the quarrying of stone for building purposes and for statuary we have no indication that this was a commercial undertaking. Stone was only used in quantity for public monuments and its quarrying and transportation were presumably state enterprises. Extensive quarries tunnelled into the hillside following seams of sandstone are to be seen at Meroe (col. pl. 10), but these were presumably the exception and usually open quarrying methods would have been preferred. For hard stone the granite quarries at Tumbus were utilised (col. pl. 11).[67] Limestone was required to produce the lime mortar used as rendering on buildings constructed of mud brick, red-brick and stone. Sources are not common, but one has been noted at Jebel Gir several kilometres to the north of Meroe.[68] Close to the eastern hafir at Musawwarat es Sufra a large number of pits, set into a plaster floor, were connected with the production of plaster.[69] Some of this was mixed with ground red-brick, forming the waterproof material known by the Romans as *opus signinum*.

Mineral resources and metalworking

Sudan today is not rich in mineral resources. In the eastern desert, particularly in the Wadis el Allaqi and Gabgaba, there were rich seams of gold and these were extensively worked by the Egyptians, Ptolemies and the Romans. There is no evidence for any Kushite presence in that area. Pliny notes that the route from Napata to the Red Sea passed through a rich gold producing area, suggesting one source for Kushite gold.[70] There is also gold in the Nile valley itself. The Egyptians mined this gold in the area between Kerma and Buhen and perhaps also in the area of Abu Hamed.[71] Again, there is no evidence for the working of these mines by the Kushites nor of the gold fields on the Upper Blue Nile near Fazougli. Gold objects, considering the amounts which were presumably robbed long ago, are abundant in Kushite royal tombs, but the source of this gold is unknown.

To judge from the Kushite royal inscriptions, gold was in plentiful supply during the XXVth Dynasty.[72] Taharqo boasts that he gave large amounts of the metal to the Temple of Amun at Kawa. Nastasen, who ruled 300 years later, captured large amounts of gold from his enemies in the eastern desert.[73] If the eastern desert remained the main source of gold for the Kushites, we may assume that extraction by force was only one of the means by which Kushites had access to this material: trade with the desert dwellers would have been a more reliable option.

At Buhen from early in the Old Kingdom the Egyptians were extracting and smelting copper ores. This activity ceased at the end of the Old Kingdom. How much copper was available within the confines of the Kingdom of Kush is unclear, but no important deposits of copper ore are known in the area today.[74] Although the Kushites certainly did produce copper-alloy vessels and other artefacts, it has been suggested that much of the raw material may have been imported from the north in ingot form. At Meroe a crucible used for melting copper-alloy was found associated with an area of iron working.[75]

The earliest evidence for the use of iron by the Kushites for utilitarian objects dates to the earlier part of the sixth century BC.[76] An iron spearhead, found in the tomb of Taharqo, was originally wrapped in gold foil, indicating the very special nature of the object and suggesting the great value attached to it.[77] In the early royal tombs iron is excessively rare and only appears in foundation deposits beneath the pyramids at Nuri at the time of Harsiyotef. That jewellery was made from iron does not appear to reflect its high value when it was still a scarce commodity, as the use of iron for jewellery continued throughout the Kushite period. In the later Kushite period iron became commonplace and was used for a wide range of artefacts.

Evidence for the production of iron is one of the most outstanding features of the site at Meroe, where there are massive mounds of slag. This led one of the earlier observers to describe Meroe as the 'Birmingham of Africa'[78] and the Kushites have been seen as playing a fundamental role in the dissemination of metalworking from the Mediterranean world into sub-Saharan Africa. The pivotal role of Kush in this process is now doubted as is the scale of iron production at Meroe itself.[79]

Iron was being worked at Meroe by the fifth century BC at the latest and continued into the period AD 300–500.[80] Recent work has shown that the iron was not extracted from the abundant local ferruginous sandstone, but from an ore, the source of which has yet to be located.[81] Smelting was undertaken in small furnaces which may have been domed or had a shaft-like funnel. The necessary heat was achieved by forcing air into the furnace using pot bellows, the tuyères entering the furnace a little above its floor. An arched opening allowed access into the furnace. A number of the furnaces found at Meroe were enclosed within a rectangular red-brick building. The repeated use of these installations has been thought to be indicative of the existence of an organised specialist industry.[82]

Other centres of iron production have been claimed, associated with the temples at Taba, Kawa and Napata,[83] although the evidence is unclear.

Transport

Trade is directly related to the transportation facilities available. In the ancient world the cost of transport by water was vastly cheaper than by land. The availability of water transport, therefore, affected the viability of trade, particularly in bulky, heavy or low-valued goods. There is no reason to doubt that similar cost factors pertained in the Kingdom of Kush.

The suitability of the Nile for transport varies along its course. In the reach from Abu Hamed to el Debba, where the direction of the current and the prevailing wind coincide, movement upstream is virtually impossible for vessels under sail. Elsewhere boats were able to float downstream with the current or sail upstream before the north wind which blows virtually all the year round. Local movement of people and goods in the favourable reaches of the river is to be expected and at high water sailing through some of the cataracts was possible. Inscriptions record Kushite kings travelling by water, and Pliny and Juvenal mention the use of water transport by the Ethiopians [Kushites] to bring trade goods to Aswan. Swift Ethiopian barges are also recorded on a Greek inscription from Philae.[84] Whether the absence of other direct evidence for the use of boats indicates their lack of importance is uncertain. The rarity of representations of them in Kushite art, in contrast to the situation in pharaonic Egypt, has been thought to indicate that they were not commonly used.[85]

The Kushite kings were not averse to relocating sculpture, particularly of the New Kingdom, to adorn their temple complexes. Amanislo was responsible for transporting the two red granite lions originally erected by Amenophis III[86] at Soleb, upstream to Jebel Barkal. These objects, weighing two tons each, must have been moved by water. Granite from Tumbus was frequently used for sculpture, and the two massive sarcophagi of Aspelta and Anlamani were brought from there to Nuri, again presumably by water. The small statue of Amenophis II originally from Kumma[87] may have made its journey to Wad ben Naqa by land.

Long-distance trade goods, of necessity, will have gone by land at least for part of their journey. The Egyptians used donkeys as beast of burden on their expeditions to Nubia and the Kushites may have used the same animal or the camel. There is no evidence either way, although the rarity of representations of the camel in Kushite art casts doubts on its presence in large numbers. Wheeled vehicles did exist and a number of different types are depicted on reliefs (fig. 75). Relief blocks from the temple at Sanam show two-wheeled chariots and high-sided carts with four and with six wheels.[88] Wheeled vehicles were used to carry the sacred barks in procession, and on the chapel wall of Beg.N.6 at Meroe they carry the coffin of the queen and a shrine.[89] In these contexts the discovery of a finely decorated yoke in Beg.N.5 and a wooden spoked wheel in Temple KC.102 can be understood.[90] For crossing the desert, however, wheeled vehicles would have been far from ideal. The only 'made' road known is at Jebel Barkal.

Three main cross-desert routes may be postulated, across the Bayuda from Meroe to Jebel Barkal, the Maheila Road from Jebel Barkal to Kawa and the Korosko Road from Abu Hamed to Korosko. The first of these was certainly used and a journey along it is recorded in some detail by Nastasen on his stela.[91] The importance of the Meheila Road had been cited as the reason for the growth and importance of the sites at Napata and Kawa at points where it rejoins the river. Whether the Korosko Road was also a major route is unclear. Certainly no major Kushite site is known at Abu Hamed and there is very little evidence for Kushite activity in this region of the Nile valley. This matter is

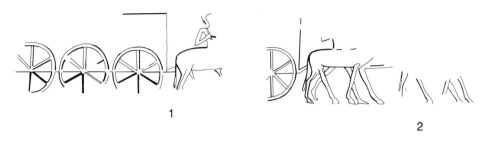

75 *Wheeled vehicles*
   1, 2 and 4 Temple of Amun, Sanam. (After Griffith 1922)
   3 Beg.N.6, Meroe. (After Lepsius 1849–59)

of some importance as the marginalisation of the Napata region and the increased prominence of Meroe has been linked to the flow of trade down the Nile to Abu Hamed and then on across the desert to Egypt via Korosko.[92]

The brief records left by Kushite officials at Philae make it clear that cross-desert routes were usually used for travel between Egypt and Meroe if speed and directness were desired. Fear of losing the way preyed heavily on the minds of some of these travellers.[93]

Other caravan routes may be postulated to the east and west of the Nile, but there is very little evidence for their use by the Kushites or by their suppliers of raw materials. Pliny is our only source of information about a route from Napata to the Red Sea along which rainwater storage facilities were provided.[94] The Red Sea trade had been dominated by the rulers of Egypt, be they pharaohs, Ptolemaic kings or Roman emperors. Increasingly in the later Kushite period Axum was the major conduit by which products from central Africa reached the Mediterranean world.[95] The competition between Axum and Kush, together with the increased poverty of the Roman Empire, which would have reduced the demand, may have been important factors in the reduction of Kushite trade.

Internal trade

The question of the nature and volume of trade in the Kushite state is complex. In the absence of a monetary economy, the level of economic activity is difficult to gauge. For internal trade to have existed at all, certain sectors of the population needed to produce a surplus which they could use themselves for barter or which they could pay in taxes to a higher authority who could then engage in barter. It is likely that the same legal fiction existed in Kush as in Egypt where all land belonged to the crown. Some scholars are of the opinion that the Kushite economy functioned as a redistributive system: surplus produce, collected as taxes, was then redistributed by the state. Others have seen the bulk of society working the land at subsistence level, contributing nothing to the state and receiving nothing from the state.[96] A number of buildings have been identified as magazines where agricultural produce may have been stored, but in the more southerly parts of the kingdom the very humid rainy season will have made the long term storage of foodstuffs difficult. In the so-called Western Palace at Faras, which is probably a magazine, a number of *ostraca* were found which look like tax receipts or records of the delivery of certain types of produce.[97]

Amongst the Kushite population there would have been a number of individuals who were not primary food producers. These included members of the army, of the adminstration, the priesthood, and the royal family. We have no evidence to indicate how these people were paid. There must also have been an artisan class involved in the manufacture of pottery and other artefacts and also such specialists as architects, builders and sculptors. Many of these individuals would have been closely connected with the court. However, the abundance of fine pottery, for example, indicates that a sizeable proportion of the population was able to obtain luxury items.

The level of wealth, implicit in the quality and quantity of grave goods, appears to have been much higher in northern Nubia than in the south. This has been related to the advantageous position of that area close to the border with Egypt. Exactly how the wealth was disseminated has never been satisfactorily explained as Lower Nubia is, relatively speaking, a much less productive area than the rest of Kush. It is unlikely that any trade in luxury raw materials from central Africa passing through Kush would have generated wealth along the way only in the north. In any event, this trade is likely to have been a state monopoly. A military and administrative presence would have tended to foster local prosperity, but there is no reason why these factors should have especially favoured the north.

Today the presence of luxury items in impoverished areas – be they a video camera, a colour TV, or a Toyota land cruiser – is invariably the result of wealth brought home by migrant workers. There is abundant evidence from the medieval period for large numbers of Nubians in Egypt, many of them enrolled in the armies of the Fatimids.[98] A similar situation may have pertained in Kushite times where the inhabitants of Lower Nubia were much more favourably placed to undertake work in Egypt than their fellow countrymen to the south. Graffiti on the walls of the temples at Dakka and Philae indicate the large number of Kushite pilgrims visiting them. These people, the majority of whom presumably lived in Lower Nubia, will have been in a good position to purchase luxury items of foreign manufacture.[99]

Tomb robbing was endemic in Kush, as in other places where very high-value objects were buried with the dead. The interval between the burial and the robbing of the tomb may sometimes have been extremely short. Many fine objects still remain in these tombs, where they have been discarded by the robbers who were presumably mainly interested in gold. Clearly 'fences' were not available to dispose of the artistically extremely fine metalwork and glass objects which were made of base materials, but there must have been some means by which gold could be recirculated into the economy with a profit accruing to the thief.

International trade

Imports
There is abundant evidence for the influx of foreign goods into Kush. The presence of large quantities of pottery from Egypt – of types which were traded not for their own sake, but for the contents which they contained – documents a trade in wine, olive oil and honey. These pottery containers have been found as far south as Wad ben Naqa.[100] An amphora, found in tomb Beg.N.28 at Meroe, from Tubusuctu in Mauritania Caesariensis (Tiklat in Algeria)[101] indicates the long-distance nature of this trade.

In Lower Nubia utilitarian pottery was also imported in considerable quantities, the trade in these bulky, low-value goods being facilitated by the use of water transport along the river between the First and Second Cataracts. The Second Cataract formed the southern limit of trade in low-value goods, the cost of transporting them through the further cataracts rendering the enterprise unviable.[102]

Other objects imported for their aesthetic appeal are common finds in the royal tombs and in the tombs of the aristocracy, particularly at Meroe. These objects include some extremely fine ceramics, noteworthy amongst them being the rhyton of Sotades from Beg.S.24 at Meroe.[103] Metal-work is also well represented and includes fine bronze and silver ware from throughout the Mediterranean. It may only have been the ruler who had the necessary hard currency to partake in long-distance international trade and the presence of these objects in non-royal contexts may relate to the distribution of objects as payment for services rendered.

Objects may also have entered Kush as gifts. It has been suggested that rulers sent embassies to their neighbours after their accession and these would have carried gifts. In the Roman period it was customary for embassies bearing rich gifts to be sent to the courts of allied and client kingdoms. An inscription on one of the pyramid chapels at Meroe has been interpreted as meaning that the occupant received presents from the 'Pharaoh of the West', i.e. the Roman emperor.[104] To differentiate the objects which arrived in Kush as gifts from those which were traded is far from easy. However, several categories of object, including silver vessels decorated with special iconography and luxury glassware which does not appear to have been traded over long distances within the Roman empire, are likely to have been gifts.[105]

For the fitments at his new temple at Kawa, Taharqo was able to procure cedar from Lebanon[106] and this timber would have been transported mainly through Kushite territory. As late as the beginning of our era newly felled Lebanese cedar was still available: within pyramid Beg.N.22 at Meroe a large timber 150 mm in diameter was found which has been dated by radiocarbon analysis to between 15 BC and AD 75.[107]

As well as gifts the Romans, particularly in the later empire, brought peace to their frontiers by providing subsidies to the peoples immediately beyond. We have no direct evidence for this practice on the southern frontier of Egypt, but it may have provided another avenue by which wealth entered the Kingdom of Kush.

During the XXVth Dynasty a considerable amount of wealth in the form of artefacts presumably entered Kush as booty. None of this wealth would have been returned to Egypt after the Kushites were ousted from there.

Exports

Close to the border in Lower Nubia some small-scale trade in foodstuffs may have been undertaken by private enterprise, but the volume of such trade is likely to have been small. The only documentary evidence for the export of bulk foodstuffs comes from a papyrus fragment which records that in the thirty-sixth year of the reign of Darius (486/5 BC) people were sent from Elephantine into Nubia to procure grain.[108]

The export trade would have been under state control. Direct evidence for this trade is strictly limited. Better documented eras furnish a range of goods which we can assume the Kushites supplied to the Mediterranean world, but the quantities involved are unknown. The volume of the trade, in the absence of any quantifiable evidence for it, depends on the perception of scholars as to the importance of trade in the Kushite economy. One modern authority has stated that 'the economic mainstay of the Meroitic [Kushite] state was the export of certain raw materials of which the country was uniquely possessed: gold, ivory, slaves, and to a lesser extent other exotic products of the tropics.'[109] The rise of Axum certainly robbed Kush of any claim to uniquely possess and have access to the goods of central Africa, as did the earlier trade along the Red Sea with the Land of Punt.

It was the lure of gold which led to long-term Egyptian interest in the eastern desert but, as noted above, there is no evidence that this area, apart from during the XXVth Dynasty, ever lay under Kushite control.

At Wad ben Naqa two of the other trade items, ebony and elephant ivory, were found stock-piled in a store room of the palace.[110] In room 15 of 'the Treasury' at Sanam, also, large numbers of elephant tusks were found, which had been badly fire damaged.[111] Whether these were for local consumption or for the export trade is unknown. Kushite ivory, more likely spoils of war or tribute, was used by the Persian king Darius to decorate his palace at Susa in Iran.[112] The literary sources make it clear that the Ptolemies obtained war elephants from Kush[113] and some of these may have been supplied via trade contacts with the Kushites. However, an inscription from the Red Sea port of Adulis set up by Ptolemy III indicates that the Ptolemies procured their own war elephants: 'The paramount King Ptolemaios ... went to war with Asia accompanied by troglodytic and Ethiopian elephants which his father and he himself, as the first ones, have captured from those countries.'[114]

The Kushites may not have needed to range far to the south for these animals. Pliny notes that rhinoceroses and elephants were to be found around Meroe in the AD 60s.[115] At least some of the elephants may have been trained by the Kushites, who certainly had the necessary expertise as is shown by the presence of elephants docilely 'leading' prisoners on the north-west wall of the Lion Temple at Musawwarat and the depiction of a king riding an elephant also from that site.[116]

The large numbers of slaves captured by the Egyptian pharaohs in the lands to the south of the First Cataract are proudly noted in inscriptions. In the seventh century AD the terms of the Baqt, a treaty between the Muslims of Egypt and the Christian king of Makuria in the Dongola Reach, includes an annual tribute of 400 slaves from Nubia. In the nineteenth century the Sudan was notorious for its slave trade, which largely lay in the hands of the Nubians. We would expect the Kushites also to have been involved in the slave trade, but the scale of this trade is unknown to us. Only a handful of slaves of Kushite origin are known in Egypt in the Graeco-Roman period.[117] Archaeologically, slavery is always extremely difficult to trace and no artefacts or structures connected with the Kushite slave trade have been identified.

The export of Kushite objects to the peoples living to the east, west and south is virtually unknown. A very small number of objects of Kushite manufacture have been found within the Axumite kingdom and Kushite material was reaching the 'native' settlement at Jebel Moya and the nearby site at Jebel Seqadi in the Gezira.[118] The extreme rarity of Kushite goods beyond the bounds of the kingdom, if it is not entirely the result of the lack of archaeological fieldwork, indicates that the Kushites obtained the riches of central Africa not by trade but by expropriation.

Archaeological investigations designed to furnish information on the Kushite economy – be it agriculture, animal husbandry or manufacturing processes – did not have the glamour of temple and tomb excavations. In the past most of the evidence we have for the economy has been a by-product of work concentrating on other aspects of Kushite cultural remains. Meroe has been a notable exception and interest in this is continuing. Until further work of this type occurs elsewhere in the kingdom we will not be in a position to make a valid assessment of the nature and relative importance of the many Kushite economic activities.

CHAPTER EIGHT

The Arts and the Art of Writing

The origins of Kushite art, like the origins of the Kushites themselves, are obscure. The earliest examples of Kushite artistic expression date to the period when their culture was rapidly adopting the canons prevalent in Egypt. Throughout their history the Kushite artists were continually borrowing from the current artistic trends in Egypt. Although influences from Egypt were of paramount importance, Kushite art still retained a distinctive character of its own. Kushite artists were clearly not simply purloining ideas but also adapting them, presumably to their own artistic traditions. Our ignorance of the very earliest Kushite art denies us the opportunity of observing these traditions in isolation.

Kushite art is of particular interest not only on account of its constant assimilation of new artistic canons but on account of the selective manner in which styles and motifs were adopted. Kushite artistic expression is given great prominence by historians and archaeologists of the period. Its development is one of the major features used to subdivide the continuum of Kushite history into the Napatan and Meroitic periods.

When the Kushites conquered Egypt they had direct access to an artistic tradition already over two thousand years old. They also had the wealth and the skilled artists available to embark on a programme of artistic embellishment of their kingdom. Art is a potent tool of propaganda and most of the invaders of Egypt have made use of the traditional artistic modes of expression to cloak their regimes with the legitimacy of rule and to camouflage their foreignness. The Kushite rulers of the XXVth Dynasty were less foreign than many who were later to control Egypt and they appear to have quickly been able to integrate themselves into its culture. Their sense of security is reflected in their rather idiosyncratic art. Although they assumed many of the trappings of Egyptian kingship they retained a number of distinctive features of insignia, clothing and physical features which made their non-Egyptian character plain for all to see.

Sculpture and relief decoration

Early Kushite sculpture in the round is not particularly abundant, making it difficult to form assumptions on the prevailing styles employed. So much may have depended on the accident of survival, accentuating the individuality shown by particular artists working in different parts of the kingdom. Certain features, however, are characteristic.

The tendency to hark back to Old Kingdom and Middle Kingdom models is an unusual feature which has not been satisfactorily explained. One might have expected that the pharaohs of the New Kingdom would have been more logical role models for the Kushites to adopt. It was, after all, under the New Kingdom that much of the territory of the later Kushite state was dominated by Egypt, and when many of the large religious monuments – still surviving in the eighth century BC – were built. Although Kushite artists were strongly influenced by these earlier styles, often to the extent that some confusion may occur when attempting to date a given piece on stylistic grounds, they were not producing slavish copies. Their work has a vitality of its own and marks a renaissance of pharaonic art.

Early Kushite sculpture is characterised by a 'brutal realism'[1] which often does little to flatter the individual so portrayed. The granite sphinx of King Taharqo found in the Temple of Amun at Kawa illustrates this point (fig. 76). The facial features of the king are in stark contrast to the idealised representations of earlier encumbents of the throne of the Two Lands. The round face, the high cheekbones and the pronounced folds at the base of the nose – the so-called Kushite folds – and the thick lips are all recurring features of the sculpture of this period.[2] Although many of the features seen in Kushite sculpture are less than flattering, it has been doubted that these are actual portraits but 'the sculpture [referring to the Taharqo sphinx] must be viewed as a provincial expression of kingship as embodied in the person of a particular ruler.'[3] True portraiture may, however, be observed on a number of representations of Shabaqo where the king is shown with 'a low forehead, extremely round full cheeks, and a little knob of a chin'.[4] In the field of private sculpture of the late XXVth and early XXVIth Dynasties realism is more common[5] and individuals are portrayed 'warts and all'.

The major military reverses suffered by the Kushites at the hands of the Assyrians, which led to their withdrawal from Egypt, is not reflected in the sculpture of the succeeding period. This is clearly demonstrated in the series of colossal statues recovered from Temple B800 at Jebel Barkal by Reisner. The earliest in the series is of Taharqo (fig. 77), the latest of Aspelta. They thus span a period of some 120 years, yet it is only a slight variation in the treatment of the eyes on Aspelta's statue that suggests that it is of a different period.

Relief sculpture follows similar models to those employed for sculpture in the round. The harking back to Old and Middle Kingdom styles is particularly noticeable. In the Temple of Amun at Kawa constructed by workmen brought by Taharqo from Memphis especially for the task, this is very clear. Among the reliefs on the walls of the first court of the temple the scenes of the king as a sphinx trampling the foes, and a woman with her two sons adoring, are virtually identical to the scene in the mortuary chapels of Sahura and Pepy II, even down to the same names being used.[6] The attention paid to the modelling of musculature again suggests the influence of Old Kingdom sculpture, although the influence of contemporary Assyrian reliefs has also been suggested.[7] The

77 *Taharqo. (Courtesy of the National Museum, Khartoum, photo D. A. Welsby)*

Although Archaic Greek sculpture was developed from Egyptian models, Greek art rapidly diverged and assumed a character of its own. This Greek style of art was introduced into Egypt following the conquest of the country by Alexander in 332 BC. The Ptolemaic Dynasty, one of the three main players in the Hellenistic period in the Eastern Mediterranean, maintained a predilection for this Hellenic artistic canon. Traditional Egyptian art was influenced by these new artistic modes of expression and in its turn Kushite art followed suit. This amalgam of Kushite and Hellenistic art is one of the hallmarks of 'Meroitic' culture. The arrival of the Romans in Egypt added yet another influence both to Egyptian and to Kushite art. It has been suggested, with some plausibility, that other influences came from the Near East, and also, with little justification, from India.[9]

Later Kushite art is characterised by stylistic disunity. For example, the two granite colossi which were erected in front of the Temple of Amun at Tabo (fig. 24) must be contemporary and must have been carved in the same locality. Yet they vary considerably in detail, one being more typically 'Meroitic' with the large bulging eyes in the flat face and with the mouth curving upwards as though in a smile. The other has almond-shaped eyes and a straight mouth with 'more tube-like lips'.[10]

The art of this period has been divided into five stylistic groups, one of which displays new traits which are identified as Meroitic (Group III), and one encompassing a new type of representation, the *ba*-statue (Group IV). Group I continues the traditions of the earlier Kushite period; Group II marks a renaissance of Egyptian forms; and Group V is a perhaps short-lived flowering of Hellenistic art, principally from Alexandria.

Sculpture of Group V is largely confined to the water sanctuary, the so-called 'Royal Baths' at Meroe. One of the most interesting of this group is a reclining figure carved from Nubian sandstone and coated with a thick layer of plaster which has then been painted.[11] The reclining attitude of the statue can be readily paralleled in Roman art.

These groups, although varying considerably in character, retain a number of common features which allow them to be grouped together under the single heading of 'Meroitic' art. Among these characteristics are human figures depicted with unusually broad, generally level shoulders, long columnar necks and round heads. Another is the predilection for depicting women of stout proportions, well illustrated by two female statues from Meroe[12] and by representations of Kushite queens, as for example on the pylon of the Lion Temple at Naqa (fig. 6).

This period was one of artistic innovation and we see a number of compositions used for the first time or in novel ways. Among these are column statues most frequently of the gods Arensnuphis and Sebiumeker, who are found flanking the entrances to temples (for example at Musawwarat es Sufra, Temple 300). The column base at the same site, formed by four alternating figures of a lion and an elephant, is unparalleled in Egyptian art.[13] At Jebel Barkal (fig. 47) and Wad ben Naqa, column statues of Bes survived into the nineteenth century.[14]

Similar innovations are to be seen in reliefs. Of particular interest is the representation of the Lion God Apedemak on the external back wall of his temple at Naqa (fig. 69). The composition has placed the god in a dilemma as he is receiving Queen Amanitore and the prince from the right and King Natakamani from the left. The artist solved the problem by merging two bodies together, with two arms, one leg and one face to each side. To mask the awkward point of junction of the two faces a third face looking out from the wall has been provided. This is not a triple headed god derived from the Indian pantheon as has been suggested[15] but an ingenious solution to this artistic challenge. A similar solution has been used on the pylons of the temple where the prisoners held by the king and queen are symmetrically arranged looking to left and right, with an individual shown *en face* covering the point of junction.

A number of reliefs incorporate markedly Classical elements. On the south inner face of the Apedemak temple at Naqa is a god, identified as Serapis, represented full face sporting a well-developed beard (fig. 78.1). At Jebel Qeili a figure of a god is again shown full-face wearing a radiate crown (fig. 68); this correlates closely with representations of the Sun God as at Hatra in Iraq and with representations of Mithras, a god of Persian origin who was worshipped right across the Roman empire. Considerations of the date of the relief, however, suggest that Hellenistic iconography is a more likely source.[16] Another example of a god wearing a radiate crown is to be found at Naqa (fig. 78.2).[17]

From the ruins of the palace of Natakamani at Jebel Barkal a number of glazed tiles in blue, green, brown, scarlet and yellow have been found. Many of these are circular, around 35 cm in diameter and decorated with female busts shown full-face in high relief. Their Classical inspiration is clear, but they are much more devolved copies than the similar roundels from the water sanctuary at Meroe.[18]

Ba-statues sculpted in the round are a peculiarly Kushite art form, although the beliefs behind the concept of the *ba*, the soul of the deceased, are firmly rooted in Egyptian religious practices. On Egyptian religious papyri the *ba* is represented as a human-headed bird. The Kushite representations, which are almost totally confined to northern Nubia, are given progressively more human forms. The earliest examples have the bird's body with a stylised human head. At the other extreme the figure is almost totally human in form, with the wings of the bird adopting more the form of a cloak which trails down behind the individual (fig. 34). The facial features develop until they achieve the status of real portraiture. Among the fine series from the cemetery at Karanog are several which preserve the sun disc on the head; traces of paint indicate that the figures were gaudily painted (col. pl. 5).[19]

Wall painting

The visual distinction between wall painting and relief decoration, which is so apparent today, was by no means as clear cut when these artistic works were first executed. As was commonplace in many of the cultures of the ancient world, reliefs and also sculpture in the round were often covered in brightly coloured paint, producing what to our eyes is a garish end result. The Kushites were fully integrated into this tradition and a

78 *Classically-inspired representations of gods in the Lion Temple, Naqa.*
  1 Serapis
  2 God wearing a radiate crown
  (After Lepsius 1849–59)

small number of reliefs and statues have preserved traces of their painted decoration. This was used to enhance the sculptured details, and sometimes additional details were added solely in paint. This practice was maintained throughout the Kushite period. Some of the earliest remains of relief decoration and painted plaster were found in the tomb Ku.7 at el Kurru, which probably belonged to Kashta's queen.[20]

Painted decoration also was used on its own but has rarely survived. From the early Kushite period that which was found in the tomb of Tanwetamani at el Kurru is by far the best preserved. As with the reliefs the scenes are in Egyptian style. The king, wearing the Kushite cap with double uraeus and diadem, is depicted with reddy-brown skin.[21] The mud brick temple built by Taharqo at Qasr Ibrim had its rather poor building material covered by plaster and painted. Fragments of this plaster 'bearing Egyptian motifs' were found in the building. A structure inserted into the building on its conversion into a Christian church has preserved *in situ* extensive remains of painting. On the white background the brightly painted scene shows Taharqo identified by a cartouche in Egyptian hieroglyphs, making an offering to a god or goddess.[22]

In the Royal City at Meroe, Garstang discovered extensive remains of wall paintings in Building M.292, which may have been a temple. The bronze head of the Roman emperor Augustus was found buried immediately in front of this building. Although the paintings no longer survive, watercolours made of them at the time of their discovery give some indication of the wide range of colours employed. The scenes appear to represent a king, queen and other members of the royal family giving thanks to a god. Among the bound prisoners considerable attention to detail is given to skin colour, clothing and ornamentation, which is by no means as clear on the reliefs surviving to us. One of the prisoners has been identified as a Roman.[23]

Further paintings were discovered in three temples M.720, KC.102 and KC.104 during excavations in 1975–6. Although only preserved as fragments, some scenes from the decoration of M.720 could be reconstructed. They appear to follow the standard temple decoration theme: members of the ruling family confronting gods. One shows a male and female before a red-robed god, probably Arensnuphis, and probably with Isis behind. The other shows a group of figures before a male god. The elaborate nature of the costumes is noteworthy. The paintings have been executed on a white background, initially outlined in red and corrected in black. The technique employed in the painting in Temple KC.104 is rather different. First the whole wall was covered in a red wash, then the figures were outlined in a deeper red, and then the background was overpainted in grey-blue. The material from KC.102 is non figurative.[24]

Domestic buildings were also decorated with painted wall plaster. At Ash Shaukan the relatively humble dwellings had mud-rendered internal walls painted in white, with the edges of the niches and windows picked out in red imitating frames of wood. In one house a band of decoration around the walls may represent timber joists and floor beams – here in a vaulted room![25] One of the rooms in the so-called castle at Karanog was decorated with a scene of a man on horseback attacking a camel, a crocodile, a jackal and a ship.[27] Although the building appears to be late Kushite, the date of the painting is less certain.

Painted decoration was also used on the exterior of buildings, as for example on the latest Kushite pyramids in the northern cemetery at Meroe, where the rough stonework was rendered and painted red and yellow with a band of blue stars along the base.[26] The palace of Natakamani at Jebel Barkal had its external walls enlivened with pilasters and vertical semi-circular mouldings, variously painted in blue, red and yellow, which must have made a very striking effect against the white background.[28] The faience (glazed tile) roundels already mentioned were inserted into this wall.

A large number of funerary stela from northern Nubia are decorated entirely with paint, although relief decoration also occurs.

The use of rendering and painted decoration must have been a much cheaper alternative to relief decoration. It was quicker and easier to execute and could be applied to any type of wall. For stelae and sculpture poor quality stone could be effectively masked by the application of the plaster and paint.

Recent excavations at Qasr Ibrim have for the first time made us aware of the importance of textiles (col. pl. 12) and wooden objects in the internal decoration of buildings.[29] Temple 6 at Ibrim appears to have been ransacked and then demolished perhaps
as late as the sixth century AD. The demolished walls sealed a large amount of the
temple furnishings and the extremely dry conditions on the site preserved all the
organic remains. Among these furnishings were two blue dyed curtains and three
cotton-bordered, tapestry woven cloths. Twenty-four wooden plaques bearing painted
scenes of animals, often with the creature facing a cup on a high base with two ladles
hanging from the rim, were also recovered. These are pierced for suspension. The mud
brick walls were either whitewashed or covered with a thin layer of pink cement,
against which the textiles and wooden plaques may have been hung.

Minor artistic works

Many of the influences that can be observed on large stone artistic compositions can
also be noted on smaller objects. The Kushites used metal, ceramic and organic materials for artistic work. In a number of cases Kushite products are so faithfully copied
from Egyptian, Hellenistic or Graeco-Roman models that their origin is called into
question. Frequently, however, Kushite traits can be easily recognised. What is striking is the quality of a number of the undoubted Kushite pieces. Among these one may
single out a crystal ball surmounted by a head of the goddess Hathor in gold. The head
is very Egyptian in character, but no parallels to this piece are known.[30] A very large
cast-bronze object in the form of a squatting goose is totally Egyptian in concept, yet
here it is used to form the leg of a typically Kushite funerary bed.[31]

A particularly fine piece is a spoon made from faience in the form of a swimming girl
holding a basin in her outstretched hands. Although the type has a long history, her
Kushite origin is suggested by her extremely broad hips, a feature of Kushite ladies,
and by her coiffure.[32]

The predilection for representing Kushite women of stout proportions has already
been mentioned. Several small, very crude statuettes of terracotta have this feature.[33]
Such steatopygous female figures, often of abstract form, and bearing tattooed decoration, were produced in Nubia from the Neolithic period onwards. The Kushite examples dating to the later period of the kingdom once again testify to the survival of
traditions in Nubia over millennia. The depiction of steatopygous females in the monumental art may reflect this underlying artistic practice.

The finest artistic products are almost invariably recovered from burials. What few
traces remain indicate the lavish nature of the royal grave goods, but in most cases these
burials have been thoroughly plundered. It is thus extremely fortunate that the reigning queen Amanishakheto decided to bury her everyday jewellery not in her tomb
chamber but, uniquely as far as we know, within the body of her pyramid at Meroe.[34]
It was only the unspeakable vandalism of the Italian doctor Guiseppe Ferlini in 1834
which led to their discovery. He was determined to find treasure and, after initial frus-

trations at Wad ben Naqa, Naqa, Musawwarat es Sufra and Meroe, he turned his attentions to the Meroe pyramids. He then proceeded to demolish one of the best preserved of the pyramids, which until his day had survived to a height of 28 m.

The cache consisted mainly of jewellery in great profusion. Much of this material is of gold, with fused glass being commonly used as infill in the design. Other objects are of silver, glass, gemstones, wood and copper-alloy. A few of the pieces had been imported from the Hellenistic world, including three gems set into seal rings of local manufacture, cameos, earrings and bronze bowls. The bulk of the material, however, is clearly Kushite in design and manufacture. The quality of the pieces is extremely good and their value, from the point of view of both their artistic merit and the religious iconography they depict, is high. The waning of pharaonic Egyptian artistic influence can clearly be seen, while Hellenistic motifs and forms are much more prevalent. These are so closely copied on occasion as to suggest the possibility that some of the objects were made by Greek craftsmen resident in Kush.

The modes of manufacture combine the 'ancient' and the 'modern'. Much of the decoration involves the *cloisonné* technique: in some cases the coloured glass has been poured into the 'cells' in a molten state, while elsewhere the glass has been cut to shape and inserted into the cell. The former technique was only developed in Egypt under the Ptolemies, the latter was a much older Egyptian method.

One of the dominant themes in the monumental reliefs, the wall paintings and on the jewellery of Amanishakheto is derived from religious iconography. In the larger compositions on temple walls a favourite subject is the presentation of the ruler, under the protection of Isis, and his/her family to a procession of gods.

Scenes of triumph over the enemies of the state are also frequently seen. One of the commonest compositions of the genre shows the figure of a god, a king or a queen holding a group of prisoners by their hair in one hand while the victor proceeds to smite them with an axe or sword. Other scenes, used as decorative friezes, show bound prisoners in a variety of attitudes, being trodden underfoot or under the control of war elephants (fig. 12). The Jebel Qeili relief is unusual in the realism with which it portrays the scene in which prisoners are seen tumbling head over heels down the mountainside where they were presumably being thrown to their deaths (fig. 68). Jebel Qeili would have formed an ideal venue for such a mode of execution or sacrifice; Jebel Barkal would have been even better.

Many of these scenes were the stock in trade of Egyptian artists of a much earlier period and the Kushites' predilection for borrowing ready-made scenes has led to the bizarre spectacle of their rulers being depicted in the act of smiting enemies who, in the original, are Kushites![35] The wide range of iconographic motifs found in Kushite art suggests that the sculptors had access to pattern books which contained illustrations of the motifs that had been employed in Nubia and Egypt at all periods. Hence we can find on the same monument scenes drawn from the repertoire of sculptors who lived many hundreds of years apart.[36]

Secular art is rather rare and is largely confined to pottery. Early Kushite pottery was not used as a vehicle for artistic expression and in this it follows the traditions of pharaonic Egypt.[37] In pharaonic Egypt art was the preserve of the richer strata of society and of the religious establishment. This sector of the population presumably did not appreciate pottery as an art form. In the later Kushite period there developed a fine pottery industry whose products rivalled the best available in the Mediterranean world.

This pottery is found in great profusion, and substantial collections have been recovered from cemetery sites, particularly in northern Nubia at Faras and Karanog. However, it is not confined to cemeteries and the motifs employed do not indicate that it was designed solely for a religious market. The range of motifs used is extremely wide and it gives an insight into how the Kushites viewed their world in a way that the more formal monumental art cannot. Much of the inspiration for the decoration is drawn from the natural world.

Plant motifs, particularly the vine scroll, clearly reflect the influence of Hellenistic art. Human figures, as for example the dancing fauns on a narrow mouthed jar from Karanog[38] and the satyr and naked woman on a beaker from Meroe,[39] are also derived from the same source.

Other figurative compositions are more idiosyncratic (col. pl. 9). Among the human figures is one engaged in pastoral activities: a man holding a switch follows behind a massive dog and two other quadrupeds. Bound prisoners appear on several pots and one storage vessel is decorated on the shoulder with an unfortunate individual being devoured by a large cat.[40] This latter motif is common on sculpture in the round and on relief decoration. Animal figures abound and these include antelopes, giraffes, frogs, crocodiles, snakes, birds and mythical beasts. The most unusual of these are the two snakes entwined on the inner surface of a bowl from Faras and a bird within a bowl from Karanog (fig. 70).[41]

Attempts have been made, with some degree of success, to attribute particular styles to schools of potters and occasionally to individual painters, as is commonplace in the study of ancient Greek ceramics.[42] Among the schools of painters is the 'academic school', where the repertoire of specific motifs is carefully delineated by lines. However, it is the careful execution of the painting which is the most characteristic feature of the style. Painters who adhered to this style decorated a range of pottery forms. Another school shows a predilection for the vine leaf motif. Within this group individual painters have been recognised, among them the 'Altar Painter' and the 'Antelope Painter'. The continued study of this painted pottery should allow significant progress to be made on a number of questions, particularly those relating to the chronology of the pottery, its place of manufacture and the trade in these wares. At present this work is in its infancy.

The extremely fine eggshell wares are often decorated with stamped motifs. Co-existing with these fine stamped and painted wares is a class of black burnished ware with impressed, punched or incised decoration. This style of decoration shows little foreign influence, but rather, represents the indigenous Nubian traditions. Its products

79 *Graffito of the god Apedemak on a wall in the Great Enclosure at Musawwarat es Sufra.*
(D. A. Welsby)

can thus be paralleled in pottery from Nubia dating from the C-Group and Kerma periods if not earlier. It is this sort of pottery that we find surviving beyond the end of the Kushite period at a time when the fine wares had vanished from the market, being swamped by the ceramics made and decorated in the late Roman tradition.

Another form of popular art is to be found scratched onto the walls of the Great Enclosure at Musawwarat es Sufra. Here there is a very large number of graffiti, both figural and inscriptional. These can only be dated by their subject matter and clearly range from the Kushite period to the present day. Among the inscriptions are Meroitic cursive texts, an inscription carved by Frederick Cailliaud in 1821, and another by the Royal Prussian Expedition of Lepsius.

Of the figural graffiti a number show Kushite gods, with Apedemak figuring prominently (fig. 79). Small horned altars are also common. Many of the others show animals such as giraffes, elephants, felines and dogs chasing hares. A large number of these may be Kushite and correspond to the popularity of animals on painted pottery. One erotic scene is presumably also Kushite.[43]

Kushite language and writing

Literacy in the Kushite state developed rapidly, having been borrowed wholesale from Egypt. As with much else in Kushite culture, the early writings are indistinguishable from that of contemporary Egypt. It was presumably the educated priesthood who introduced the Kushites to the Egyptian spoken and written word and this was closely followed by the Kushite conquest of Egypt itself. Egyptian was the Kushite religious, diplomatic and administrative language not only in Egypt but also apparently throughout their whole domain.

All inscriptions known from this early period found south of Aswan are identical in form to those set up by the Kushites in Egypt. The inscriptions are confined either to religious texts or are royal inscriptions set up in religious establishments. Clearly these were for the consumption of a very small sector of the population, and perhaps principally for the gods through their spokesmen, the priests. It is highly unlikely that a large section of the population was conversant in Egyptian. We can only assume that one or more local languages were spoken by the bulk of the population. Of these hypothetical languages only Meroitic was ever written down. Inscriptions in Egyptian hieroglyphs continued to be written in Kush at least as late as the first century AD.

Many of these inscriptions use texts borrowed from a wide range of sources leading to the suggestion that there must have been extensive archives of Egyptian texts available in Kush, and presumably people – be they Egyptians or Egyptian trained – skilled in the reading and carving of these texts.[44] In later periods the grasp of Egyptian was clearly slipping away. The tomb of Arqamani, Beg.N.7, contains one of the last intelligible texts in a funerary context, although meaningless imitations of Egyptian hieroglyphs are found later.[45] However, there were on occasion periods when the quality of the Egyptian texts is markedly higher, as under Natakamani and Amanitore.[46]

The Meroitic language

It is only from several hundred years after the founding of the Kushite state that we have any evidence for the indigenous language.

We have little information on the language generally spoken by the Kushites before Meroitic was written down. By that time it was a fully developed language with an extensive vocabulary which appears to make relatively little use of Egyptian loan words.

This would suggest that it was already of some considerable antiquity and it certainly is not derived from Egyptian. A study of early Kushite names suggests that they are 'Meroitic' names. Kashta (or more properly Kushto) in Meroitic means 'The Kushite',[47] while *mak* (god), *malo* (good) and *mote* (child) occur as components of many names.[48]

In 1921 George Reisner, then undertaking excavations in the Kushite royal cemeteries and temples wrote: 'Unfortunately the texts of the Meroitic inscriptions are as yet practically sealed books to us. But it is, no doubt, only a question of a few years now before the Meroitic inscriptions from Barkal must yield their historical information.'[49]

Now, over seventy years later, this hope has still not been realised. The greatest scholar of Meroitic, Francis Llellwyn Griffith, made considerable progress with the deciphering of the scripts and went some way to providing an understanding of some specific types of inscriptions. However, by virtue of Griffith's genius he soon exhausted the possibilities for advancement of the study with the limited material available and little further progress has been achieved.[50]

No bilingual texts of sufficient length have come to light since the time of Griffith nor has any related language yet been found. The state of play in 1973, which is just as applicable today, was summarised by Trigger: 'Should Meroitic, like Sumerian, prove to be unrelated to any other known language and no further sources of bilingual information be forthcoming, the chances of ever adequately understanding the language are vanishingly small.'[51]

Early scholars of the language hoped that it may have been related to Old Nubian but this has been shown not to be the case, although both are agglutinative, lack gender and have the place of inflections taken by post-positions and suffixes. Whether it was related to the language of the Kerma culture is another unknown, as no inscriptions in Kerman have come to light.

In the funerary texts the scheme is so clear that it is relatively easy to pick out names and titles and even to hazard a meaning for entire phrases. It was the study of the large numbers of these texts from the cemeteries at Karanog and Shablul that enabled Griffith to recognise a considerable number of personal names, titles, toponyms and a few other words. With other types of inscription the results were much less satisfactory. This is graphically illustrated by Griffith's comments on the stela of Akinidad from Hamadab: 'The rest of the inscription . . . is a maze of words almost without clues to its general meaning'.[52]

Of phonology we know even less, but there are indications that the written language could vary to some extent from the spoken. Vowels, for example, tend on occasion not to be written even at the beginning of words; there is considerable interchange of similar letters used to write the same word; and certain consonants, although apparently enunciated, were not written in particular letter combinations. This information has been culled from a study of transliterations of Meroitic words into other ancient languages. Every symbol represents the consonant plus the vowel 'a' unless it is followed by the symbol for another vowel. Where a consonant appears without an associated vowel the symbol for 'e' is provided.[53]

Meroitic hieroglyphs

The earliest written form of Meroitic employed a hieroglyphic alphabet, most of the signs used being borrowed from Egyptian. Like Egyptian it is most usually written in columns. Unlike Egyptian hieroglyphs, the Meroitic version forms an alphabet of twenty-three characters comprising four vowel signs (a, e, i, o), fifteen consonants and four syllabic signs (ne, se, te, to).[54] Also unlike Egyptian it is to be read in the direction that the figures face, whatever that may be. Thus with hieroglyphic inscriptions written in the more common columnar format the signs are usually to be read right to left as on the rare horizontal inscriptions, but sometimes for aesthetic effect the symbols could be turned round to face the other way, occasionally leading to confusion by the workman.

The words are separated by double (or rarely triple) dots, a feature not found in Egyptian hieroglyphic, hieratic or demotic writing. The texts written in Meroitic hieroglyphs are formal and limited in range, and contain many inaccuracies. Also the quality of execution of the hieroglyphs themselves is frequently so poor as to lead to ambiguity.

The sign values of Meroitic hieroglyphs have been ascertained from the study of those inscriptions where both Meroitic and Egyptian versions occur on the same inscription. Griffith made extensive use of the inscription on a bark stand from Wad ben Naqa where the cartouches of the king and queen contain their names in both forms. His work has stood the test of time.

Inscriptions written in Meroitic hieroglyphs have been found from Aswan to Soba East. The earliest securely dated example comes from the reign of Queen Shanakdakhete in the early second century BC.[55] The hieroglyphic alphabet was clearly designed to resemble Egyptian inscriptions. It was used for royal inscriptions of a monumental character into the final years of the Kushite kingdom. In the north of the country a stone lion from Qasr Ibrim, of King Yesbokheamani datable to *c.*AD 283–300, carries an inscription in Meroitic hieroglyphs.[56] Far to the south a bronze bowl bearing an inscription which includes the title *qore*, ruler, has recently been found in a grave beneath one of the large tumuli at el Hobagi.[57] If the bowl was not being reused, and in the light of the associated Kushite funerary practices this seems unlikely, it indicates that this system of writing continued into the post-pyramidal age.

The hieroglyphic alphabet is almost invariably used for monumental texts and its use for writing in other contexts is extremely rare. An interesting illustration of unfamiliarity with the hieroglyphs was found at Mediq in Lower Nubia where a graffito giving the names of Khalême and Pakhême was begun in hieroglyphs but had to be completed using the cursive alphabet.[58]

In the royal cemeteries at Meroe some inscriptions are totally in Egyptian hieroglyphs, others have the royal name in Meroitic hieroglyphs and the rest in Egyptian, while yet others are totally in Meroitic hieroglyphs. Eventually even the majority of royal texts were written in the cursive.

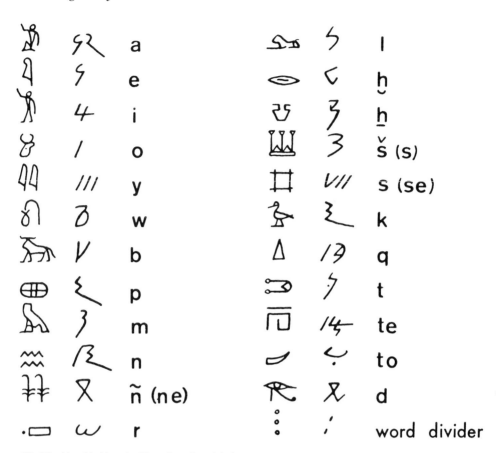

80 *The Meroitic hieroglyphic and cursive alphabets.*

Meroitic cursive

Although frequently referred to as cursive, the term is inappropriate as, apart from one letter, the signs are always spaced apart. Griffith preferred the term demotic but as cursive is now the generally accepted designation it will be adhered to here. There is a close relationship between the Meroitic hieroglyphic and cursive alphabets. Cursive spellings correspond to hieroglyphic sign by sign. Griffith first recognised this by comparing the very standardised opening formulae on altars and stelae in the two scripts. In these standardised texts there are other points of similarity which allow further sign equivalents to be ascertained (fig. 80).

There is considerable variation in the forms of the letters, even in good texts, leading to some danger of confusion. There are also marked variations in letter forms over time, with the earlier signs having a greater resemblance to hieroglyphs. Griffith divided the variations into three styles – archaic, transitional and late – and assigned rough chronological limits for the use of each style.

According to Griffith the Meroitic cursive alphabet was not a natural descendant of old Egyptian and only four of the letters resemble the equivalent Egyptian demotic signs, with some of the others perhaps being derived from hieroglyphic. Griffith considered that 'It must be an intentional and more or less artificial selection, such as might have been made, probably by some foreign adviser, at any time after the Semitic alphabet had been invented.'[59]

Griffith further suggested that the cursive alphabet may have had a long history of being used for writing on papyrus and skins before it was applied to stone. Cursive writing on pottery is not demonstrably earlier than its first appearance on stone inscriptions. Recent work at Qasr Ibrim has yielded a rich hoard of papyrus, many examples of which are in Meroitic cursive. This material is very difficult to date, but there is no reason to think that any of these pieces indicate the use of the cursive script at an earlier date than that evidenced from the lapidary inscriptions.

The presence of at least two letters in Old Nubian which are derived from the Meroitic cursive alphabet suggests that Meroitic was written until late in the history of the kingdom.[60] The latest inscription known may be that of Kharamadêye at Kalabsha,[61] although a spear blade bearing a short cursive inscription was recovered from an X-Group grave at Qustul.[62]

Numbers in Meroitic
Numerals used in Meroitic were derived from Egyptian and, like the Egyptians, the Kushites used a decimal system. Numbers 1 to 4 and even on occasion as high as 8 were represented by corresponding numbers of simple upright strokes, although ciphers were probably usually used for numbers above 4. Subdivisions of units are known on the decimal system and these were indicated by dots placed before the number: a group of nine dots, for example, arranged in a square pattern three by three, represented nine-tenths of a unit (fig. 81). Other subdivisions suggest that the duodecimal system may also have been used for some units. These units presumably include units of weights and measures. A symbol representing $\frac{1}{2}$ has also been noted.[63]

Literacy

Diodorus wrote that, although in Egypt hieroglyphs were only known by the priests, among the Ethiopians all used their native hieroglyphic script.[64] With only twenty-three signs, clearly it would have been much easier to learn Kushite than Egyptian hieroglyphs.

The presence of the numerous tombstones suggests that literacy was not the prerogative of the very few. Yet it must be remembered that it is only relatively rich burials which were marked by inscribed stelae. On a number of monuments throughout Kush the presence of graffiti, and the discovery of *ostraca* on a number of sites, particularly in Lower Nubia, indicate that the humbler members of Kushite society both were literate and used an identical form of Meroitic. Of what other language or languages they spoke when going about their everyday business we have no evidence. At Qasr Ibrim,

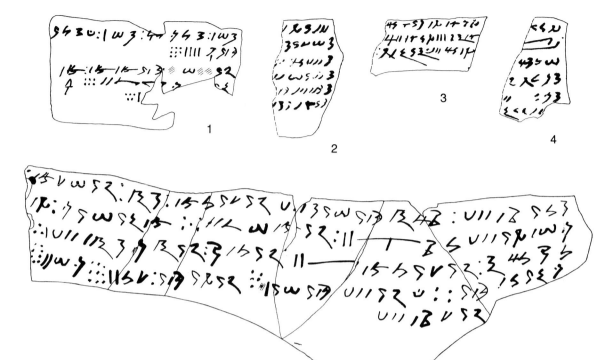

81 *Ostraca bearing Meroitic cursive texts. (After Griffith 1925b)*
1 from Buhen
2–5 from Faras

Meroitic cursive has been found on *ostraca*, papyrus, wooden tablets and on a gourd.[65]

Fragments of at least one page-sized illustration and an inscribed wooden tag, probably a book label, from Jebel Adda indicate that it is only the unfortunate vagaries of survival that has so far denied us access to Kushite books and literature.[66]

The Kushites' knowledge of other languages and systems of writing apart from Egyptian and Egyptian hieroglyphs does not appear to have been widespread. Egyptian demotic and Greek, which were current in Egypt for much of the Kushite period, are only found in Lower Nubia, apart from a very few exceptions. Only one inscription in Latin is known from Kush, at Musawwarat es Sufra.[67] There is literary and archaeological evidence for the presence of native Greek speakers at Meroe and some common language of communication must have been available to them. Diodorus records that the king whom he calls Ergamenes, a contemporary of Ptolemy II, had had a Greek education and had studied philosophy.[68] Clearly there must have been at least one Greek teacher in the capital at that time. The Greek alphabet written around a column drum at Meroe may witness an attempt to teach that language.[69] The ambassadors sent to Philae and beyond also must have had the services of translators fluent in both Meroitic and Greek. The most likely source of these will have been at the interface between the Kushites and Egypt in Lower Nubia.

CHAPTER NINE

The Decline and 'Fall' of the Kushite Kingdom

The fall of mighty empires and kingdoms is always an intriguing subject. The questions asked are usually why, how and when did these events, which appear from a distance of time to be cataclysmic, take place. The answers are rarely simple and this is particularly the case with the demise of the Kushite kingdom. Its end is shrouded in as much mystery as its beginnings well over a thousand years before.

It is clear, certainly, that no natural disaster stimulated these events. The Nubia of the early medieval period was a very similar place, with the same potential for agriculture and settlement as that of the late Kushite period. The people were also largely the same and there is little evidence for massive movements of population. In the past the theory of mass migration was held to account for the collapse of the kingdom, but such mass movement theories are now out of fashion in archaeology the world over. Continuity is seen as the normal state of cultural development. To some extent the end of the Kushite state is now discounted altogether!

Whatever theories we propound concerning the events and developments in Nubia from the third century AD into the sixth century AD, they are bound to be inadequate. Any evidence for dramatic change is brought into question by the strong evidence for continuity. None the less, the early medieval kingdoms known to us from the writings of the Byzantine ecclesiastical historians of the sixth century AD existed in a world very different from that of the late Kushite period.

Modern theories relating to the demise of the Kushite state are principally based on a small amount of literary and epigraphic evidence. Literary and epigraphic sources relate to the situation in the north, epigraphic sources to the situation in the south.

Lower Nubia

The Byzantine historian Procopius, writing in the mid-sixth century AD, records that Diocletian withdrew the frontier to the First Cataract and called upon the Nobatae to occupy and defend the vacated territory against the hostile desert tribes collectively called the Blemmyes.[1] There is no mention in this account of the Kushites and it is generally assumed that they were in no position to play any part in the occupation of the old Roman province.

Although there are some obvious errors in Procopius' account, the sequence of events has rarely been challenged. A close scrutiny of what little additional literary evidence there is indicates that probably at least as late as AD 336, the Kushites were still a force to be reckoned with in the affairs of Lower Nubia. A joint embassy to the emperor Constantine, probably on the occasion of his tricennalia, the thirtieth anniversary of his accession to power, came from the Ethiopians (Kushites) and the Blemmyes.

With the withdrawal of the Roman frontier to the First Cataract, it may have been the Kushites who stepped in to fill the political vacuum, the situation recorded by Procopius being more relevant to his own time when the Kushites had faded into history. The archaeological evidence may be interpreted to support the argument for a Kushite presence in the fourth century. The discovery of a stone lion at Qasr Ibrim bearing the name of the Kushite king Yesbokheamani (Amani-Yeshbehe),[2] who is generally dated to the period AD 283–300, and the presence of his name Philae and in the Lion Temple at Meroe, indicate the territorial integrity of the Kushite state at this time.[3] It has been suggested that the Kushite cemetery at Sayala post-dates AD 298,[4] but as this is based on a study of the associated artefacts no certainty is possible. As will be noted below, evidence for continuity in the archaeological record effectively masks the evidence for political discontinuity.

Particularly intriguing is the long inscription in Meroitic cursive carved on the wall of the temple at Kalabsha. Although most of the sense of the text cannot be ascertained, the opening formula seems clear and begins with the phrase 'Kharamazêye, the king'.[5] The form of the letters suggest that this inscription is of very late date. No royal pyramid at Meroe is available for this king and he may well have been a local ruler in the north, perhaps even one of the kings buried at Ballana and Qustul. His use of Meroitic puts him firmly into the Kushite period. The king considered himself as a Kushite ruler and ascribed his victory to the state gods of Kush. He, however, appears to be one among a number of either hostile, subject or allied kings. A date in the later fourth century AD has been suggested for the inscription.[6] King Silko, whose inscription is also inscribed on the Kalabsha temple wall, may be a successor of Kharamadêye. His inscription, however, is written in Greek, one of the main languages of medieval Nubia.

Upper Nubia

Of crucial importance to our understanding of events in the south is the inscription set up by the Axumite, King Aezana, at Axum. This inscription is a record of a campaign by the king, after he had been converted to Christianity, against a number of different tribes. As well as the names of these tribes, it includes a large number of toponyms and details of the length of the journeys between one place and another.[7] It is an extremely detailed document, but to derive any useful information from it one has to identify the places it mentions on the ground. This is far from easy.

Initially it was assumed that it recorded a campaign into the Nile valley against the Noba, who had occupied towns belonging to the Kushites. This has found general favour and the invasion of the Middle Nile has largely passed into the accepted history of the decline of the Kushite state. The arrival of Aezana and his army has been seen as one of the major factors bringing about the fall of the kingdom. Perhaps of more significance than the presence of Aezana is the mention of the Noba occupying tracts of land and towns in the heartland of the Kushite kingdom. Clearly, it has been argued, the kingdom was in terminal decline by this date, the decline being the result of infiltration by the Noba into its territory.

Dissenting voices to this very plausible scenario have been few indeed. Nowhere in the inscription is there sufficient topographical information to allow us to identify with certainty particular places on the ground. The reconstruction of the campaign and of the geo-politics of the area is derived from the supposed identification of the tribes, rivers and settlements in the inscription with those known from other sources. Hence the Noba are the same as the Noba of Eratosthenes, who were reported to be living to the west of the Nile in the third century BC. The Kasu are identified as the Kushites. The River Takkaze is the Atbara and the Sida is the Nile. The confluence of the two must, therefore, be at the site of the modern town of Atbara, and Sayce dutifully located there the remains of the altar erected by Aezana at the confluence of the Takkaze and the Sida. Other archaeologists have been unable to locate any such structure. The town of Alwa has been peripatetic, being assigned to Meroe, Soba East, the later capital of the Kingdom of Alwa, and to a site to the north of Meroe.[8]

The validity of these identifications is hard to judge. Most appear plausible in the context of a campaign in the Nile valley. However, if one does not make the initial assumption that the Nile valley was the theatre of operations, there is a body of evidence which suggests most strongly that Aezana in actual fact never set foot in the Nile valley, but conducted his campaign against the tribes in the Ethiopian highlands, with the immediate neighbours of the Axumite kingdom.[9] This argument is based partly on a correlation of the timescale of the campaign, as noted in the inscription, with the probable starting point and routes available. The argument also rests on the recognition of the tribes noted in the inscription with those known from other sources to inhabit the areas to the north and west of Axum around the confluence of the Takkaze and Atbara rivers.

This alternative scenario is very attractive, the only real objections to it coming from Meroe where two Axumite inscriptions have been found. The first of these was discovered in 1909 during Garstang's excavations in the Royal City; the second was found close to Temple KC.102 in 1975/76. The former piece was identified by Sayce as part of a stela, the latter as part of a throne. It was customary for the Axumites to erect thrones in their homeland, but also as victory monuments in conquered territory.[10] The Aezana inscription records how the king set up a throne of this type at the confluence of the Sida and the Takkaze. In this context the presence of the two Axumite inscriptions at Meroe has been accepted as indicating that Axumite armies occupied the city.

It is clear that these inscriptions must have been erected in an area which was controlled by the Axumites, however briefly. Were they brought from elsewhere or were they originally set up at Meroe? This is the crux of the problem. As neither was found *in situ* we cannot be certain of their original context.

The most enthusiastic supporters of Axumite intervention on the Middle Nile argue that, as Aezana was already king of the Kasu at the time of his campaign against them and the Noba, Meroe must have been conquered and hence Kush was tributary to Axum before the time of Aezana. Aezana's campaign is seen as one of several Axumite campaigns in or near Kushite territory and indicates an extended period of Axumite domination of the still existent Kushite monarchy.[11] The presence of a graffito written in Old Abyssinian or Sabaean characters low down on the wall of the Temple of Tarharqo at Kawa[12] led to the tentative suggestion that the northern limit of the Axumite advance was in the Dongola reach.[13] The identification of the person who made this graffito, and the graffito on the chapel of pyramid Beg.N.2 at Meroe, with soldiers of an Axumite army is totally unfounded.

The inscriptions and graffiti noted above and an Axumite coin, perhaps of mid or later fourth century date,[14] are the only traces of the presence of Axumites in the Kingdom of Kush. No artefacts of Axumite type have been recovered from the kingdom, which must call into question the possibility of a long-term Axumite presence there. We would not, however, necessarily expect to find artefacts connected with an Axumite army on campaign.

The end of the kingdom

Whatever the truth of the Axumite contacts with Kush during the fourth century AD we no longer accept the view put forward by Arkell that 'Meroe town was sacked and the kingdom destroyed by an army sent by Ezana, who probably used the excuse of some border incident ... to put an end to a trade rival whose increasing weakness, poverty, and inefficiency had left her at his mercy.'[15]

Although the Kushite civilisation – as evidenced by the construction of elaborate cult monuments and fine royal pyramids – seems to have reached its apogee in the first and second centuries AD, there is evidence for great prosperity, particularly observable in Lower Nubia, during the third and perhaps into the fourth century AD.

Our perception of the decline of the Kushite heartland is based largely on the decline in the grandeur of the royal tombs and tomb monuments at Meroe. There is no doubt that from the first to the fourth centuries AD the royal tombs became smaller and the pyramids both became smaller and were constructed of much cheaper materials. The lime mortar rendering of all the pyramids, however, will have effectively hidden the differences between those constructed of red-brick or rough stone from those constructed of finely dressed cut stone blocks. The process is, furthermore, by no means a simple linear progression and what is assumed to have been the latest pyramid is considerably larger than many of its distant predecessors.[16]

The decline in the wealth of the monarch and the royal family need not reflect a decline in the wealth of the state. Haycock has summed up the situation thus: 'Possibly what was happening was not a process of general impoverishment, but simply the complete royal autocracy was giving way before the growth of a rich and powerful nobility.'[17] It has been observed that the later burials of non-royal personages in the western cemetery at Meroe are extremely rich, implying that in the late Kushite state the ruler was surrounded by a powerful and wealthy noble class who reduced the ruler's share of the wealth available.

The latest Kushite ruler who can be related to an absolute chronology is Teqerideamani, who was king in AD 253 and was subsequently buried beneath pyramid Beg.N.28. The date of the latest royal burial, beneath pyramid Beg.N.25 in the northern cemetery at Meroe, is uncertain.[18] Reisner put it at AD 339 and was followed by Dunham. Hintze has suggested that it may be as early as AD 320. These scholars identified four royal burials as post-dating that of Teqerideamani, others have identified at least seven.[19] Whatever the precise date, the absence of later royal tombs in that cemetery has been taken to indicate that the incumbent of Beg.N.25 was the last ruler of Kush and, by implication, that the end of the Kushite state was contemporary with his death.

He most certainly was not the ultimate Kushite ruler, as it can only have been his successor who carried on the age-old traditions of royal burial. The latest royal tombs at Meroe have the pyramid constructed over the grave entrance; not only the burial, therefore, but also the pyramid with its chapel and reliefs were constructed by the next incumbent of the Kushite throne. This individual did not choose to be buried in the northern cemetery and the absence of any evidence for a new cemetery with pyramids suggests that he did not choose to be buried under a pyramid. The tradition of burial under pyramids seems to have continued for several decades in the western cemetery. Pyramid Beg.W.130 has been dated to the second half of the fourth century AD.[20]

For some considerable time less exalted Kushites had been buried in graves marked by tumuli and a large tumulus within an enclosure was observed by Lepsius at Meroe.[21] As at the dawn of Kushite history the tumulus now took over as one of the symbols of power, although the earlier rituals associated with death were retained. The large tumulus at Meroe is now no longer visible and its precise location is uncertain. We are, therefore, denied the opportunity to excavate and observe the burial of what may have been the latest ruler to have been interred at Meroe in what has been termed the post-pyramidal period.

With the arrival of the tumulus as the preferred tomb monument of all sectors of society we are entering what has until recently been called the X-Group in Lower Nubia and the post-Meroitic in Upper Nubia. This is the point where, in the past, it would have been convenient to bring this account of the Kingdom of Kush to a close. In the present stage of our research it is no longer acceptable to take this view.

When an account of the Kushites should end is unclear As one commentator on the end of the Kushite state has eloquently stated: 'The chief question ... seems to be whether Meroe went with a "bang" or a "whimper".'[22] The 'bang' would require some natural disaster, violent internal upheaval or a catastrophic invasion from outside. Even in these scenarios it would only be the political and religious organisation which would be likely to disintegrate; at least some cultural continuity would be assured to however limited an extent. As we have noted above, there is no evidence for such a disaster. It is therefore to the 'whimper' scenario that we must turn.

The terms X-Group and the post-Meroitic relate to cultures which are broadly contemporary. They have much in common. They have both been thought to immediately post-date the Kushite kingdom. They both make use of a number of artefacts which are rather different to those of the late Kushite period, yet they both retain some of the Kushite symbols of kingship and funerary rituals.

What we appear to be witnessing in the archaeological record is the gradual break-up of the Kushite state into perhaps two major territorial units which may have coexisted with, or controlled to some extent, a number of smaller units. This need not indicate the arrival of new groups into the Kushite territory, but the fragmentation of the state as central control weakened. The Nile valley south of Egypt is not an area conducive to the maintenance of a single polity. The valley is divided up by the cataracts into discrete zones and this can only have fostered an independent spirit. The success of the Kushites in establishing a far-flung kingdom and their ability to sustain it for over a thousand years is the anomalous situation; the break-up of the kingdom is a return to the more natural state.

Our knowledge of the political situation within the area of the Kushite kingdom is derived from the location of those cemeteries which contain larger than average tumuli. The largest tumuli are to be found in the cemeteries at Ballana and Qustul, which lie immediately across the river from each other a little downstream from Abu Simbel. Other very large tumuli are to be found at el Hobagi 65 km south-west of Meroe on the west bank of the river and at Jebel Qisi. Lesser but still substantial tumuli are known at Gemai, Firka, Kosha, Wawa, Zuma, and Tanqasi downstream of the Fourth Cataract, Khizeinah and Hagar el Beida in the Abu Hamed reach and Sururab south of the Sixth Cataract.[23]

No major settlement site has been found in the vicinity of any of these tumuli fields, so the direct relationship between the major centres of the late Kushite state and those of a later period is unclear. There is evidence on the other hand for the continued occupation of the fortresses of Qasr Ibrim and Jebel Adda, at Faras and at a number of village sites elsewhere in the north.

The situation at Meroe is unclear, with little evidence for the occupation of the site at this period. However, the latest occupation is the most prone to destruction by wind and water erosion and this may be partly responsible for the apparent lack of deposits from this period. The mid-fourth century Axumite coin was found below the second building level in a domestic quarter of the city.[24] In Temple M.720 there was considerable evidence for squatter occupation with much pottery, grindstones and food debris including date stones, dom nuts and sorghum. Immediately to the east of Temple KC.102, and post-dating the destruction of that temple, was a mass burial of over thirty bodies of adults and children which appear to have been dismembered before burial.[25] The presence of large cemeteries to the east of the city of this date suggests that a settlement of considerable size did exist. Contemporary burials found in a number of Meroe's temples indicate that the formal observance of the state religion had ceased. At Kawa the settlement appears to have finally succumbed to the wind-blown sand which had threatened to bury it throughout its long history.

When state control weakened to the point where the kingdom fragmented, the major dividing line lay in the vicinity of the Third Cataract. The area to the north was typified by a profusion of artefacts which remained heavily influenced by contemporary Egyptian models. In the area to the south these influences were markedly less pronounced. This remained the situation until the seventh century AD when the areas upstream and downstream of the Third Cataract were reunited on the assimilation by the medieval Kingdom of Makouria of its northern neighbour, the Kingdom of Nobatia.

Continuity and change

In the fourth and fifth centuries we are faced with the apparent contradiction of strong evidence for continuity and equally strong evidence for change. Some aspects of Kushite life continued into this period while others disappeared entirely. Many of the discontinuities are in actual fact a re-emergence of very ancient local traditions. The most obvious of these is the use of tumuli as royal funerary monuments. This is the type of royal funerary monument we see at Kerma in the cemetery of the Kerma kings, and at el Kurru in the burials of the early Kushite rulers. The presence of sacrificial victims, both human and animal, was a very prevalent feature of the Kerma period, which continued throughout the Kushite period, and was spectacularly revealed by the excavations at Ballana and Qustul in the 1930s.[26] Bed burials are a further manifestation of the longevity of burial customs.

The burials at el Hobagi, perhaps of the direct successors of the Kushite royal house of Meroe, follow precisely Kushite funerary ritual, as witnessed by the presence of the libating and censing vessels and the veneration of Isis without any discernible foreign influences. No longer is the power of the ruler displayed in the triumphal processions carved on the walls of the offering chapels but by the inclusion of their triumphal panoply – among which are spears, axes, maces and quivers – within the grave.[27] Sacrificial burials of animals and humans are common to both phases. At Ballana and Qustul the royal nature of the burials is confirmed in no uncertain terms by the presence of bodies which were still wearing their crowns at the time of their discovery. The evidence for the rank of the individuals at el Hobagi is less certain, although one grave contained a bronze bowl with a Meroitic hieroglyphic inscription recording a *qore*, a king.[28] The excavator has argued that whatever the status of these individuals, the material buried with them indicates that they were holders of royal power, although whether kings in their own right or princes wielding delegated authority is unclear.[29]

At Qasr Ibrim a temple which had been in use for over a millenium appears to have survived well into the X-Group. Its final demise came when it was systematically ransacked and then demolished.[30] Another temple on the site, Temple 1, a well-built stone structure with an entrance between two pylons giving access into a single chamber, was constructed not earlier than the mid-fourth century AD.[31] A mud brick temple at Buhen may have continued in use into the post-Meroitic period and a mud and red-brick structure, perhaps also a temple, at Soba East was constructed at that time.[32]

At a more mundane level, evidence for continuity of settlement has been noted on a number of sites, in some cases with the same dwellings being occupied throughout this period of 'change'.[33] Cemeteries also remained in use and the typically Kushite burial monument, the pyramid, has at Jebel Adda been found erected over graves containing typically 'X-Group' pottery types.

Evidence for discontinuity has been noted in the ceramic assemblage. In Upper Nubia the fine wheel-made ceramics disappear to be replaced by much coarser hand-made vessels of different form. This is certainly the sequence, but the two types of pottery are not as mutually exclusive as used to be thought. At el Kadada graves have been excavated where the wheel-made 'Kushite' and the hand-made 'post-Meroitic' wares are found side by side.[34] This situation is mirrored at the other end of the post-Meroitic period where characteristic pottery types of that phase are found with characteristic pots of the medieval Christian phase.[35] In the north the wheel-made wares become overwhelmed by the influence of late Roman Egyptian pottery types and decorative motifs, a trend which one can observe to a limited degree as originating in the late Kushite period.[36]

The model which appears to be most suitable to explain the contradiction between continuity and change incorporates a number of mechanisms into what should be seen as a dynamic process. The Kushite civilisation was not static. Its roots may have been in the indigenous culture of the central Nile valley, but it progressively assimilated cultural influences from Egypt in particular. Egypt was the source of pharaonic civilisation, but it also acted as a conduit for the other major civilisations of the Mediterranean, those of the Greeks, the Hellenistic world and the Romans. At the same time there was a gradual assimilation of peoples from the east and west into the Nile valley, most notably the Noba. These peoples will have been partly acculturated and influences emanating from them, like those coming from the north, will have been instrumental in bringing about developments in Kushite culture. Cultural development is a continuum throughout Nubian history, the pace of change fluctuating and being particularly rapid at certain points in time. The 'end' of the Kushite state is one of these periods of more rapid change where it is easy for us, using the very imperfect methods available to the archaeologist, only to see the situation before and after the change rather than to be able to document its course in detail.

We can attempt to elucidate the reasons for the rapid period of cultural change between the fourth and the sixth centuries AD. The territorial integrity of the state depended on the strength of the monarchy and of the state institutions, particularly the army and the religious establishment. As we have already seen, the pre-eminence of the monarch may have been eroded by the emergence of a large and powerful nobility. The wider distribution of wealth will have reduced the amount of wealth available for the monarch to display patronage and thereby maintain loyalty to the crown.

These problems may also have been exacerbated by a diminution of the wealth-generating potential in the state. The decline of trade has been seen by many scholars as the reason for the reduction of the economic well-being of the Kushite monarch and hence of the monarch's control over the state. Since early in the Old Kingdom the Nile valley was an important route by which the exotic goods from sub-Saharan Africa reached Egypt and the Middle East. Kush did not, however, have a monopoly on this trade as the Egyptians opened another route down the Red Sea. It was this latter route which prospered and may have supplanted the Nile route by the Late Kushite period. Major players in this Red Sea trade in the early centuries AD were the Axumites and their good connections with the Roman world were demonstrated by the conversion of their king Aezana to Christianity in the middle of the fourth century.

The increasing poverty of Roman Egypt will have reduced its market potential and this, combined with increased competition from Axumite sea-borne trade, may have had a fatal effect on trade along the river.

Another related factor is the increasing aggression of the desert tribes against the civilisations on the Nile, be they Roman or Kushite. Increased aggression against Kush presumably gave the Kushites the stark choice faced by their Roman neighbours, either to vastly increase their army at a crippling cost to their economy or to succumb to invasion and occupation. Within the Roman world the greatly increased army, and the concomitant increase in taxation and bureaucracy necessary to support it, together with the physical destruction wrought by barbarian groups and a diminution in trade caused by the state of almost continual warfare on certain frontiers, contributed markedly to the disintegration of the empire.

We have very little direct evidence to evaluate how the Kushites responded to a not dissimilar situation. As already noted we know little of the military defence of the Kushite kingdom although the appearance of a number of forts, perhaps datable to the fourth century, may indicate an attempt to combat the military threat. The success of the desert raiders at this time has been attributed to their use of the camel which allowed increased mobility. However, attacks on Kush by desert tribes was not a new phenomenon. Such activities are recorded throughout Kushite history and notable successes were scored, as with the looting of the temples at Kawa during the reign of Talakhamani and the invasion of the area around Meroe in the fifth century BC. There is also increasing evidence for the presence of the camel in the area from a much earlier date. It was not that the threat was new, but that the Kushites may no longer have had the resources or will to combat the invaders. The gradual infiltration of the state by these same desert peoples may have partly contributed to this.

The racial origin of the kings and queens buried at Ballana and Qustul and of those individuals buried at el Hobagi and elsewhere is uncertain.[37] Their adherence to Kushite funerary ritual and their retention of a number of the Kushite symbols of power indicate that they considered themselves Kushite rulers. One of the few of these rulers known to us by name, Silko, describes himself in an inscription on the wall of the temple of Kalabsha as 'King of the Nobades and all the Ethiopians [Kushites]'.[38] The main intrusive group are the Blemmyes, who appear to have attempted to move *en masse* into the Nile valley with some degree of success, although they were ultimately ousted by the riverine groups during the fifth century AD.

By the mid-sixth century AD, within the territory of the old Kushite state, three kingdoms had consolidated their power. It was the adoption by their rulers and progressively by their citizens of Christianity that sounded the death-knell of Kushite culture. This marks the most radical cultural change experienced by the dwellers along the Middle Nile since the first arrival of the Egyptians millennia before. As in Egypt, Christianity eclipsed the old pharaonic religion and with it a whole way of life. The changes its adoption brought about properly belong to an account of the history of the medieval Kingdoms of Nubia. With the mid-sixth century AD we may thus finally bring to a close our account of the Kushites.

APPENDIX

The Rulers of Kush

This list of the rulers of Kush is largely based on that published by Wenig in 1978. However, for the earliest rulers data has been drawn from Kendall. How closely this list approximates to the true situation is unclear.

A number of these rulers have now been radically re-dated and other individuals who are not included in the 'king-list' have been accepted as rulers. As a result not all the data within the body of the text is consistent with this list of the rulers of Kush. If these new interpretations of the evidence are correct their implications for the order and dating of the other rulers has not yet been assessed.

(Ku.=el Kurru, Nu.=Nuri, Bar.=Barkal, Beg.=Meroe)

Generation	Name	Tomb	Date
A	'Lord A'	Ku.Tum.1	890–840 BC[1]
B	'Lord B'	Ku.Tum.6	865–825 BC
C	'Lord C'	Ku.14	815–795 BC
D	'Lord D'	Ku.11	795–785 BC
E	Alara	Ku.9(?)	785–760 BC
1	Kashta	Ku.8	760–747 BC
2	Piye	Ku.17	747–716 BC
3	Shabaqo	Ku.15	716–702 BC
4	Shebitqo	Ku.18	702–690 BC
5	Taharqo	Nu.1	690–664 BC[2]
6	Tamwetamani	Ku.16	664–653 BC
7	Atlanersa	Nu.20	653–643 BC
8	Senkamanisken	Nu.3	643–623 BC
9	Anlamani	Nu.6	623–593 BC
10	Aspelta	Nu.8	593–568 BC
11	Aramatelqo	Nu.9	568–555 BC
12	Malonaqen	Nu.5	555–542 BC
13	Analmaaye	Nu.18	542–538 BC
14	Amani-natake-lebte	Nu.10	538–519 BC
15	Karkamani	Nu.7	519–510 BC

16	Amaniastabarqo	Nu.2	510–487 BC
17	Siaspiqa	Nu.4	487–468 BC
18	Nasakhma	Nu.19	468–463 BC
19	Malowiebamani	Nu.11	463–435 BC
20	Talakhamani	Nu.16	435–431 BC
21	Irike-Amanote[3]	Nu.12	431–405 BC
22	Baskakeren	Nu.17	405–404 BC
23	Harsiyotef	Nu.13	404–369 BC
24	?	Ku.1	369–353 BC
25	Akhratan	Nu.14	353–340 BC
26	Amanibakhi	Nu.?	340–335 BC
27	Nastasen	Nu.15	335–315 BC
28[4]	Aktisanes	Bar.11	
29	Aryamani	Bar.14	
30	Kash … merj Imen	Bar.15	315–270 BC
31	Irike-Piye-qo	?	
32	Sabrakamani	?	
33	Arkamani-qo	Beg.S.6	270–260 BC
34	Amanislo	Beg.S.5	260–250 BC
35	Aman … tekha	Beg.N.4	250–235 BC
36	Arnekhamani	Beg.N.53	235–218 BC
37	Arqamani	Beg.N.7	218–200 BC
38	Tabirqo (=Adikhalamani?)	Beg.N.9	200–190 BC
39	? king	Beg.N10	190–185 BC
40	? king	Beg.N.8	185–170 BC
41	Shanakdakhete	Beg.N.11	170–150 BC
42	? king	Beg.N.12	150–130 BC
43	Naqyrinsan	Beg.N.13	130–110 BC
44	Tanyidamani	Beg.N.20	110–90 BC
45	? king	Bar.2	
46	? queen	Bar.4	90–50 BC
47	Nawidemak	Bar.6	
48	Amanikhabale	Beg.N.2	50–40 BC
49	Teriteqas[5]	Beg.N.14	
50	Amanirenas	Beg.N.21	40–10 BC
51	Akinidad	?	
52	Amanishakheto	Beg.N.6	10–1 BC
53	Natakamani[6]	Beg.N.22	
53.1	Amanitore	Beg.N.1	AD 1–20
53.2	Arikhankharer	Beg.N.5	
53.3	Arikakahtani	Beg.N.56	
54	Shorkaror	?	AD 20–30

55	Pisakar	Beg.N.15	AD 30–40
56	Amanitaraqide	Beg.N.16	AD 40–50
57	Amanitenmemide	Beg.N.17	AD 50–62
58	Amanikhatashan	Beg.N.18	AD 62–85
59	Teritnide	Beg.N.40	AD 85–90
60	Teqerideamani	Beg.N.28	AD 90–114
61	Tamelerdeamani	Beg.N.34	AD 114–134
62	Adeqetali	Beg.N.41	AD 134–140
63	Takideamani	Beg.N.29	AD 140–155
64	Tarekeniwal	Beg.N.19	AD 155–170
65	Amanikhalika	Beg.N.32	AD 170–175
66	Aritenyesbokhe	Beg.N.30	AD 175–190
67	Amanikhareqerem	Beg.N.37	AD 190–200
68	Teritedakhatey	Beg.N.38	AD 200–215
69	Aryesbokhe	Beg.N.36	AD 215–225
70	? king	Beg.N.51	AD 225–246
71	? king	Beg.N.35	AD 246
72	Teqerideamani II	?	AD 246–266
73	Maleqorobar	Beg.N.27	AD 266–283
74	Yesbokheamani	Beg.N.24	AD 283–300
75	? queen	Beg.N.26	AD 300–308
76	? queen	Beg.N.25	AD 308–320
77[7]	?	?	AD 320–?

Notes

Introduction
1 Posener 1940, 54ff
2 Posener 1958, 45–6
3 Posener 1987, 23
4 Säve-Söderbergh 1949, 56
5 Moss 1960
6 Reisner 1922, 179

Chapter 1
1 Emery 1963, 116; 1965, 129
2 Arkell 1950, 36–9; Vercoutter 1956, 68
3 Reisner 1919, 247
4 Giorgini 1965, 116ff
5 Morkot 1991, 295
6 Kendall 1992, 46ff
7 Reisner 1920a, 62–63
8 For the short chronology see Kendall 1992; for the long see Török 1992b.
9 Säve-Söderbergh 1963, 57
10 Kendall 1992, 53
11 Reisner 1922, 176
12 Macadam 1949, 16
13 Horton 1991, 264
14 pers. comm. Dr P. Rose
15 Kendall 1992, 52–3
16 Kendall 1992, 54
17 Dunham 1963
18 Vercoutter 1961
19 Addison 1949, 251 ff.
20 Macadam 1949, 16
21 pers. comm. T. Kendall
22 Reisner 1920, 254
23 unpublished notes of Reisner; pers. comm. T. Kendall
24 Kendall 1991, 302
25 Kendall 1992, 46–49
26 Macadam 1955
27 Griffith 1922, 79ff; Jacquet-Gordon et al. 1969, 104ff
28 Giorgini 1965, 116

29 For references see Leclant 1980, 900, fn 58.
30 Robertson 1992, 45; cf. Shinnie and Bradley 1980, 16
31 Reisner 1922, 180

Chapter 2
1 Reisner 1923b
2 Morkot 1992, 35
3 Dunham 1957, 2
4 Reisner quoted in Dunham 1957, 2
5 Hintze 1973, 142
6 Hintze 1973, 135
7 Hintze 1962, 177
8 Reisner 1923b, 77
9 See Török 1987a, 49.
10 Priese 1992, 10, 45
11 Török 1987a, 48
12 For the case of Irike-Amanote and Talakhamani see Vinogradov 1992.
13 Kitchen 1973, 164–170
14 pers. comm. T. Kendall
15 in Budge 1912, 99–100
16 Diodorus III.6.7.3
17 Macadam 1949, 28
18 Budge 1907, II, 63–66
19 For these officers see the section on Politics and administration, pp. 35–7.
20 Morkot 1992, 28
21 Diodorus III.5.1–2; see the amended translation by Vinogradov 1989, 361–2.
22 Macadam 1949, 51–2
23 Török 1987a
24 Russmann 1974, 38ff
25 Macadam 1955, 112, pl. LXIV, 96–6, 102
26 Budge 1907, II 66–8
27 e.g. Piye's sister Amenirdis I (Kitchen 1973, 151)
28 Griffith 1922, 78–9

29 Budge 1907, II, 70

30 Reisner 1920, 251, 252

31 Reisner 1921, 72, 73

32 Diodorus III.6.1–4

33 Török 1992a, 118

34 Török 1992a, 116

35 Bonnet and Valbelle 1980

36 Zibelius 1972, 163ff

37 Török 1992a, 116

38 Török 1992a

39 Budge 1907, II, 82

40 Reisner 1919, 58

41 Macadam 1949, 15, 62

42 Budge 1907, II, 82

43 Török 1992a, 115; Vercoutter 1961

44 Zach 1992, 31

45 Welsby and Daniels 1991, 296–8; Welsby (forth. 1)

46 Shinnie and Bradley 1977; Wenig 1992

47 Reisner 1921, 73

48 Budge 1912, 90–1; corrected by reference to Grimal 1981, 23–4 and indices

49 Török 1979, 44

50 Török 1979, 5, 6

51 Török 1979, 89

52 Török 1984, 56

53 Macadam 1949, 55

54 For the usage of this title in the New Kingdom see Schulman 1964, 45–6; Chevereau 1994, 58–62.

55 Török 1979, 27–8, 35, 133

56 Török 1979, 101

57 Budge 1907, II, 80ff, 100ff

58 Hakim 1988, fig. 24

59 Dabrowa 1991

60 Herodotus, VII, 69

61 Shinnie and Bradley, 1980, 191

62 Strabo XVII.C.1.54, XVII.C.2.3

63 Griffith 1923, 3–4, 126

64 Emery and Kirwan 1935, 93

65 Woolley and Randall-MacIver 1910, 237, 317; O'Connor 1993, 158, no. 153

66 Griffith 1924, 3–4, 166

67 Dunham 1957, 28–9; Griffith 1925, pl. XXVII. 4

68 Dunham 1963, 194; the use of poisoned arrows by the Kushites is noted by the Greek writer Agatharchides (ref. in Burstein 1986, 17).

69 For a fine example see Millet 1963, fig. 7.

70 Dunham 1963, 155, 194; for this practice among the Huns see Coulston 1985, 243.

71 Dunham 1957, 149

72 Hintze 1979, fig. 3

73 Emery and Kirwan 1938, II, pl. 53

74 For the type see Arkell 1949, 123, fig. 10.

75 For a discussion of the archer's looses and the advantages of the Mongolian release see Coulston 1985, 275ff; for a general discussion of Kushite archer's looses see Hayes 1973.

76 Dunham 1963, 328

77 Dunham 1963, fig. 189

78 Garstang et al. 1911, pl. XXXIII. 2

79 Macadam 1949, 167

80 Shinnie 1967, pl. 33

81 Garstang et al. 1911, pl. XXXIII. 2; Dunham 1963, fig. 87f; Griffith 1925, 77; Crawford and Addison 1951, 86–7; Lenoble 1989, pl. VIIIb

82 Hintze 1962b, pl. V

83 Woolley and Randall-MacIver 1910, 34

84 Hintze 1979, figs 17, 18 and 23

85 quoted in Snowden 1970, 130

86 Hintze 1962, pl. LIIa

87 e.g. at Sanam (Griffith 1922 pl. XXIV 1,2 and 4, pl. XXXII 1)

88 Kitchen 1973, 391

89 Strabo XVII.C.1.54

90 Kendall 1992, 48, fig. 17

91 George 1914, 9

92 Woolley 1911, 15ff

93 Welsby 1992

94 Horton 1991, 265

95 Strabo XVII.C.1.54

96 Millett 1968, 47–8

97 See for example Griffith 1926, pl. XXVIII; a comparison of gates at Faras and Sheik Daud.

98 Griffith 1926, 25

99 Donadoni 1969, 29–30

100 Chittick 1955, 89–90, figs 2–4

101 Crawford 1953, 36–8

102 Lenoble 1992b, 94, pl. VI

103 A centrally placed building, set within a bastioned enclosure, was a feature of the installation at Hosh el Kab (pers. comm. P. Lenoble).

104 Crawford 1953a, 39
105 Hakim 1979, 155
106 Crawford 1953b, 8–9
107 Crawford 1953a, 18
108 Diodorus III, 8.1–5
109 Macadam 1949, 53, n.6
110 Strouhal 1992; Armelagos 1969
111 Cassius Dio LXXVI,13,1
112 Thucydides 2.48; Johannes Zonaras 12,21B (reference in Eide et al. 1994, 339)
113 Russmann 1974, 25; Török 1990, 181
114 Wenig 1978, fig. 21; Török 1990, 180
115 Wenig 1978, 70
116 Wenig 1978, no. 127–9, also the *ba*-statue no. 151
117 Wenig 1978, 228–9, no. 153
118 Randall-MacIver and Woolley 1909, pl. 20
119 Diodorus III, 5
120 Thurman and Williams 1979, 69
121 Zabkar 1975, 44–5, pl. XXIV
122 British Museum EA 72275, info. from H. Granger-Taylor
123 Adams 1989
124 Woolley and Randall-MacIver 1910, 244–5
125 Woolley and Randall-MacIver 1910, pl. 11
126 Almagro et al. 1965, 88
127 Woolley and Randall-MacIver 1910, pl. 2, 9
128 Griffith 1924, pl. LII,4 – this individual is presumably one of the enemies of Kush; Sadik Nur 1956.
129 Plumley and Adams 1974, 218
130 Hintze 1979, fig. 16
131 Macadam 1955, 79, pl. XIVb
132 Macadam 1955, 171 fig. 63
133 Hintze 1962a, 191
134 Bodley 1946; Dixon and Wachsmann 1964
135 Kendall 1989, 659
136 Woolley and Randall-MacIver 1910, pl. 109; Dunham 1963, fig. 107j–1
137 Hintze 1979

Chapter 3

1 Sudan Almanac 1964, 60–1; data from observations made from 1931–60
2 Arkell 1950, 40
3 Arkell 1950, 40
4 Crawford 1951
5 Dixon 1963
6 Leclant 1989, 42; Arkell 1950, 40
7 For a possibly similar building at Jebel Seqadi see Crawford and Addison 1951, fig. 27.
8 The Kingdom of Alwa was certainly in existence by AD 580 when the king was converted to Christianity.
9 Stone column drums were found by Sayce at Kasembar 70 km upstream and were thought by him to indicate the presence of a Meroitic site (Sayce 1909, 192).
10 Strabo XVII, C.II.3
11 Ptolemy IV, 5
12 Macadam 1949, 47, 49 fn.37
13 Macadam 1949, 58
14 in Budge 1912, 166
15 Budge 1907, II, 101–2
16 Macadam 1949, 51
17 in Budge 1912, 127, 132, 133
18 Wenig 1978, 218, but see Hofmann et al. 1989, 277–8.
19 Török 1989, 113
20 Adams 1977, fig. 48; Griffith 1911, pl. XIV, 31, 32; Hintze 1959, 189–90
21 Török 1989, 116
22 Kuper 1988
23 Adams 1973, 193
24 2 Kings XIX,9
25 Kendall 1992, 53
26 Reisner and Reisner 1934, 26
27 Priese 1978, 78
28 Arkell 1961, 121
29 Reisner 1931, 89–94
30 2 Kings XVIII, 21
31 For an alternative interpretation which has Psammetik I a vassal of Tanwetamani see Burnstein 1984.
32 Török in Eide et al. 1994, 284–6
33 Török 1989, 67
34 Sauneron and Yoyotte 1952, 157ff
35 Herodotus III: 17–25
36 Heidorn 1991, 206, 209

37 Cairo 48864
38 Török 1989, 58
39 Burnstein 1989, 225–6
40 Adams 1977, 335
41 Horton 1991, 273
42 Griffith 1912, 32
43 Török 1980b, 77–8
44 Török 1989, 60, 72
45 Arkell 1961, 159; Haycock 1972, 233ff
46 Randall-MacIver and Woolley 1911, 125–8; Griffith 1924, 118
47 Vercoutter 1970, 23, 171, 189
48 Griffith 1924
49 Horton 1991, 268
50 Monneret de Villard 1941, 2–4; Kirwan 1959, 24
51 Strabo XVII, 53–4
52 Cf. Török 1989–90, 181–2, who accepts that the style of the head suggests a date later than 25 BC for its casting and doubts that such a statue would already have been in place at Syene in 23 BC.
53 See Griffith 1917, 168. This inscription was set up by Akinidad and Amanitore, who have been dated by some scholars to 10 BC or later.
54 Strabo XVII, 53–4
55 Horton 1991, 271, fig. 3
56 Reisner 1910, vol. II, plan IX
57 Cf. Török 1989, 78–80: 1989–90, 176. Semna seems a more likely candidate for a place where the Nile deafens all those living in the neighbourhood.
58 Welsby (forth. 2)
59 Titherington 1938
60 Alexander 1988, 78
61 Hintze 1973, 131
62 Seneca VI, 8.3
63 Pliny VI, XXV, 181
64 Mattingly 1995, 712
65 Bersina 1989, 222
66 Cassius Dio LXXVI, 13, 1
67 Kirwan 1977, 24
68 Török 1989, 81–82
69 Philae inscription 416
70 Philae inscriptions 119 and 120
71 Hintze 1973, 141
72 Török 1979, 100ff
73 Paneg. Constantii
74 Török 1989, 26, 29–31

Chapter 4
1 Quirke 1992, 39
2 pers. comm. T. Kendall
3 Yellin 1994
4 pers. comm. L. Török
5 Török 1990, 7
6 Millet 1984, 118; for the temple see Millet 1967, 55–7.
7 Kendall 1986, 4
8 Priese 1992, 29–32
9 Török 1980, 84
10 in Budge 1912, 138–9
11 Garstang et al. 1911, 17–19
12 Millet 1984, 120
13 Hintze 1962a, 178
14 Trigger 1970, 11
15 Zabkar 1975, 47; see also Török 1979, 18
16 Hintze 1962b, 28
17 Zabkar 1975, 17–18
18 On Apedemak and Mahas see Zabkar 1975, 52ff; on syncretism ibid. 96ff.
19 Hintze 1967–8, 291
20 Hintze 1967–8, 292
21 Hintze 1962a, 183
22 Zabkar 1975, 95
23 Millet 1968, 180–3; Török 1979, 21
24 in Budge 1907, II, 63
25 Török 1984, 165
26 Yellin 1979; 1990, 368
27 However, it has been suggested that a number of the niches in houses at Ash Shaukan in Lower Nubia are connected with domestic cults (Jacquet 1971, 124).
28 Millet 1984, 112
29 Frend 1974, 40
30 Millet 1984, 113; Lenoble 1992a
31 Macadam 1955, 245; for foundation deposits from Nuri see Dunham 1955, pls CXXIX–CXXXIX
32 Reisner 1921, 74
33 Kendall 1992, 35
34 Reisner 1919, 240–1
35 Griffith 1923, 79–80
36 Griffith 1923, 80–1
37 Griffith 1923, 87, 88, pl. XIXb
38 Dunham 1950, 129
39 Dunham 1950, fig. 22c
40 Griffith 1923, 80
41 Sadik el Nur 1956
42 Dunham 1963, 207

43 Doll 1982, 279–80
44 Reisner 1922, 185
45 Khidir 1994
46 Griffith 1923, 82
47 Griffith 1923, 82
48 Tomandl 1987; Török 1987b, 81
49 Kendall 1992, 30
50 Reisner 1922, 185–6
51 Vila 1982, 109, fig. 4
52 Griffith 1923, 82
53 Millet 1963, 161
54 Mills 1982, pl. LXXXIV, 5
55 Budge 1907, I, 290ff; Priese 1992
56 Woolley and Randall-MacIver 1910, 14
57 Dunham 1957, 192, nos 483–6
58 Priese 1992, 16
59 Kendall 1992, 38
60 Dunham 1955, 10, pl. CXL; Taylor
    1991, fig. 53; Wenig 1978, 169–70
61 Kendall 1992, 18–19
62 Yellin 1994, 4–5; for Kerma see Bonnet
    1990, pl. 69
63 Kendall 1992, 51
64 Note the presence of small offering
    chapels associated with C-Group tumuli
    (e.g. Nordström 1962, 35).
65 Kendall 1992, 16–17
66 Woolley and Randall-MacIver 1910,
    pl. 114
67 Millet 1963, 163
68 Reisner 1923, 69
69 Reisner 1922, 181
70 Budge 1907, I, 346
71 Lenoble (forth.)
72 Lenoble (forth.)
73 Garstang 1912, 48; the identity of these
    bones as human is doubted by Török
    e.g. in Eide et al. 1994, 316.
74 Khidir 1994
75 Lenoble 1994c
76 Dunham 1950, 110, pl. 4a
77 Dunham 1950, 110
78 Budge 1907, II, 17; Török 1991, 195–6
79 Lenoble 1991, 178
80 Lenoble 1991, 175
81 Griffith 1923, 81–2
82 Bonnet and el Tayeb Mahoud 1991, 32
83 Giorgini 1966, 246ff, fig. 1
84 Woolley and Randall-MacIver 1910, 17
85 Fernandez 1980, 14

86 Bonnet and Valbelle 1987
87 Lenoble 1989; Lenoble and Sharif 1992
88 Lepsius 1853, 212–3; Hakim 1979, 152
89 Emery and Kirwan 1938
90 Millet 1963, 163
91 Lenoble and Sharif 1992
92 Driskell et al. 1989, 20
93 Dunham 1950, pls XVIII–XX; Wenig
    1978, 44
94 Reisner 1922, 185
95 Yellin 1990
96 Yellin 1982
97 Driskell et al. 1989, 20–1, pl. VIII. See
    also Hofmann 1991b.
98 Driskell et al. 1989, 21
99 Wenig 1978, 197
100 For a discussion of the *ba*-statues and for
    illustrations of many examples see
    Woolley and Randall-MacIver 1910,
    46–8, pl. 2–10; Wenig 1978, 88–9;
    Hofmann 1991, 35–41.
101 Dunham 1950, 49
102 Dunham 1950, 78

Chapter 5
1 Kendall 1992, 10–12
2 Unless otherwise stated all the data
   relating to the cemeteries at el Kurru,
   Nuri, Jebel Barkal and Meroe is derived
   from Reisner's excavations which are
   published in *The Royal Cemeteries of
   Kush*, volumes 1–5, by Dunham 1950–63.
3 The largest of the pyramids at el Kurru,
   Ku.1 measuring 26.65 m per side, is dated
   to the fourth century BC. The XXVth
   Dynasty pyramids are 11 m square
   or less.
4 Dunham 1955, pl. LX, e
5 Hinkel 1994, 60
6 Kendall 1992, 31
7 Berger 1994b
8 Hinkel 1986, 101
9 Hakim 1988, fig. 43
10 Bonnet and Valbelle 1987
11 Griffith 1924, pl. 67.5–8
12 From Faras, Griffith 1924, pl. LXVII.5;
   from Sedeinga, Berger 1994a, fig. 34
13 of Amanitaraqide according to Wenig
   1978, 17
14 Kendall 1992, 18

76 *Sphinx with the head of Taharqo, from Kawa. (BM, EA 1770)*

quality of the reliefs in the slightly later temple at Sanam is lower, indicating that the stone carvers were a different group. These were presumably locally trained and the insertion of some new motifs into the reliefs they produced is further support for this. Motifs and scenes of types unknown in Egypt serve to remind us that the Kushites were a distinct people with their own traditions.

Attempts to trace the development of sculpture and relief carving during the fifth and fourth centuries BC is severely hampered by the rarity of pieces and by their uncertain date. For example, the largest 'Napatan' sculpture known, which stands about 5.5 m high, is assigned to this time simply because there are no stylistic parallels to it among the dated sculpture of an earlier or a later period.[8]

15 One tumulus near Jebel Qisi is 41 m in diameter and 8 m high and also lies within a circular enclosure; Hakim 1979, 152.
16 Lenoble 1989
17 Lepsius 1853, 212–3
18 Williams 1991, part 2, 70, pl. 6a
19 Giorgini 1965, 116ff
20 Giorgini 1965, fig. 2
21 Williams 1991, part 2, pl. 6b
22 Crawford 1953b, 11
23 pers. comm. T. Kendall
24 Macadam 1949, 15–16
25 Garstang et al. 1911, pl. III
26 Plumley and Adams 1974, 228ff
27 Hakim 1988, 206
28 Hintze 1962, 174, 178
29 Garstang et al. 1911, pl. XX
30 Török 1976
31 Shinnie 1984
32 Adams 1965, 162, fig. 1
33 Kirwan in Macadam 1955, 208
34 Hintze 1962, 187–8
35 Garstang 1912b, 8
36 Török 1992a, 117
37 Vercoutter 1962, 273–5
38 Budge 1912, 136
39 Kendall 1991
40 Vercoutter 1962, 277ff
41 Donadoni (n.d.)
42 Shinnie and Bradley 1980, 28–9
43 Mohamed Ahmed 1992, 96
44 Woolley and Randall MacIver 1910, pls 26–27
45 Adams and Nordström 1963, 41
46 Adams and Nordström 1963, 26
47 Crawford and Addison 1951, plan in endfolder
48 Jacquet 1971
49 Woolley 1911, pls 21–3, 25; O'Connor 1993, 100–1
50 Mohamed Ahmed 1992, 103
51 Garstang et al. 1911, pl. XXIX; Török 1992a, 118
52 For these late dwellings at Kawa, in the temple of Taharqo, Kirwan in Macadam 1955, 234; at Sanam, Griffith 1922, 85, pl. V; at Jebel Barkal in Temple B500, Dunham 1970, pl. XLVIB .
53 Reisner 1918, 112, pl. XVII
54 Kirwan in Macadam 1955, 230, pl. CXIId
55 Kendall 1992, 48, fig. 17
56 Hintze 1962, 196–7; 1963, 221–4
57 Crowfoot 1911, 15
58 Kirwan in Macadam 1955, 221, 228
59 Hinkel 1985, 173–5
60 Kirwan in Macadam 1955, 211
61 Griffith 1922, 114ff, pl. L
62 Adams 1965, 162–3, fig. 1
63 Griffith 1926, 21–3, pl. XIII
64 Garstang 1912b, 5, pl. VI
65 Griffith 1925b, 219
66 Jacquet 1971, 128–9
67 Macadam 1955, 171
68 Kirwan in Macadam 1955, pl. XXXV, no. 2002
69 Michalowski 1965, 180, pl. XXXVIIIa; Plumley 1970, pl. XXIII.4
70 Jacquet-Gordon et al. 1969, 107
71 Macadam 1949, 42
72 Shinnie 1984, 503
73 Hintze 1962a, 176
74 Jacquet 1971, fig. 30
75 Macadam 1955, 85
76 Adams 1974, 274
77 Dunham 1957, 125
78 Ferlini 1838, 15
79 Hinkel 1984; 1986; 1994, 62
80 Hinkel 1991
81 Jacquet 1971, 130–1
82 Wenig 1978, 75

Chapter 6
1 Robertson 1992, 45
2 first suggested by Reisner 1922, 180
3 Ahmed 1984, 278
4 Addison 1949, 251ff
5 Crawford 1951, pl. XLa; Welsby 1991; forth. 1
6 Kendall 1991, 302
7 Kendall 1991, 310, fn. 13
8 Mohamed Ahmed 1992, 110
9 Horton 1991, fig. 5
10 Horton 1991, 272–3
11 Rose and Rowley 1989
12 Török 1990, 157
13 Török 1992a, 122–4
14 Hintze 1959, 181
15 Hintze 1979, fig. 41
16 Anon. 1991, 16
17 Hinkel 1977b

18 Hinkel M. 1991, abb. 13; Arkell suggested that some of the hafirs in the Gezira may be of Kushite date (Arkell 1932, 202).
19 Garstang et al. 1914, 11, pl. II
20 Heitzmann 1976, ref. in Robertson 1992, 41
21 Bradley 1982, 167ff
22 Kendall 1991, 310, fn. 13
23 Shinnie 1984, 504
24 Hintze 1959, 186–7
25 Emery and Kirwan 1935, 108ff., pl. 17
26 Woolley 1911
27 Adams 1965, 152
28 Török 1979, 118
29 Adams and Nordström 1963, 24–8
30 Crawford and Addison 1951
31 Recent studies suggest, however, that many of the sites used to arrive at this high figure are actually of post-Meroitic date (pers. comm. D. N. Edwards). For the rarity of Kushite settlement in the area between Gamai and Dal see Mills 1965, 12.
32 Trigger 1984, 377
33 Grzymski 1984, 289

Chapter 7

1 For a study of this relationship in the present-day Sudan see Abbas Mohammed 1973.
2 Adams 1977, 54
3 For a discussion of pastoralism in the Kushite period with ethnographic parallels see Edwards 1989, 147ff; Bradley 1992.
4 Bradley 1992, 191
5 Carter and Foley 1980, 304–5
6 Hall in Nordström 1962, 61
7 Ripinski 1985, 135
8 Robinson 1936, 65–6
9 Rowley-Conwy 1988, 246
10 Arkell 1961, 128
11 Robinson 1936, 63
12 Lepsius 1849–59, V, 28a
13 Dunham 1957, 127, fig. 28
14 For a summary of the evidence with references see Morkot 1994, 13–4.
15 Tracey and Hewison 1948, 744
16 Macadam 1949, 27
17 Allan and Smith 1948, 631
18 Trigger 1965, 123

19 Adams 1977, fig. 56
20 Adams 1977, 346
21 On Tabo information from Prof. C. Bonnet; for Meinarti see Adams 1965, 164, fig. 1. In the light of the absence of Kushite material in the Wadi el Khowi one may doubt that *saqia* of that period exist there; see Arkell 1948, 16.
22 Shinnie 1976, 91
23 Allan and Smith 1948, 628; Tracey and Hewison 1948, 745–6
24 Hintze 1963, 222
25 For Tripolitania see Gilbertson et al. 1984; for the Negev see Evenari et al. 1982.
26 Ireland 1948, 82
27 A system of this type, provisionally dated to the Kerma period has been recognised in the Wadi Farjar near the Third Cataract; see Edwards and Salih 1992, 58.
28 Hinkel 1985, 173–5
29 In the Sudan today it only grows on the upper slopes of Jebel Marra in Darfur and in the Red Sea Hills (Andrews 1948, 46, 55).
30 Macadam 1949, 36, 38 note 53
31 Kirwan in Macadam 1955, 220
32 Macadam 1955, 220. A series of tanks found at Meroe have been claimed as a wine-press but there is little to recommend this suggestion – see Shinnie and Bradley 1980, 66–7, pl. 32–3, fig. 24; Bradley 1984, 206; 1992, 170.
33 For a general discussion see Adams 1966.
34 Adams 1965, 163–4, pl. XXXIVb; Adams 1966, fig. 2
35 Adams 1966
36 Thurman and Williams 1979, 36
37 in Budge 1912, 137
38 Strabo XVII, 1
39 Rowley-Conwy in Adams et al. 1983, 59
40 Shinnie 1954, 73
41 Clark and Stemler 1975
42 Shinnie 1989, 23
43 Plumley 1970, 15, pls XXIII.1, .2
44 Hewes 1964, 179
45 Adams 1981, 3
46 Carter and Foley 1980, 303

47 Bonnet and Mohamed Ahmed 1991, XI
48 in Budge 1912, 68
49 cf. Adams 1973, 189, 202
50 For the production of the fine wares at Meroe see Török 1989, 99; cf. Adams 1973, 205–6.
51 Robertson 1992, 47
52 pers. comm. Prof. S. Wenig
53 Adams 1973, 204
54 Bonnet and Mohamed Ahmed 1991, XI, pl. 1; Mohamed Ahmed 1992, 75ff
55 Adams 1962, 64
56 Edwards and Salih 1992, 82
57 Garstang 1912, 46
58 For possible coverings see Adams 1986 I, 31.
59 See for example the Black Burnished I industry of south-west England which traded throughout Roman Britain from the early second until the mid-fourth century AD; Gillam 1976.
60 Kirwan in Macadam 1955, 213
61 Griffith 1922, 87–9, pl. XVII
62 Jacquet 1971, 127
63 Török 1989, 102
64 pers. comm. Dr H. Cool
65 McWhirr 1979
66 Garstang 1913, 76
67 For the unfinished granite statue, probably of XXVth dynasty date, lying in the quarry see Dunham 1947, 64 and pl. XII.1.
68 Hinkel 1989, 831, fn. 11
69 Hintze 1962, fig. 15, 197–9
70 Pliny VI.XXXV.189
71 Vercoutter 1959, 128ff.
72 Vercoutter 1959, 137–8
73 in Budge 1907, II, 101–2
74 el Sayed el Gayar and Jones 1989
75 Tylecote 1982, 36
76 Wainwright 1945, 9–10
77 Dunham 1955, 12; Shinnie 1971, 93
78 Sayce 1912, 55
79 Trigger 1969
80 Shinnie 1971, 94; Shinnie and Kense 1982, 24
81 Wenig 1993, 11
82 Shinnie and Kense 1982, 22–3, fig. 1
83 Wainwright 1945, 24

84 in Török 1984, 51, 53
85 Adams 1981, 8
86 For a discussion of the date of these pieces see Edwards 1939–40.
87 Finneiser in Arnst et al. 1991, 78
88 Griffith 1922, pl. XXXII
89 Yellin 1990, 364
90 Dunham 1957, 124–5
91 Wainwright 1947
92 Adams 1977, 304
93 Millet 1968, 2; Haycock 1967, 116, fn. 1
94 Pliny VI.XXXV.189
95 For a summary of this trade see Munro-Hay 1991, 172ff.
96 Adams 1981, 9
97 Griffith 1925, 219
98 Vantini 1981, 129–31
99 Török 1989, 63
100 Vercoutter 1962, fig. 33
101 Dunham 1957, 186; Hofmann 1991b, 241–2
102 Adams 1973, 192
103 Dunham 1963, 387–9
104 Sayce in Garstang et al. 1911, 4
105 Török 1989, 58, 61, 95, 102
106 Macadam 1949, 36
107 Hinkel 1994, 62
108 Spiegelberg 1931, 1–2
109 Adams 1918, 9
110 Vercoutter 1962, pl. XXb
111 Griffith 1922, 117, pl. LIIIb
112 Wainwright 1952, 76
113 See Török 1984, 49.
114 *Corpus Inscriptionum Graecarum* 5127
115 Pliny VI.XXXV.185
116 Hintze 1962, pl. LIIa; Shinnie 1967, fig. 27
117 Török 1984, 54
118 Shinnie 1971, 99; Crawford and Addison 1951

Chapter 8
1 Bothmer 1960, XXXVIII
2 Wenig 1978, 49
3 Wenig 1978, 53
4 Russmann 1974, 15
5 See Wenig 1978, figs 28 and 29.
6 Macadam 1949, 21, note 51
7 Russmann 1974, 22–3

8 Wenig 1978, 55
9 Arkell 1961, 166; cf. Zabkar 1977
10 Wenig 1978, 86
11 Wenig 1978, fig. 61
12 Garstang 1913, pl. IX
13 Wenig 1978, fig. 38
14 Linant de Bellefonds drawing; Cailliaud 1826, pl. X
15 Arkell 1961, 166
16 Rostkowska 1982
17 Hofmann 1978, fig. 15
18 Donadoni n.d. 3, figs 6–15; Wenig 1978, 274, no. 215
19 Woolley and Randall-MacIver 1910, pl. 1ff.
20 Kendall 1992, 36
21 Wenig 1978, fig. 21
22 Plumley and Adams 1974, 229, pl. XLIV.1
23 Shinnie and Bradley 1981
24 Bradley 1984b
25 Jacquet 1971, 127
26 Hinkel 1994, 60
27 Woolley 1911, 20
28 Donadoni n.d., 2
29 Driskell et al. 1989
30 Wenig 1978, 180, no. 93
31 Wenig 1978, 179, no. 91
32 Wenig 1978, 177, no. 90; 178
33 See Wenig 1978, 220–1
34 Priese 1992
35 Török 1989, 111
36 For a detailed discussion of this see Török 1989, 110ff
37 Adams 1973, 202
38 Woolley and Randall-MacIver 1910
39 Wenig 1978, 278, no. 220
40 Griffith 1924, 163, pl. LII, 4
41 Griffith 1924, 162, pl. LI, 7; Woolley and Randall-MacIver 1910, 58
42 Wenig 1978, 97–8
43 Hintze 1979, fig. 6
44 Török 1989, 56; Doll 1982, 279–80
45 Adams 1977, 311
46 Griffith 1911, 67–8
47 Abdalla 1989, 876; Trigger 1964, 193
48 Priese 1978, 75
49 Reisner 1921, 74
50 Much of what follows is derived from Griffith's studies to be found particularly

in Randall-MacIver and Woolley 1909, 43–54, and Griffith 1911b
51 Trigger 1973, 245
52 Griffith 1917, 169
53 Hintze 1978, 94
54 Leclant 1978, 111
55 Hintze 1960, 127
56 Plumley 1966, 12
57 Reinold and Lenoble 1994, 2
58 Hintze 1961, 283
59 For the contrary view see Priese 1973, 300–3.
60 Trigger 1973b, 339
61 Griffith 1912, 27ff
62 Emery and Kirwan 1938, I, 224
63 Griffith 1916, 22ff
64 Diodorus III, 3.5
65 Adams 1982, 211
66 Millet 1974, 52
67 Hintze 1964
68 Diodorus III, 6.3
69 Shinnie 1967, 23

Chapter 9
1 Procopius I, XIX, 29–30
2 Plumley 1966, 12
3 Hintze 1973, 141; Török 1980b, 85
4 Török 1978
5 Griffith 1912, 27
6 Millet 1974, 54–5
7 For an English translation see Kirwan 1960, 163–5.
8 For a recent discussion see Török 1988, 35
9 Behrens 1986; Bechhaus-Gerst 1991
10 Hägg 1984, 440
11 Burstein 1981, 49
12 Macadam 1949, 117–18
13 Kirwan 1957, 40
14 For this dating for the type see Munro-Hay 1991, 192; Török dates it to the fifth century at the earliest (1988, 43–4).
15 Arkell 1961, 171–2
16 Török 1988, 39
17 Haycock 1967, 111
18 For this burial see Dunham 1957, 198–9.
19 Török 1988, 33
20 Török 1974
21 Lepsius 1853, 212–3
22 Bradley 1984, 196
23 Lenoble 1992c, 11

24 Shinnie 1970, 18: Shinnie and Bradley 1980, 185
25 Shinnie 1984, 501, 503
26 Emery and Kirwan 1938
27 Lenoble 1994a; 1994b; Lenoble et al. 1994
28 Lenoble and Sharif 1992, 634, fig. 6
29 Lenoble 1994b, 112–3
30 Driskell et al. 1989
31 Alexander 1994; for the dating derived from pottery in the foundation trenches of the building, pers. comm. Dr P. Rose.
32 Randall-MacIver and Woolley 1911, 125–6; Welsby (forth. 1)
33 e.g. at Arminna, Trigger 1965, 133
34 Lenoble 1992c, 10
35 Welsby 1991, 279
36 Adams 1986, 51
37 See Lenoble 1994b, 113–14
38 Török 1988, 56

Appendix
1 The 'dates' given for the tombs of Lords A to D are the date range within which the construction of the tombs is most likely to have taken place. These are not absolute dates for the reigns of these men.
2 The only securely dated reign.
3 In earlier literature referred to as Amani-nete-yerike.
4 The succession in generations 28–32 is unclear.
5 This king, his queen and offspring are now thought by some scholars to date to after 10 BC.
6 Now dated by some scholars to the mid-first century AD.
7 The builder of the pyramid over tomb Beg.N.25.

Bibliography

Abbreviations

ANM Archéologie du Nil Moyen, Lille 1986–

BzS Beiträge zur Sudanforschung, Wien-Mödling 1986–

JARCE Journal of the American Research Centre in Cairo, Cairo 1962–

JEA Journal of Egyptian Archaeology, London 1914–

LAAA Liverpool Annals of Archaeology and Anthropology, Liverpool 1908–48

MNL Meroitic Newsletter, Paris 1968–

SARSN Sudan Archaeological Research Society Newsletter, London 1991–

SNR Sudan Notes and Records, Khartoum 1918–

ZAS Zeitschrift für Ägyptische Sprache und Altertumskunde, Berlin 1863–

Bibliography

Abbas, Mohammed 1973 'The Nomad and the Sedentary: Polar Complementaries – not Polar Opposites', in C. Nelson (ed.) *The Desert and the Sown. Nomads in the Wider Society*, Institute of International Studies, Research paper no. 21, University of California, Berkeley

Abdalla, A. M. 1989 'Napatan-Meroitic continuity: Kush and Kushiteness/Meroiticness' *Meroitica* 10, 875–84

Adams, N. K. 1989 'Meroitic high fashion: examples from art and archaeology', *Meroitica* 10, 747–55

Adams, W. Y. 1962 'Archaeological Survey on the West bank of the Nile – Pottery Kiln Excavations', *Kush* 10, 62–75

Adams, W. Y. 1965 'Sudan Antiquities Service Excavations at Meinarti, 1963–64', *Kush* 13, 148–76

Adams, W. Y. 1966 'The Vintage of Nubia', *Kush* 14, 262–83

Adams, W. Y. 1973 'Pottery, Society and History in Meroitic Nubia', *Meroitica* 1, 177–219

Adams, W. Y. 1977 *Nubia: Corridor to Africa*, London and Princeton

Adams, W. Y. 1981 'Ecology and Economy in the Empire of Kush', *ZAS* 108, 1–11

Adams, W. Y. 1986 *Ceramic Industries of Medieval Nubia*, Lexington

Adams, W. Y., J. A. Alexander and R. Allen 1983 'Qasr Ibrim 1980 and 1982' *JEA* 69, 43–60

Adams, W. Y. and H.-Å. Nordström 1963 'The Archaeological Survey of the West Bank of the Nile: Third Season', *Kush* 11, 10–46

Addison, F. 1949 *Jebel Moya*, The Wellcome Excavations in the Sudan, vols 1 & 2, London, New York and Toronto

Addison, F. 1956 'Second Thoughts on Jebel Moya', *Kush* 4, 4–18

Ahmed, K. A. 1984 *Meroitic Settlement in the Central Sudan*, BAR Int. Ser. 197, Oxford

Alexander, J. A. 1988 'The Saharan divide in the Nile Valley: the evidence from Qasr Ibrim', *African Archaeological Review* 6, 73–90

Alexander, J. A. 1994 'Islamic Archaeology: the Ottoman Frontier on the Middle Nile' *SARSN* 7, 20–6

Allan, W. N. and R. J. Smith 1948 'Irrigation in the Sudan' in Tothill (ed.) 1948, 593–631

Almagro, M., R. Blanco Caro, M. A. Gracia-Guinea, F. Presedo Velo, Pellicer Catalan, and J. Teixidor 1965 'Excavations by the Spanish Archaeological Mission in the Sudan, 1962–63 and 1963–64' *Kush* 13, 78–95

Andrews, F. W. 1948 'The Vegetation of the Sudan', in Tothill (ed.) 1948, 32–61

Anon. 1991 *Meroe, Naga, Musawwarat es Sufra*, Khartoum

Arkell, A. J. 1932 'Funj Origins' *SNR* 15, 201–50

Arkell, A. J. 1948 'The Historical Background of Sudanese Agriculture', in Tothill (ed.) 1948, 9–17

Arkell, A. J. 1949 *Early Khartoum*, London, New York and Toronto

Arkell, A. J. 1950 'Varia Sudanica' *JEA* 36, 24–40

Arkell, A. J. 1961 *A History of the Sudan to 1821*, 2nd edn, London

Armelagos, G. J. 1969 'Diseases in Ancient Nubia', *Science* 163, 255–9

Arnst, C.-B., Finneiser, I. Müller, H. Kischkewitz, K.-H. Priese and G. Poethke 1991, *Das Ägyptisches Museum*, Berlin

Bechhaus-Gerst, M. 1991 'Noba Puzzles: Miscellaneous Notes on the Ezana Inscriptions', in D. von Mendel and U. Claudi (eds), *Ägypten im Afro-Orientalischen Kontext*, Koln, 17–25

Behrens, P. 1986 'The "Noba" of Nubia and the "Noba" of the Ezana inscription: a matter of confusion (Part I)', *Afrikanistische Arbeitspapiere* 8, 117–126

Berger, C. 1994a 'Sedeinga', in B. Gratien and F. Le Saout (eds), *Nubie: Les Cultures Antiques du Soudan*, Lille, 209–13

Berger, C. 1994b 'Les Couronnements des Pyramides Méroïtiques de Sedeinga', in Bonnet (ed.) 1994, 135–7

Bersina, S. Y. 1989 'Milanese Papyrus No. 40', *Meroitica* 10, 217–24

Bodley, N. B. 1946 'The Auloi of Meroë', *American Journal of Archaeology* 50.2, 217–40

Bonnet, C. (ed.) 1992 *Études Nubiennes*, vol. 1, Geneva

Bonnet, C. (ed.) 1994 *Études Nubiennes*, vol. 2, Geneva

Bonnet, C. and S. Mohamed Ahmed ed Din 1991 'A potter's workshop of the Napatan period and some Christian tombs', *Genava* 39, XI–XII

Bonnet, C. and M. el Tayeb Mahmoud 1991 'Une tombe méroïtique du cimetière de la ville antique', *Genava* 39, 29–34

Bonnet, C. and D. Valbelle 1980 'Un Prêtre d'Amon de Pnoubs enterré à Kerma', *Bull. Inst. Française d'Archéologie Orientale* 80, 1–12

Bonnet, C. and D. Valbelle 1987 'Un objet inscrit, retrouvé dans un bâtiment napatéen à Kerma (Soudan)', *Cahier de Recherches de l'Institut de Papyrologie et d'Égyptologie de Lille* 9, 25–30

Bothmer, B. V. 1960 *Egyptian Sculpture of the Late Period 700 BC to AD 100*, Brooklyn

Bradley, R. J. 1982 'Varia from the City of Meroe' *Meroitica* 6, 195–211

Bradley, R. J. 1984a 'Meroitic Chronology', *Meroitica* 7, 163–70

Bradley, R. J. 1984b 'Wall Paintings from Meroe Townsite', *Meroitica* 7, 421–3

Bradley, R. J. 1992 'Nomads in the Archaeological Record', *Meroitica* 13

Budge, E. A. W. 1907 *The Egyptian Sudan*, London

Budge, E. A. W. 1912 *Egyptian Literature II: Annals of Nubian Kings*, London

Burstein, S. M. 1981 'Axum and the Fall of Meroe', *JARCE* 18, 47–50

Burstein, S. M. 1984 'Psamtek I and the End of Nubian Domination in Egypt', *SSEAJ* 14, no. 2, 31–4

Burstein, S. M. 1986 'The Ethiopian War of Ptolemy V: an Historical Myth?', *BzS* 1, 17–23

Burstein, S. M. 1989 'Kush and the external world: a comment', *Meroitica* 10, 225–30

Cailliaud, F. 1826 *Voyage à Meroe*, Paris

Carter, P. L. and R. Foley 1980 'A Report on the Fauna from the Excavations at Meroe, 1967–1972', in Shinnie and Bradley 1980, 298–312

Cassius Dio Cocceianus *Roman History*, trans. E. Cary, Loeb edn. 1982

Chevereau, P.-M. 1994 *Prosopographie des Cadres Militaires Égyptiens du Nouvel Empire*, Paris

Chittick, H. N. 1955 'An Exploratory Journey in the Bayuda Region', *Kush* 3, 86–92

Clark, D. and A. Stemler 1975 'Early Domesticated Sorghum from Central Sudan', *Nature* 254, 588–91

Coulston, J. C. 1985 'Roman Archery Equipment' in Bishop, M. C. (ed.) *The Production and Distribution of Roman Military Equipment* BAR Int. Ser. 275, 220–366

Crawford, O. G. S. 1953a *Castles and Churches in the Middle Nile Region*, Sudan Antiquities Service Occasional Papers no. 2, Khartoum

Crawford, O. G. S. 1953b 'Field Archaeology of the Middle Nile Region', *Kush* 1, 2–29

Crawford, O. G. S. and F. Addison 1951 *Abu Geili*, The Wellcome Excavations in the Sudan vol. 3, London, New York and Toronto

Crowfoot, J.W. 1911 *The Island of Meroë*, London

Dabrowa, E. 1991 '*Dromedarii* in the Roman Army: a note', in V. A. Maxfield and M.J. Dobson, (eds) *Roman Frontier Studies 1989*, Exeter

Davies, W.V. (ed.) 1991 *Egypt and Africa*, London

Diodorus Siculus, trans. C.H. Oldfather, Loeb edn 1979

Dixon, D.M. 1963 'A Meroitic Cemetery at Sennar (Makwar)', *Kush* XI, 227–34

Dixon, D.M. and K.P. Wachsmann 1964 'A Sandstone Statue of an Auletes from Meroë', *Kush* 12, 119–25

Doll, S.K. 1982 'Identity and Significance of the texts and decoration on the sarcophagi of Anlamani and Aspelta', *Meroitica* 6, 276–80

Donadoni, S. (1969) 'Les Débuts du Christianisme en Nubie' *Mémoires de l'Institut d'Égypte* 59, 25–33

Donadoni, S. (n.d.) *Excavations of the University of Rome at 'Natakamani Palace' Jebel Barkal*, re-print from *Kush* XVI, Rome

Driskell, B.N., N.K. Adams and P.G. French 1989 'A Newly Discovered Temple at Qasr Ibrim', *ANM* 3, 11–54

Dunham, D. 1947 'Four Kushite Colossi in the Sudan', *JEA* 33, 63–5

Dunham, D. 1950 *The Royal Cemeteries of Kush I: El Kurru*, Cambridge, Massachusetts

Dunham, D. 1955 *The Royal Cemeteries of Kush II: Nuri*, Boston, Massachusetts

Dunham, D. 1957 *The Royal Cemeteries of Kush IV: Royal Tombs at Meroe and Barkal*, Boston, Massachusetts

Dunham, D. 1963 *The Royal Cemeteries of Kush V: West and South Cemeteries at Meroe*, Boston, Massachusetts

Dunham, D. 1970 *The Barkal Temples*, Boston, Massachusetts

Dunham, D. and J.M. A. Janssen 1960 *Semna Kumma, Second Cataract Forts*, Boston, Massachusetts

Edwards, D.N. 1989 *Archaeology and Settlement in Upper Nubia in the 1st Millenium AD*, BAR Int. Ser. 537, Oxford

Edwards, D.N. and Ali Osman M. Salih 1992 *The Mahas Survey 1991: Interim Report and Site Inventory*, Mahas Survey Report no. 1

Edwards, I.E.S. 1939–40 'The Prudhoe Lions', *LAAA* 26, 3–9

Eide, T., T. Hägg, R.H. Pierce and L. Török 1994 *Fontes Historiae Nubiorum*, vol. I, Bergen

Emery, W.B. and L.P. Kirwan 1935 *The Excavations and Survey Between Wadi es-Sebua and Adindan 1929–1931*, Cairo

Emery, W.B. and L.P. Kirwan 1938 *The Royal Tombs of Ballana and Qustul*, Cairo

Evanari, M., L. Shanon and N. Tadmor 1982 *The Negev: The Challenge of a Desert*, 2nd edn, Harvard

Ferlini, J. 1838 *Relation Historique des Fouilles Opérées dans la Nubie*, Rome

Fernandez, V. 1980 'Excavations at the Meroitic Cemetery of Emir Abdallah (Abri, Northern Province, The Sudan): Some aspects of the pottery and its distribution' *MNL* 20, 13–22

Frend, W. H. C. 1974 'The Podium Site at Qasr Ibrim', *JEA* 60, 30–59

Garstang, J. 1910 'Preliminary Note on the Expedition to Meroë in Ethiopia', *LAAA*, 3, 57–70

Garstang, J. 1912a 'Second Interim Report on Excavations at Meroë in Ethiopia: Part I The Excavations', *LAAA*, 4, 45–52

Garstang, J. 1912b *Excavations at Meroë, Sudan, 1912: Guide to the Eleventh Annual Exhibition of Antiquities Discovered*, Liverpool

Garstang, J., A. H. Sayce and F. Ll. Griffith 1911 *Meroë, the City of the Ethiopians*, Oxford

Garstang, J., W. J. Pythian-Adams and A. H. Sayce 1914 'Fifth Interim Report on Excavations at Meroë in Ethiopia', *LAAA*, 7, 1–24

George, W. S. 1914 'Fourth Interim Report on Excavations at Meroë in Ethiopia: Part 2 Architecture and General Results', *LAAA*, 6, 9–21

Geus, F. 1982 'La nécropole méroïtique d'el Kadada', *Meroitica* 6, 178–88

Geus, F. and F. Thill (eds) 1985 *Mélanges offerts à Jean Vercoutter*, Paris

Gilbertson, D. D., P. P. Hayes, G. W. W. Barker and C. O. Hunt 1984 'The UNESCO Libyan Valleys Survey VII: An Interim Classification and Functional Analysis of Ancient Wall Technology and Land Use', *Libyan Studies* 15, 45–70

Gillam, J. P. 1976 'Coarse Fumed Ware in North Britain and Beyond', *Glasgow Archaeological Journal* 4, 57–80

Giorgini, M. S. 1965 'Première Campagne de Fouilles à Sedeinga 1963–1964', *Kush* 13, 112–30

Griffith, F. Ll. 1911a *Meroitic Inscriptions, Part I*, Archaeological Survey of Egypt, Memoir 19, London

Griffith, F. Ll. 1911b *Karanòg: The Meroitic inscriptions of Shablûl and Karanòg*, University of Pennsylvania Museum, Eckley B. Coxe Junior Expedition to Nubia, vol. VI, Philadelphia

Griffith, F. Ll. 1912 *Meroitic Inscriptions, Part II*, Archaeological Survey of Egypt, Memoir 20

Griffith, F. Ll. 1916 'Meroitic Studies', *JEA* 3.1, 22–30

Griffith, F. Ll. 1917 'Meroitic Studies IV', *JEA* 4, 159–73

Griffith, F. Ll. 1922 'The Oxford Excavations in Nubia', *LAAA*, 9, 67–124

Griffith, F. Ll. 1923 'Oxford Excavations in Nubia XVIII: The Cemetery of Sanam', *LAAA* 10, 73–171

Griffith, F. Ll. 1924 'Oxford Excavations in Nubia', *LAAA*, 11, pt.3–4, 115–80

Griffith, F. Ll. 1925a 'Oxford Excavations in Nubia', *LAAA*, 12, pt.3–4, 57–172

Griffith, F. Ll. 1925b 'Meroitic Studies V', *JEA* 11, 218–24

Griffith, F.Ll. 1926 'Oxford Excavations in Nubia: Meroitic Antiquities at Faras and other sites', *LAAA*, 13, pt.1–2, 17–37

Grimal, N.C. 1981 'Quatre Stèles Napatéennes au Musée du Caire JE. 48863-48866, *MIFAO* 106

Grzymski, K. 1984 'Population Estimates from Meroitic Architecture', *Meroitica* 7, 287–9

Hägg, T. 1984 'A New Axumite Inscription in Greek from Meroe', *Meroitica* 7, 436–41

Hakem, A.M.A. 1979 'University of Khartoum Excavations at Sarurab and Bauda, North of Omdurman', *Meroitica* 5, 151–6

Hakem, A.M.A. 1988 *Meroitic Architecture: A Background to an African Civilization*, Khartoum

Haycock, B.G. 1967 'Later Phases of Meroïtic Civilisation', *JEA* 53, 107–20

Haycock, B.G. 1972 'Landmarks in Cushite History', *JEA* 58, 225–44

Hayes, R.O. 1973 'The Distribution of Meroitic Archer's Rings: An Outline of Political Borders' *Meroitica* 1, 113–22

Heidorn, L.A. 1991 'The Saite and Persian Period Forts at Dorginarti', in Davies (ed.) 205–19

Heitzmann, R. 1976 *The Temples of Kush: An examination of form and ideas*, MA Thesis, University of Calgary

Herodotus *The Histories*, trans. H.Cary, London 1891

Hewes, G.W. 1964 'Gezira Dabarosa: Report of the University of Colorado Nubian Expedition, 1962–63 Season', *Kush* 12, 174–87

Hinkel, F.W. 1977a *Auszug aus Nubien*, Berlin

Hinkel, F.W. 1977b 'Ein neues Triumphabild der meroitischen Löwen', *Aegyptus und Kush* 13, 175–82

Hinkel, F.W. 1981 'Pyramide oder Pyramidenstumpf?', *ZÄS* 108, 105–24

Hinkel, F.W. 1982 'An Ancient Scheme to Build a Pyramid at Meroe', in P.Van Moorsel (ed.), *New Discoveries in Nubia*, Leiden (45–50)

Hinkel, F.W. 1984 'Das Schaduf als konstruktives Hilfsmittel', *Meroitica* 7, 462–8

Hinkel, F.W. 1985 'Alim-El Hosh-Shaq el Ahmar', in Geus and Thill (eds), 163–80

Hinkel, F.W. 1986 'Reconstruction Work at the Royal Cemetery at Meroe', in Krause (ed.), 99–108

Hinkel, F.W. 1989 'Examination of Meroitic mortar and plaster', *Meroitica* 10, 827–34

Hinkel, F.W. 1991 'Proportion and Harmony: The Process of Planning in Meroitic Architecture', in Davies (ed.) 1991, 220–33

Hinkel, F.W. 1994 'Les Pyramides de Meroé', *Les Dossiers d'Archéologie* 196, 60–3

Hinkel, M. 1991 'Hafire im antiken Sudan', *ZÄS* 118, 32–48

Hintze, F. 1959 'Preliminary Report on the Butana Expedition 1958', *Kush* 7, 171–96

Hintze, F. 1960 'Die meroitische Stele des Königs Tañyidamani aus Napata', *Kush* 8, 125–62

Hintze, F. 1961 'Drei meroitische Graffiti aus Unternubien', *Kush* 9, 282–4

Hintze, F. 1962a 'Preliminary Report on the Excavations at Musawwarat es Sufra 1960–1', *Kush* 10, 170–202

Hintze, F. 1962b *Die Inschriften des Löwentempels von Musawwarat es Sufra*, Berlin

Hintze, F. 1963 'Musawwarat es Sufra: Preliminary report on the Excavations of the Institute of Egyptology, Humboldt University, Berlin, 1961–62 (Third Season)', *Kush* 11, 217–26

Hintze, F. 1964 'The Latin Inscription from Musawwarat es Sufra', *Kush* 12, 296–98

Hintze, F. 1967–68 'Musawwarat es Sufra: Report on the Excavations of the Institute of Egyptology, Humboldt University, Berlin, 1963–66 (Fourth–Sixth Seasons)', *Kush* 15, 283–98

Hintze, F. 1973 'Meroitic Chronology: Problems and Prospects', *Meroitica* I, 127–44

Hintze, F. 1978 'The Kingdom of Kush: The Meroitic Period', in S. Hochfield and F. Riefstahl (eds) *Africa in Antiquity I: The Essays*, Brooklyn, 89–105

Hintze, U. 1979 'The Graffiti from the Great Enclosure at Musawwarat es Sufra', *Meroitica* 5, 135–50

Hofmann, I. 1991a 'Der Wein- und Ölimport im meroitischen Reich', in Davies (ed.) 1991, 234–45

Hofmann, I. 1991b 'Steine für die Ewigkeit Meroitische Opfertafeln und Totenstelen', *BzS* Beiheft 6, Wren-Mödling 1991

Hofmann, I., H. Tomandl and M. Zach 1989 'Beitrag zur Geschichte der Nubier', *Meroitica* 10, 269–98

Horton, M. 1991 'Africa in Egypt: New Evidence from Qasr Ibrim', in Davies (ed.) 1991, 264–77

Ireland, A. W. 1948 'The Climate of the Sudan', in Tothill (ed.) 1948, 62–83

Jacquet, J. 1971 'Remarques sur l'architecture domestique à l'époque Méroitique', *Beiträge zur Ägyptischen Bauforschung und Altertumskunde* 12, 121–31

Jacquet-Gordon, H., C. Bonnet and J. Jacquet 1969 'Pnubs and the Temple of Tabo on Argo Island', *JEA* 55, 103–11

Kendall, T. 1989 'Ethnoarchaeology in Meroitic Studies', *Meroitica* 10, 625–745

Kendall, T. 1991 'The Napatan Palace at Gebel Barkal: A first look at B1200', in Davies (ed.) 1991, 302–13

Kendall, T. 1992 'The Origin of the Napatan State, Part 1 – The evidence for the Royal Ancestors at el-Kurru', 7th International Conference for Meroitic Studies, pre-circulated papers

Khidir, F. Abdel Hamid Salih 1994 'The Excavation of Tumulus KE5 at Kawa, Sudan', *SARSN* 7, 26–9

Kirwan, L. P. 1957 'Tanqasi and the Noba', *Kush* 5, 37–41

Kirwan, L. P. 1959 'The International Position of Sudan in Roman and Medieval Times', *SNR* 40, 23–37

Kirwan, L. P. 1960 'The Decline and Fall of Meroe', *Kush* 8, 163–73

Kirwan, L. P. 1977 'Rome beyond the Southern Egyptian Frontier', *Proc. British Academy* 63, 13–31

Kitchen, K. A. 1973 *The Third Intermediate Period in Egypt*, Warminster

Krause, M. (ed.) 1986 *Nubische Studien*, Mainz am Rhein

Kuper, R. 1988 'Neuere Forschungen zur Besiedlungsgeschichte der Ostsahara', *Archäologisches Korrespondenzblatt* 18 (2), 127–42

Leclant, J. 1978 'The present position in the deciphering of Meroitic script', in UNESCO 1978, 107–20

Leclant, J. 1980 'Kuschitenherrschaft', *Lexicon der Ägyptologie* 3, 893–901

Leclant, J. 1989 'Meroé et Rome', *Meroitica* 10, 29–46

Lenoble, P. 1989 '"A New Type of Mound-Grave" (Continued): Le Tumulus à enciente d'Umm Makharaqa, près d'el Hobagi (A.M.S. NE-36-0/7-0-3)', *ANM* 3, 93–120

Lenoble, P. 1991 'Chiens de païens: une tombe postpyramidale à double descenderie hors de Méroé', *ANM* 5, 167–188

Lenoble, P. 1992a 'Cônes de Déjections Archéologiques dans des Djebels à Cimetières Tumulaires proches de Méroé', *BzS* 5, 73–91

Lenoble, P. 1992b 'Documentation tumulaire et céramique entre 5e et 6e cataractes', in Bonnet (ed.) 1992, 79–97

Lenoble, P. 1992c 'The "End" of the Meroitic Empire: The Evidence from Central Sudan', *SARSN* 3, 9–12

Lenoble, P. 1994a 'À propos des tumulus d'El Hobagi et de Ballana-Qustul', *MNL* 25, 51–2

Lenoble, P. 1994b 'Le rang des inhumés sous tertre à enceinte à El Hobagi', *MNL* 25, 89–124

Lenoble, P. 1994c 'Une monture pour mon royaume: Sacrifices triomphaux de chevaux et de méhara d'el Kurru à Ballana', *ANM* 6, 107–130

Lenoble, P. (forth.) 'Les "Sacrifices Humains" de Meroe, Qustul et Ballana'

Lenoble, P. and Nigm el Din Mohammed Sharif 1992 'Barbarians at the gates? The royal mounds of El Hobagi and the end of Meroe', *Antiquity* 66, 626–35

Lenoble, P., R.-P. Disseaux, Abd el Rahman Ali Mohammed, B. Ronce and J. Bialais 1994 'La fouille du tumulus à enceinte à El Hobagi', *MNL* 25, 53–88

Lepsius, C. R. 1849–59 *Denkmäler aus Aegypten und Aethiopien* (Plates), Berlin

Lepsius, C. R. 1853 *Discoveries in Egypt, Ethiopia and the Peninsula of Sinai in the years 1842–1845*, 2nd edn K. Mackenzie, London

Lepsius, C. R. 1897–1913 *Denkmäler aus Aegypten und Aethiopien* (Text), Leipzig

Macadam, M. F. L. 1949 *The Temples of Kawa I: The Inscriptions*, London

Macadam, M. F. L. 1955 *The Temples of Kawa II: History and Archaeology of the Site*, London

Mattingly, D. J. 1995 *Tripolitania*, London

McWhirr, A. 1979 'Tile Kilns in Roman Britain', in A. McWhirr (ed.) *Roman Brick and Tile: Studies in Manufacture, Distribution and use in the Western Empire*, BAR S68, Oxford

Michalowski, K. 1965 'Polish Excavations at Faras – Fourth Season 1963–64', *Kush* 13, 177–89

Millet, N.B. 1963 'Gebel Adda, Preliminary Report, 1963', *JARCE* 2, 147–64

Millet, N.B. 1967 'Gebel Adda, Preliminary Report, 1965–66', *JARCE* 6, 53–64

Millet, N.B. 1968 *Meroitic Nubia*, PhD thesis, Yale University

Millet, N.B. 1974 'Writing and Literacy in Ancient Sudan', in Abdelgadir Mahmoud Abdalla (ed.), *Studies in the Ancient Languages of the Sudan*, Khartoum, 49–58

Millet, N.B. 1984 'Meroitic Religion', *Meroitica* 7, 111–21

Mills, A.J. 1965 'The Reconnaissance Survey from Gemai to Dal – A Preliminary Report for 1963–64', *Kush* 15, 1–12

Mills, A.J. 1982 *The Cemeteries of Qasr Ibrim*, Oxford

Mohammed Ahmed S. el Din 1992 *L'agglomération napatéenne de Kerma*, Paris

Morkot, R. 1991 'Nubia in the New Kingdom: The limits of Egyptian Control', in Davies (ed.) 1991, 294–301

Morkot, R. 1992 'Kingship and Kinship in the Empire of Kush, Part 2', 7th International Conference for Meroitic Studies, pre-circulated papers

Morkot, R. 1994 'The Foundations of the Kushite State', 8th International Conference of Nubian Studies, pre-circulated papers

Moss, R. 1960 'The Statue of an Ambassador of Ethiopia from Kiev', *Kush* 8, 269–71

Munro-Hay, S.C. 1991 *Aksum: An African Civilisation of Late Antiquity*, Edinburgh

Nordström, H-Å 1962 'Excavations and Survey in Faras, Argin and Gezira Dabarosa', *Kush* 10, 34–61

O'Connor, D. 1993 *Ancient Nubia, Egypt's Rival in Africa*, Philadelphia

Pliny, *Naturia Historia*, trans. vol. I–VI, IX–X, H.Rakham, Loeb edn 1952; vols VII–VIII, W.H.S.Jones, Loeb edn 1956

Plumley, J.M. 1966 'Qasr Ibrim 1966', *JEA* 52, 9–12

Plumley, J.M. 1970 'Qasr Ibrim 1969', *JEA* 56, 12–18

Plumley, J.M. and W.Y.Adams 1974 'Qasr Ibrim, 1972', *JEA* 60, 212–38

Posener, G. 1940 *Princes et Pays d'Asie et de Nubie*, Brussels

Posener, G. 1958 'Pour une Localisation du Pays Koush au Moyen Empire', *Kush* 6, 39–68

Posener, G. 1987 *Cinq Figurines d'envoûtement*, Cairo

Priese, K.-H. 1973 'Zur Entstehung der meroitischen Schrift', *Meroitica* 1, 273–306

Priese, K.-H. 1992 *The Gold of Meroe*, New York and Mainz am Rhein

Procopius *De Bello Persico* trans. H.B.Dewing, Loeb edn 1914

Quirke, S. 1992 *Ancient Egyptian Religion*, London

Quirke, S. and J.Spencer 1992 *The British Museum Book of Ancient Egypt*, London

Randall-MacIver, D. and C.L.Woolley 1909 *Areika*, University of Pennsylvania Museum, Eckley B.Coxe Junior Expedition to Nubia, vol. I, Oxford

Randall-MacIver, D. and C.L.Woolley 1911 *Buhen*, University of Pennsylvania Museum, Eckley B.Coxe Junior Expedition to Nubia, vol. VIII, Oxford

Reinold, J. and P.Lenoble 1994 'Engraved bronze vessels from el Hobagi', *Nubian Letters* 21, 1–3

Reisner, G.A. 1910 *The Archaeological Survey of Nubia: Report for 1907–1908*, Cairo

Reisner, G.A. 1918 'The Barkal Temples in 1916', *JEA* 5, 99–112

Reisner, G.A. 1919 'Discovery of the Tombs of the Egyptian XXV Dynasty at El-Kurruw in Dongola Province', *SNR* 2, 237–54

Reisner, G.A. 1920a 'Note on the Harvard-Boston Excavations at El-Kurruw and Barkal in 1918–1919', *JEA* 6, 61–4

Reisner, G.A. 1920b 'The Barkal Temples in 1916', *JEA* 6, 247–64

Reisner, G.A. 1921 'Historical Inscriptions from Gebel Barkal', *SNR* 4, 59–75

Reisner, G.A. 1922 'The Pyramids of Meroe and the Candaces of Ethiopia', *SNR* 5, 173–96

Reisner, G.A. 1923a 'Kerma I–III', *Harvard African Studies* 5

Reisner, G.A. 1923b 'The Meroitic Kingdom of Ethiopia: a Chronological Outline', *JEA* 9, 34–78

Reisner, G.A. 1931 'Inscribed Monuments from Gebel Barkal', *ZAS* 66, 76–100

Reisner, G.A. and M.B.Reisner 1934 'Inscribed Monuments from Gebel Barkal II', *ZAS* 69, 24–39

Ripinski, M. 1985 'The Camel in Dynastic Egypt', *JEA* 71, 134–41

Robertson, J.H. 1992 'History and Archaeology at Meroe', in J.Strener and N.David (eds.) *An African Commitment: Papers in honour of Peter Lewis Shinnie*, Calgary

Robinson, A.E. 1936 'The Camel in Antiquity', *SNR* 19, 47–69

Rostkowska, B. 1982 'The God's representation from Jebel Qeili', *Meroitica* 6, 289–90

Rose, P. and P.Rowley-Conwy 1989 'Qasr Ibrim Regional Survey: Preliminary Report', *ANM* 3, 121–30

Rowley-Conwy, P. 1988 'The Camel in the Nile Valley: new Radiocarbon Accelerator (AMS) dates from Qasr Ibrim', *JEA* 74, 245–8

Russmann, E.R. 1974 *The Representation of the King in the XXVth Dynasty*, Brussels and Brooklyn

Sadik Nur 1956 'Two Meroitic Pottery Coffins from Argin in Halfa District', *Kush* 4, 86–7

Sauneron, S. and J.Yoyotte 1952 'La Campagne nubienne de Psammetique II et sa signification historique', *Bull. Inst. Française d'Archéologie Orientale* 50, 157–207

Säve-Söderbergh, T. 1949 'A Buhen Stela (Khartum No. 18)', *JEA* 35, 50–8

Sayce, A.H. 1909 'A Greek Inscription of a King(?) of Axum found at Meroe', *Proc. Soc. Biblical Archaeology* 31, 189–203

Sayce, A.H. 1912 'Second Interim Report on the Excavations at Meroë in Ethiopia: Part 2 The Historical Results', *LAAA* 4, 53–65

el Sayid el Gayar and M.P. Jones 1989 'A possible source of copper ore fragments found at the Old Kingdom town of Buhen', *JEA* 75, 31–40

Schulman, A.R. 1964 *Military Rank, Title, and Organisation in the Egyptian New Kingdom*, Berlin

Shinnie, P.L. 1954 'Excavations at Tanqasi, 1953', *Kush* 2, 66–85

Shinnie, P.L. 1967 *Meroe: A Civilisation of the Sudan*, London

Shinnie, P.L. 1970 'Excavations at Meroe', *MNL* 5, 17–19

Shinnie, P.L. 1971 'The Sudan', in P.L. Shinnie (ed.) 1971, *The African Iron Age*, Oxford, 89–107

Shinnie, P.L. 1976 'Comments', *Meroitica* 2, 89–93

Shinnie, P.L. 1984 'Excavations at Meroe 1974–1976', *Meroitica* 7, 498–504

Shinnie, P.L. 1989 'The Culture of Meroe and its Influence in the Central Sudan', *Sahara* 2, 21–30

Shinnie, P.L. and R.J. Bradley 1977 'A New Meroitic Royal Name', *Meroitic Newsletter* 18, 29–31

Shinnie, P.L. and R.J. Bradley 1980 'The Capital of Kush 1', *Meroitica* 4, Berlin

Shinnie, P.L. and R.J. Bradley 1981 'The Murals from the Augustus Temple, Meroe' in Simpson and Davis (eds) 1981, 167–72

Shinnie, P.L. and F.J. Kense 1982 'Meroitic iron working', *Meroitica* 6, 17–28

Simpson, W.K. and W.M. Davis (eds) 1981 *Studies in Ancient Egypt, the Aegean and the Sudan*, Boston, Massachusetts

Snowden, F.M. 1970 *Blacks in Antiquity: Ethiopians in the Greco-Roman Experience*, Cambridge, Massachusetts

Spiegelberg, W. 1931 *Die demotischen Papyri Loeb*, Munich

Strabo, *The Geography*, trans. W. Falconer, London 1889

Strouhal, E. 1992 'Palaeodemography of Kush', 7th International Conference for Meroitic Studies, pre-circulated papers

Taylor, J.H. 1991 *Egypt and Nubia*, London

Thucydides, *The Persian Wars*, trans. R. Warner 1954, Penguin edn 1972

Thurman, C.C.M. and B. Williams 1979 *Ancient Textiles from Nubia*, Chicago

Titherington, G.W. 'A Roman Fort in the Sudan', *SNR* 1923, 331–2

Tomandl, H. 1987 'Tradierung und Bedeutung eines religiösen Motivs von meroitischen bis zur christlichen Periode', *BzS* 2, 107–26

Török, L. 1974 'An Archaeological Note on the Connection between the Meroitic and Ballana Cultures', *Studia Aegyptiaca* 1, 361–78

Török, L. 1976 'Traces of Alexandrian Architecture in Meroe: A Late Hellenistic Motif in History', *Studia Aegyptiaca* 2, 115–30

Török, L. 1978 'Zum Problem der "römischen" Gräberfelder in Sayala (Nubien)', *AAASH* 30, 431–5

Török, L. 1979 'Economic Offices and Officials in Meroitic Nubia (A Study in Territorial Administration of the Late Meroitic Kingdom)', *Studia Aegyptiaca* V, Budapest

Török, L. 1980a 'Meroitic Religion: Three Contributions in a Positivistic Manner', *Meroitica* 7, 156–82

Török, L. 1980b 'To the History of the Dodekaschoinos between *ca.* 250 B.C. and 298 A.D.', *ZÄS* 107, 76–86

Török, L. 1984 'Economy in the Empire of Kush: A Review of the Written Evidence', *ZÄS* 111, 45–69

Török, L. 1987a *The Royal Crowns of Kush: A Study in Middle Nile Valley regalia and iconography in the 1st millenia B.C. and A.D.*, BAR Int. Ser. 338, Oxford

Török, L. 1987b 'Meroitic Painted Pottery: Problems of Chronology and Style', *BzS* 2, 75–106

Török, L. 1988 *Late Antique Nubia*, Budapest

Török, L. 1989 'Kush and the External World', *Meroitica* 10, 49–215

Török, L. 1989–90 'Augustus and Meroe', *Orientalia Suecana* 38–9, 171–90

Török, L. 1990 'The Costume of the Ruler in Meroe: Remarks on its Origins and Significance', *ANM* 4, 151–202

Török, L. 1991 'Iconography and Mentality: Three Remarks on the Kushite Way of Thinking', in Davies (ed.) 1991, 195–204

Török, L. 1992a 'Ambulatory Kingship and Settlement History: A study of the contribution of archaeology to Meroitic history', in Bonnet (ed.), 111–26

Török, L. 1992b 'The Origin of the Napatan State: The Long Chronology of the el-Kurru Cemetery', 7th International Conference for Meroitic Studies, pre-circulated papers

Tothill, J.D. (ed.) 1948 *Agriculture in the Sudan*, Oxford

Tracey, C.B. and J.W. Hewison 1948 'Northern Province', in Tothill (ed.) 1948, 736–61

Trigger, B.G. 1965 *History and Settlement in Lower Nubia*, Yale University Publications in Anthropology, 69

Trigger, B.G. 1967 *The Late Nubian Settlement at Arminna West*, New Haven and Philadelphia

Trigger, B.G. 1969 'The Myth of Meroe and the African Iron Age', *African Historical Studies* II, 23–50

Trigger, B.G. 1970 *The Meroitic Funerary Inscriptions from Arminna West*, New Haven and Pennsylvania

Trigger, B.G. 1973 'Meroitic Language Studies: Strategies and Goals', *Meroitica* 1, 243–72

Trigger, B.G. 1984 'History and Settlement in Lower Nubia in the Perspective of Fifteen Years', *Meroitica* 7, 367–80

Tylecote, R.F. 1982 'Metal working at Meroe, Sudan', *Meroitica* 6, 29–42

UNESCO 1978 *The peopling of Ancient Egypt and the deciphering of Meroitic script*, Paris

Vantini, G. 1981 *Christianity in the Sudan*, Bologna

Vercoutter, J. 1959 'The Gold of Kush', *Kush* 7, 120–53

Vercoutter, J. 1961 'Le Sphinx d'Aspelta de Defeia', *Mélanges Mariette* (Bibliothèque d'études 32), 97–104

Vercoutter, J. 1962 'Un Palais des "Candaces", contemporain d'Auguste', *Syria* 39, 263–99

Vercoutter, J. 1970 *Mirgissa I*, Paris

Vila, A. 1982 'Analyse de sépultures péri-Napatéenes à Abri', *Meroitica* 6, 105–22

Vinogradov, A.K. 1989 'Diodorus on the election of Kings of Meroe', *Meroitica* 10, 353–64

Vinogradov, A.K. 1992 'On the supposed coregency of Irikeamannote with Talakhamani', *Sesto Congreso Internazionale di Egittologia*, vol. I, 635–41

Wainwright, G.A. 1945 'Iron in the Napatan and Meroitic Ages', *SNR* 26, 5–36

Wainwright, G.A. 1947 'The Position of Ast-Raset', *JEA* 33, 58–62

Wainwright, G.A. 1952 'The Date of the Rise of Meroe', *JEA* 38, 75–77

Welsby, D.A. 1991 'Early Medieval and Pre-Medieval Soba', in Davies (ed.) 1991, 278–85

Welsby, D.A. 1992 'ULVS XXV: The *Gsur* and Associated Settlements in the Wadi Umm el Kharab: An Architectural Survey', *Libyan Studies* 23, 73–99

Welsby, D.A. (forth. 1) 'Meroitic Soba', *Meroitica*

Welsby, D.A. (forth. 2) 'Roman Camps and other defended enclosures in Nubia'

Welsby, D.A. and C.M.Daniels 1991 *Soba: archaeological research at a medieval capital on the Blue Nile*, BIEA monograph series no. 12, London

Wenig, S. 1978 *Africa in Antiquity: The Catalogue*, New York

Wenig, S. 1992 'Ein "neuer" alter Königsname', 7th International Conference for Meroitic Studies, pre-circulated papers

Wenig, S. 1993 'Recent Archaeological Work at Meroe and Musawwarat es Sufra', *SARSN* 4, 10–12

Woolley, C.L. 1911 *Karanòg: The Town*, Philadelphia

Woolley, C.L. and D.Randall-MacIver 1910 *Karanòg: The Romano-Nubian Cemetery*, Philadelphia

Williams, B.B. 1991 *Meroitic Remains from Qustul Cemetery Q, Ballana Cemetery B, and a Ballana Settlement*, Oriental Institute Nubian Expedition VIII, Chicago

Yellin, J.W. 1979 'A Suggested Interpretation of the Relief Decoration in the Type B Chapels at Begrawiyah North', *Meroitica* 5, 157–64

Yellin, J.W. 1982 'Abaton-style milk libation at Meroe', *Meroitica* 6, 151–5

Yellin, J. W. 1990 'The Decorated Pyramid Chapels of Meroe and Meroitic Funerary Religion', *Meroitica* 12, 361–74

Yellin, J. W. 1994 'Egyptian Religion and the Formation of the Napatan State', 8th International Conference for Nubian Studies, pre-circulated papers

Zabkar, L. V. 1975 *Apedemak, Lion God of Meroe*, Warminster

Zabkar, L. V. 1977 'Some Particular Features in the Representations of Apedemak', *Aegyptus und Kush* 13, 487–506

Zach, M. 1992 'Das Hathor-Relief aus Soba-Ost: Ein Beitrag zu Fragen der meroitischen Religion', *Aegyptus Antiqua* 8, 27–32

Zibelius, K. 1972 *Afrikanische Orts- und Völkernamen in hieroglyphischen und hieratischen Texten*, TAVO, Beih. Reihe B. 1, Tübingen

Index